Bullies, Victims, and Bystanders

Lisa H. Rosen · Shannon R. Scott · Samuel Y. Kim
Editors

Bullies, Victims, and Bystanders

Understanding Child and Adult Participant Vantage Points

Editors
Lisa H. Rosen
Department of Psychology and Philosophy
Texas Woman's University
Denton, TX, USA

Shannon R. Scott
Department of Psychology and Philosophy
Texas Woman's University
Denton, TX, USA

Samuel Y. Kim
Department of Psychology and Philosophy
Texas Woman's University
Denton, TX, USA

ISBN 978-3-030-52938-3   ISBN 978-3-030-52939-0 (eBook)
https://doi.org/10.1007/978-3-030-52939-0

© The Editor(s) (if applicable) and The Author(s), under exclusive license to Springer Nature Switzerland AG 2020
This work is subject to copyright. All rights are solely and exclusively licensed by the Publisher, whether the whole or part of the material is concerned, specifically the rights of translation, reprinting, reuse of illustrations, recitation, broadcasting, reproduction on microfilms or in any other physical way, and transmission or information storage and retrieval, electronic adaptation, computer software, or by similar or dissimilar methodology now known or hereafter developed.
The use of general descriptive names, registered names, trademarks, service marks, etc. in this publication does not imply, even in the absence of a specific statement, that such names are exempt from the relevant protective laws and regulations and therefore free for general use.
The publisher, the authors and the editors are safe to assume that the advice and information in this book are believed to be true and accurate at the date of publication. Neither the publisher nor the authors or the editors give a warranty, expressed or implied, with respect to the material contained herein or for any errors or omissions that may have been made. The publisher remains neutral with regard to jurisdictional claims in published maps and institutional affiliations.

Cover illustration: Rawpixel

This Palgrave Macmillan imprint is published by the registered company Springer Nature Switzerland AG
The registered company address is: Gewerbestrasse 11, 6330 Cham, Switzerland

Contents

1. **Bullying Through Different Perspectives: An Introduction to Multiple Vantage Points** ... 1
   Samuel Y. Kim, Lisa H. Rosen, Shannon R. Scott, and Briana Paulman

2. **The Vantage Point of a Bully** ... 17
   Lara Mayeux and Molly O'Mealey

3. **The Vantage Points of Assistants and Reinforcers** ... 45
   Claire P. Monks and Sarah E. O'Toole

4. **The Outsider Vantage Point** ... 79
   Greg R. Machek, Jaynee L. Bohart, Ashlyn M. Kincaid, and Emily A. Hattouni

5. **The Defender Vantage Point** ... 117
   Stephanie S. Fredrick, Lyndsay Jenkins, and Cassandra M. Dexter

6	The Vantage Point of a Victim *David Schwartz, Luiza Mali, and Annemarie Kelleghan*	143
7	Role of Adults in Prevention and Intervention of Peer Victimization *Jina Yoon, Sheri Bauman, and Colleen Corcoran*	179
8	Bullying Through the Eyes of the Peer Group: Lessons Learned Through Multiple Vantage Points *Lisa H. Rosen, Shannon R. Scott, Samuel Y. Kim, and Meredith G. Higgins*	213

Index 249

Notes on Contributors

Sheri Bauman, Ph.D. is Professor of Counseling at the University of Arizona. She earned her Ph.D. in counseling psychology from New Mexico State University in 1999. Before then, she worked in K-12 schools for 30 years, as a teacher and school counselor, and is also a retired licensed psychologist.

Jaynee L. Bohart is a graduate student in the University of Montana's school psychology doctoral training program and is currently examining the relative importance of peer and parental influences on self-reported attitudes towards bullying.

Colleen Corcoran, Ed.S. is a doctoral candidate in School Psychology at the University of Arizona. As a Nationally Certified School Psychologist, she provides psychological services at Vail Public Schools, Vail, AZ. Her research interest includes victimization, school climate, and social support for LGBTQ youth.

Cassandra M. Dexter, B.S. is a graduate student at Central Michigan University. Her primary research interest is bystander behavior in bullying behavior, with her thesis focused on differences in self-reported bystander intervention across types of bullying (i.e., physical, verbal, and relational).

Stephanie S. Fredrick, Ph.D. is Assistant Professor in the Department of Counseling, School, and Educational Psychology and Associate Director of the Alberti Center for Bullying Abuse Prevention in the Graduate School of Education at the University at Buffalo. Her research focuses on risk and protective factors for youth involved in bullying.

Emily A. Hattouni, M.A. is a graduate student in the University of Montana's school psychology doctoral training program who engages in research related to mindfulness, both for students and pre-service teachers.

Meredith G. Higgins is in the Counseling Psychology Doctoral program at Texas Woman's University. She is currently serving as project manager for a research project focused on child and parental health and adjustment in the context of peer victimization.

Lyndsay Jenkins, Ph.D. is Assistant Professor at Florida State University in the M.S./Ed.S. School Psychology and Combined Ph.D. in Counseling and School Psychology programs. Her research interests focus on bullying and victimization, defending behaviors in youth and adolescents, as well as social and emotional barriers to academic achievement.

Annemarie Kelleghan is a doctoral candidate in Clinical Science (Clinical Psychology) and a Masters of Public Health (MPH) student at the University of Southern California. Her research interests include adolescent peer relationships and social environments and their impact on adolescent mental health, substance use, and adjustment to health problems.

Samuel Y. Kim, Ph.D. is Assistant Professor and Director of the Specialist in School Psychology Program at Texas Woman's University. His areas of research interest include peer victimization, assessment, and the experience of Korean Americans.

Ashlyn M. Kincaid is a graduate student in the University of Montana's school psychology doctoral training program doing research on how to support at-risk children in foster care and other alternative placements.

Greg R. Machek, Ph.D. is Associate Professor in the Department of Psychology at the University of Montana. He serves as a core member of the university's school psychology graduate program and has interests in mitigating peer aggression in the schools through components of multitiered models of support.

Luiza Mali is a doctoral candidate in Clinical Science (Clinical Psychology) at the University of Southern California. Her research focuses on understanding children's peer relationships, meta-cognition, developmental disorders, emotional functioning, and academic achievement. She is currently completing her predoctoral internship in pediatric psychology at Children's Hospital of Orange County (CHOC).

Lara Mayeux, Ph.D. is Associate Professor of Psychology at the University of Oklahoma. Her primary research focuses on friendships, peer status, and aggressive behavior in adolescence. Her interdisciplinary research interests include health risk behavior in youth and coping and resilience among direct tornado survivors.

Claire P. Monks, Ph.D. is a Professor of Developmental Psychology at the University of Greenwich. Her research focuses on the development of aggressive behavior among children and young people. She has carried out research examining peer-directed aggression in the early years of school, cyberbullying during elementary school, and aggression within young people's dating relationships.

Molly O'Mealey is a Ph.D. candidate at the University of Oklahoma. Her research interests involve childhood and adolescent peer relationships. Her dissertation research focuses on the cognitive and social mechanisms involved in friendships, particularly friendship formation, downgrading, and dissolution.

Sarah E. O'Toole, Ph.D. is Research Fellow at the University of College London. She is a developmental psychologist with a research interest in the interplay of social and cognitive development in early childhood. Her previous research has focused on the role of executive function in aggressive behavior.

Briana Paulman is a doctoral student in the School Psychology program at Texas Woman's University. Her research interests include body image, social influences, and neuropsychological functioning in children and adolescents.

Lisa H. Rosen, Ph.D. is Associate Professor and Director of the Undergraduate Psychology Program at Texas Woman's University. Her research focuses on children's peer relations. Her recent work centers on how parents and teachers can best support victimized youth.

David Schwartz, Ph.D. is an associate professor of psychology at the University of Southern California. His research focuses on children's peer relationships. He has published extensively on social adjustment with peers and bully/victim problems in school peer groups. Dr. Schwartz has been involved in research on social rejection, popularity, friendship, and social media use among youth.

Shannon R. Scott, Ph.D. is Professor and Department Chair of the Psychology and Philosophy Department at Texas Woman's University. Her research focuses on body image, weight stigma, and anti-fat attitudes as well as examining the consequences of peer victimization.

Jina Yoon, Ph.D. is Professor in School Psychology at the University of Arizona. She is a Nationally Certified School Psychologist (NCSP) and is also licensed as a psychologist in Arizona. Her research focuses on social relationships and classroom processes in the school contexts, including peer victimization and teacher-student relationships.

1

Bullying Through Different Perspectives: An Introduction to Multiple Vantage Points

Samuel Y. Kim, Lisa H. Rosen, Shannon R. Scott, and Briana Paulman

Demetra and Sophia walk down the hallway of the school talking about their last class. As they pass Mr. Simone's class, Nash knocks Demetra down for the fourth time that week. Sophia quickly walks down the hallway away from both of them. As Nash kicks her, Demetra curls up in a ball not only to block Nash's kicks, but also to block the sound of Rafferty cheering Nash on and throwing books at her. She meets the eyes of Ajani who watches and giggles from the crowd. Rachel walks up and sees Demetra on the ground. She yells at everyone to stop and calls Mr. Simone's name as she helps Demetra up from

---

S. Y. Kim (✉) · L. H. Rosen · S. R. Scott · B. Paulman
Psychology and Philosophy, Texas Woman's University, Denton, TX, USA
e-mail: SKim18@twu.edu

L. H. Rosen
e-mail: LRosen@twu.edu

S. R. Scott
e-mail: SScott@twu.edu

© The Author(s) 2020
L. Rosen et al. (eds.), *Bullies, Victims, and Bystanders*,
https://doi.org/10.1007/978-3-030-52939-0_1

the ground. Rachel escorts Demetra to Mr. Simone's classroom and stays with her until Demetra's parents arrive.

Imagine the above scenario that was adapted from one of the author's lived experiences with names changed. As can be seen from this vignette, bullying is a complex series of events that can involve and impact more than just a bully and victim. Traditionally, research has focused on the bully-victim dyad, and as such, the focus would be solely on Nash and Demetra. However, as was first articulated in the pioneering work of Salmivalli, Lagerspetz, Björkqvist, Österman, and Kaukialnen (1996) and clearly evident in the above scenario, bullying is largely a group process in which bystanders can help fuel or combat bullying. The students in this scenario take on multiple roles including those that support the bully as evident in the actions of the assistant to the bully (Rafferty) and the reinforcer of the bully (Ajani). However, bystanders can also behave in ways that support the victim as seen in the behavior of the defender (Rachel). Still, peers can behave in ways that do not explicitly assist the bully or victim as in the case of the outsider (Sophia) who distances herself both physically and emotionally. Teachers, such as Mr. Simone, and other significant adults also have the potential to influence bullying dynamics. Each chapter in this book highlights a particular participant role. By viewing bullying through the eyes of each individual role, this book provides an in-depth exploration of bullying as a group process with special attention to implications for prevention and intervention.

Definition and Forms of Bullying

Most people feel that they know bullying when they see it, but it is critical to understand how bullying is defined in the research literature. The most common definition of bullying is based on Dan Olweus' (1993) seminal work in which he proposed three essential components to bullying: (1) a power imbalance, (2) repetition, and (3) an intention to harm. The first component, imbalance of power, can refer to either the bully having greater physical power (e.g., size, strength) or social power (e.g., popularity, social hierarchy). Second, the behavior must be repetitive; bullying is not considered a singular incident, but rather is behavior that occurs on a continued basis. Finally, the bully acts with an intention to harm his or her victim. Although other definitions have been proposed, the work of Olweus forms the basis of definitions put forth by the American Psychological Association and the National Association of School Psychologists (Hymel & Swearer, 2015). The contributors in this book refer back to this classic definition.

Bullying behaviors can take different forms, which further adds to the complexity of understanding bullying (Gladden, Vivolo-Kantor, Hamburger, & Lumpkin, 2014). Even though teachers tend to think of physical bullying (Bauman & Del Rio, 2006), bullying can also take the forms of verbal attacks, relational bullying, and property damage (Hymel & Swearer, 2015; Mynard & Joseph, 2000; Olweus, 2010). More recently, attention has also been aimed at understanding cyberbullying (Hinduja & Patchin, 2009).

Researchers have sought to differentiate these forms of bullying (Gladden et al., 2014; Mynard & Joseph, 2000; Rosen, Scott, & DeOrnellas, 2017). Physical bullying refers to a direct physical attack on an individual such as hitting, pinching, kicking, or biting. Verbal bullying, on the other hand, refers to the use of language to inflict harm on another (e.g., teasing and name-calling). Social bullying can be more nuanced, and although teachers often consider this a less serious form (Bauman & Del Rio, 2006), it can be quite hurtful to victims (Paquette & Underwood, 1999). Social bullying, similar to what has been termed relational or indirect bullying, is intended to harm the victim's social status or relationships (Underwood, 2003). Common forms of social aggression include social exclusion and gossip (Paquette & Underwood, 1999). Social aggression may become more common and take more complex forms in adolescence as greater importance is devoted to popularity (Pouwels, Lansu, & Cillessen, 2018; Underwood, 2003). Though not as frequently examined, property damage can be considered a form of bullying, which involves destruction or any change to the property that is carried out with the intention of harming someone (Mynard & Joseph, 2000).

Cyberbullying involves aggression through electronic devices (e.g., cell phones and social media; Hinduja & Patchin, 2009), and many contributors to this book identify this as an area for future research on participant roles. Cyberbullying presents a number of conceptual and practical challenges (Volk, Dane, & Marini, 2014). For example, identifying a power imbalance can be difficult as the traditional metric of physical size is not apparent. Those who perpetrate cyberbullying may have greater power in their ability to reach a wide audience quickly. However, perpetrators of cyberbullying can act anonymously, which further makes it difficult to discern power imbalances and can contribute to aggressors feeling more empowered. Importantly, cyberbullying can occur at any time—day or night—and without geographical limitations, which may lead to victims feeling more vulnerable (Hinduja & Patchin, 2009). Further, the potential for cyberbullying to unfold in front of a wide audience can translate into a larger number of bystanders, whether or not they wish to be involved (Cohen-Almagor, 2018).

Prevalence of Bullying

Bullying is not a rare phenomenon, and consequently, is of serious concern to educators and parents (Rosen et al., 2017). However, answering the question of how common bullying is can be quite a difficult endeavor. Reported prevalence rates have varied greatly with estimates of bullying perpetration ranging from 10 to 90% of students and estimates of bullying victimization ranging from 9 to 98% of students (Modecki, Minchin, Harbaugh, Guerra, & Runions, 2014). A number of explanations have been proposed for this wide variability including differences in how bullying perpetration and victimization are measured as well as sampling issues (Cook, Williams, Guerra, Kim, & Sadek, 2010; Hymel & Swearer, 2015; Leff, Kupersmidt, Patterson, & Power, 1999; Modecki et al., 2014).

Although there is substantial variability in prevalence rates, many researchers draw from the work of Nansel and colleagues (2001) who surveyed a large, nationally representative sample of American students. Approximately 30% of the 15,686 participants reported moderate to frequent involvement in bullying. Of these students, 13% reported bullying perpetration, 11% reported bullying victimization, and 6% reported both bullying perpetration and victimization.

To further examine prevalence rates, Modecki and colleagues (2014) conducted a meta-analysis of 80 studies. Whereas Nansel and colleagues (2001) focused on estimates of moderate to frequent bullying involvement, Modecki and colleagues sought to identify mean prevalence rates of traditional bullying and cyberbullying. The mean prevalence rate of traditional bullying perpetration (35%) was higher than the mean prevalence rate of cyberbullying perpetration (16%). Correspondingly, the mean prevalence rate of traditional bullying victimization (36%) was higher than the mean prevalence rate of cyberbullying victimization (15%).

In examining these prevalence rates, it is important to note that researchers have commonly focused on the bully-victim dyad. These findings highlight the importance of examining the role of the bystander, which is more common than either the victim or bully role (Salmivalli et al., 1996). As noted by many contributors, the vast majority of bullying episodes (85–88%) occur in front of an audience (Craig & Pepler, 1997; Hawkins, Pepler, & Craig, 2001). Consequently, it is critical to understand the prevalence of different bystander roles. Throughout this book, contributors discuss prevalence rates for the different bullying roles with attention to differences based on gender and age.

Impact of Bullying

In the opening vignette, most would focus on the ramifications of the experience for Demetra. However, this book seeks to understand the impact of bullying on each participant's role. More is known about the associations with adjustment for the victim and bully role while the other roles have received less research attention. We briefly outline these associations here, and contributors will provide a more in-depth examination in the following chapters.

A large body of research has documented negative adjustment difficulties for victims (Hymel & Swearer, 2015; Sigurdson, Wallander, & Sund, 2014). Longitudinal investigations suggest that being bullied in childhood can also predict adult maladjustment (McDougall & Vaillancourt, 2015). As will be outlined later, both concurrent and longitudinal research indicates that victimization is associated with internalizing symptoms, such as depression and anxiety (Brunstein Klomek, Marrocco, Kleinman, Schonfeld, & Gould, 2007; Prinstein, Boergers, & Vernberg, 2001; Storch, Brassard, & Masia-Warner, 2003; Storch & Masia-Warner, 2004). Beyond internalizing symptoms, victimization is associated with externalizing problems such as delinquency and substance use (Sullivan, Farrell, & Kliewer, 2006). In addition, victimization has been linked with physical health; victimized youth report increased somatic complaints, decreased quality of sleep, and disrupted eating behavior (Hatzinger et al., 2008; Nishina & Juvonen, 2005; van den Berg, Wertheim, Thompson, & Paxton, 2002). Finally, victimization by peers is associated with poorer educational outcomes (Buhs, Ladd, & Herald-Brown, 2010; Hughes, Gaines, & Pryor, 2015; Kochenderfer & Ladd, 1996; Schwartz, Gorman, Nakamoto, & Toblin, 2005).

The impact of engaging in bullying behavior has also been examined. Perpetration of peer aggression may be associated with internalizing difficulties (Crick, Ostrov, & Werner, 2006; Underwood, 2011). Further, peer aggression may predict delinquency, conduct problems, and academic difficulties (Coyne, Nelson, & Underwood, 2011; Feldman et al., 2014; Smith, Polenik, Nakasita, & Jones, 2012; Underwood, 2011). Not only is there an immediate association between aggression and maladjustment in childhood and adolescence, there is also longitudinal work suggesting that maladjustment in adulthood (e.g., lower educational attainment and increased unemployment) can be predicted by being identified as a bully in adolescence (Sigurdson et al., 2014).

Beyond the bully-victim dyad, there is evidence that peers can influence victims' adjustment. For example, those who are victimized show fewer negative outcomes when more of their peers are also bullied (McDougall & Vaillancourt, 2015). Further, social support from peers can serve as a protective function (McDougall & Vaillancourt, 2015). In particular, defending behavior can play an important protective role for victimized youth (Kärnä et al., 2011; Salmivalli, 2010).

Of critical importance, research has demonstrated that witnessing peer victimization, even one episode, may be related to increased maladjustment for the bystander including anxiety, depression, substance use, and somatic complaints (Rivers, Poteat, Noret, & Ashurst, 2009). Bystanders who have previously been the victims of peer aggression may be at a greater risk for maladjustment when witnessing bullying (Werth, Nickerson, Aloe, & Swearer, 2015). The negative outcomes of bullying on victims, aggressors, and bystanders suggest the need to continue to combat bullying from a social ecological framework as will be highlighted throughout this book.

Social Ecological Framework of Bullying

Bronfenbrenner's (1979) Ecological Systems Theory has been widely applied to further our understanding of bullying (Espelage & Swearer, 2010; Lambe, Cioppa, Hong, & Craig, 2019; Lee, 2011; Rosen et al., 2017; Swearer et al., 2012). In line with a social ecological view of bullying, "children are viewed as the center of their world, and they interact with their own ecological environments. This indicates that their behaviors are influenced by not only their own traits but also by the ecological contexts with which they are interacting" (Lee, 2011, p. 4). Thus, an individual child, with his or her unique attributes (e.g., gender, age, attitudes toward aggression, personality), can be viewed as the center of nested environmental contexts, and the child's interactions with these environmental systems shape his or her development (Ettekal & Mahoney, 2017; Lambe et al., 2019; Lee, 2011). The child's immediate environment, termed the microsystem, includes the influence of peers, parents, and teachers (Ettekal & Mahoney, 2017). The most distal environmental context, the macrosystem, includes societal characteristics (e.g., individualistic/collectivist culture; Lee, 2011).

The participant role approach is consistent with a social ecological view of bullying (Lambe et al., 2019), and the contributors of this book draw extensively on this framework. Accordingly, each chapter outlines the child-level correlates of participant roles (e.g., social status, antibullying attitudes, empathy, moral disengagement, and self-efficacy). However, as highlighted by the social ecological framework, contributors also highlight important environmental influences as well as discuss how child-level and contextual factors interact. Lambe and colleagues (2019) note that "an approach that takes these multiple levels into account may help us to best understand the factors that promote defending behavior, as defending is more than a product of individual differences" (pp. 51–52). Given the importance of the adults in the school and home context, a chapter is devoted to these influences. In this chapter, important connections between microsystems, which Bronfenbrenner termed mesosystems (Ettekal & Mahoney, 2017), are described (e.g., parent-peer and parent-teacher connections). Providing a comprehensive view of environmental factors influencing bullying is of critical importance because there is "growing recognition that effective bullying prevention programs should be situated within a social-ecological framework… addressing the characteristics of the individuals involved and the multiple contexts in which they are embedded" (Holt, Raczynskib, Frey, Hymel, & Limber, 2013, p. 239). Therefore, our hope is that the focus on child-level and environmental correlates of each role can help guide prevention and intervention work.

Bullying Through My Eyes: Overview of Bullying Roles

Early work on school bullying was largely limited to the bully-victim dyad (Salmivalli & Voeten, 2004; Sutton & Smith, 1999). The innovative research of Salmivalli and colleagues brought to light the important roles bystanders can play in school bullying (Salmivalli, 1999, 2010). Even though the view of bullying as a group process has been widely adopted and has spurred a great deal of research on the different bullying roles (Ross, Lund, Sabey, & Charlton, 2017; Salmivalli & Voeten, 2004; Smokowski & Evans, 2019), less is known about the roles of assistants, reinforcers, and outsiders than the roles of bully, defender, and victim. The major aim of this book is to synthesize the growing body of research on each participant role while also highlighting the potential of teachers and parents to influence the likelihood of students adopting different roles.

Bullying roles can be viewed as a spectrum with the bully on one side and the victim on the other (Olweus et al., 2007; Ross et al., 2017). When bullying is viewed as a group process, those roles in the middle of the spectrum are of critical importance. According to the functional perspective, bullies aggress against the victim because doing so serves a particular purpose. That is, students are much more likely to engage in behavior that is reinforced than behavior that is not reinforced or met with some form of punishment by the peer group (Ross et al., 2017).

This book is organized to begin with the bully end of the spectrum, progressing to those roles that support the bully before moving to the supporters of victims. Following this brief introduction of bullying as a group process, Mayeux and O'Mealey provide a thorough overview of the first role—the bully—in Chapter 2. Monks and O'Toole highlight how the assistant and reinforcer roles encourage the bully's behavior in Chapter 3. In Chapter 4, Macheck and colleagues then address the role of outsider, which is one that does not actively support either the bully or the victim. Progressing toward the victim end of the bullying roles spectrum, Fredrick and colleagues in Chapter 5 focus on defenders who either directly or indirectly intervene in bullying episodes to aid the victim. Schwartz and colleagues describe the final bullying role—the victim—in Chapter 6. Although not a part of the bullying spectrum, Yoon and colleagues in Chapter 7 detail how teachers and parents can exert significant influence on peer dynamics in general, as well as specifically affect the participants in bullying.

The chapters in this book follow a similar format. Each chapter begins with a definition of the highlighted role. Contributors discuss both individual-level and environmental correlates associated with each role. Further, contributors outline the associations between the focus role and adjustment outcomes. Bystanders (including adults) can take on roles that either encourage the bully or support the victim, which in turn, holds important implications for anti-bullying efforts. As such, each chapter outlines suggestions for prevention and intervention framed for the particular bullying role. Chapters end with the discussion of future research directions as well as how the bullying role will likely be impacted by technological and societal changes. The final chapter in this volume draws across the different bullying roles presented to outline a road map for bullying prevention and intervention efforts.

References

Bauman, S., & Del Rio, A. (2006). Preservice teachers' responses to bullying scenarios: Comparing physical, verbal, and relational bullying. *Journal of Educational Psychology, 98*, 219–231. https://doi.org/10.1037/0022-0663.98.1.219.

Bronfenbrenner, U. (1979). Contexts of child rearing: Problems and prospects. *American Psychologist, 34*, 844–850. https://doi.org/10.1037/0003-066X.34.10.844.

Brunstein Klomek, A. B., Marrocco, F., Kleinman, M., Schonfeld, I. S., & Gould, M. S. (2007). Bullying, depression, and suicidality in adolescents. *Journal of the American Academy of Child and Adolescent Psychiatry, 46*, 40–49. https://doi.org/10.1097/01.chi.0000242237.84925.18.

Buhs, E. S., Ladd, G. W., & Herald-Brown, S. I. (2010). Victimization and exclusion: Links to peer rejection, classroom engagement, and achievement. In S. R. Jimerson, S. M. Swearer, & D. L. Espelage (Eds.), *Handbook of bullying in schools: An international perspective* (pp. 163–172). New York: Routledge.

Cohen-Almagor, R. (2018). Social responsibility on the internet: Addressing the challenge of cyberbullying. *Aggression and Violent Behavior, 39*, 42–52. https://doi.org/doi/10.1016/j.avb.2018.01.001.

Cook, C. R., Williams, K. R., Guerra, N. G., Kim, T. E., & Sadek, S. (2010). Predictors of bullying and victimization in childhood and adolescence: A meta-analytic investigation. *School Psychology, 25*, 65–83. https://doi.org/10.1037/a0020149.

Coyne, S. M., Nelson, D. A., & Underwood, M. K. (2011). Aggression in childhood. In P. K. Smith & C. H. Hart (Eds.), *The Wiley-Blackwell handbook of childhood social development* (pp. 491–509). Chichester: Wiley-Blackwell.

Craig, W., & Pepler, D. J. (1997). Observations of bullying and victimization in the schoolyard. *Canadian Journal of School Psychology, 13,* 41–60. https://doi.org/10.1177/082957359801300205.

Crick, N. R., Ostrov, J. M., & Werner, N. E. (2006). A longitudinal study of relational aggression, physical aggression, and children's social-psychological adjustment. *Journal of Abnormal Child Psychology, 34,* 131–142. https://doi.org/10.1007/s10802-005-9009-4.

Espelage, D. L., & Swearer, S. M. (2010). A social-ecological model for bullying prevention and intervention: Understanding the impact of adult communities children live. In S. R. Jimerson, S. M. Swearer & D. L. Espelage (Eds.), *The handbook of bullying in schools: An international perspective* (pp. 61–71). New York: Routledge.

Ettekal, A., & Mahoney, J. L. (2017). Ecological systems theory. Invited chapter to appear in K. Peppler (Ed.), *The SAGE encyclopedia of out-of-school learning* (pp. 239–241). Thousand Oaks, CA: SAGE.

Feldman, M. A., Ojanen, T., Gesten, E. L., Smith-Schrandt, H., Brannick, M., Totura, C. M. W., … Brown, K. (2014). The effects of middle school bullying and victimization on adjustment through high school: Growth modeling of achievement, school attendance, and disciplinary trajectories. *Psychology in the Schools, 51,* 1046–1062. https://doi.org/10.1002/pits.21799.

Gladden, R. M., Vivolo-Kantor, A. M., Hamburger, M. E., & Lumpkin, C. D. (2014). *Bullying surveillance among youths: Uniform definitions for public health and recommended data elements, Version 1.0.* Atlanta, GA: National Center for Injury Prevention and Control, Centers for Disease Control and Prevention and U.S. Department of Education.

Hatzinger, M., Brand, S., Perren, S., Stadelmann, S., von Wyl, A., von Klitzing, K., & Holsboer-Trachsler, E. (2008). Electroencephalographic sleep profiles and hypothalamic-pituitary-adrenocortical (HPA)-activity in kindergarten children: Early indication of poor sleep quality associated with increased cortisol secretion. *Journal of Psychiatric Research, 42,* 532–543. https://doi.org/10.1016/j.jpsychires.2007.05.010.

Hawkins, D. L., Pepler, D. J., & Craig, W. M. (2001). Naturalistic observations of peer interventions in bullying. *Social Development, 10,* 512–527. https://doi.org/10.1111/1467-9507.00178.

Hinduja, S. & Patchin, J. W. (2009). *Bullying beyond the schoolyard: Preventing and responding to cyberbullying.* Thousand Oaks: SAGE.

Holt, M. K., Raczynskib, K., Frey, K. S., Hymel, S., & Limber, S. P. (2013). School and community-based approaches for preventing bullying. *Journal of School Violence, 12*, 238–252. https://doi.org/10.1080/15388220.2013.792271.

Hughes, M. R., Gaines, J. S., & Pryor, D. W. (2015). Staying away from school: Adolescents who miss school due to feeling unsafe. *Youth Violence and Juvenile Justice, 13*, 270–290. https://doi.org/10.1177/1541204014538067.

Hymel, S., & Swearer, S. M. (2015). Four decades of research on school bullying. *American Psychologist, 70*, 293–299. https://doi.org/10.1037/a0038928.

Kärnä, A., Voeten, M., Little, T. D., Poskiparta, E., Kaljonen, A., & Salmivalli, C. (2011). A large-scale evaluation of the KiVa anti-bullying program: Grades 4–6. *Child Development, 82*, 311–330. https://doi.org/10.1111/j.1467-8624.2010.01557.x.

Kochenderfer, B. J., & Ladd, G. W. (1996). Peer victimization: Manifestations and relations to school adjustment in kindergarten. *Journal of School Psychology, 34*, 267–283. https://doi.org/10.1016/0022-4405(96)00015-5.

Lambe, L. J., Cioppa, V. D., Hong, I. K., & Craig, W. M. (2019). Standing up to bullying: A social ecological review of peer defending in offline and online contexts. *Aggression and Violent Behavior, 45*, 51–74. https://doi.org/10.1016/j.avb.2018.05.007.

Lee, C. H. (2011). An ecological systems approach to bullying behaviors among middle school students in the United States. *Journal of Interpersonal Violence, 26*, 1664–1693. https://doi.org/10.1177/0886260510370591.

Leff, S. S., Kupersmidt, J. B., Patterson, C. J., & Power, T. J. (1999). Factors influencing teacher identification of peer bullies and victims. *School Psychology Review, 28*, 505–517.

McDougall, P., & Vaillancourt, T. (2015). Long-term adult outcomes of peer victimization in childhood and adolescence: Pathways to adjustment and maladjustment. *American Psychologist, 70*, 300–310. https://doi.org/10.1037/a0039174.

Modecki, K. L., Minchin, J., Harbaugh, A. G., Guerra, N. G., & Runions, K. C. (2014). Bullying prevalence across contexts: A meta-analysis measuring cyber and traditional bullying. *Journal of Adolescent Health, 55*, 602–611. https://doi.org/10.1016/j.jadohealth.2014.06.007.

Mynard, H., & Joseph, S. (2000). Development of the multidimensional peer-victimization scale. *Aggressive Behavior, 26*, 169–178. https://doi.org/10.1002/(SICI)1098-2337(2000)26:2%3c169:AID-AB3%3e3.0.CO;2-A.

Nansel, T. R., Overpeck, M., Pilla, R. S., Ruan, W. J., Simons-Morton, B., & Scheidt, P. (2001). Bullying behaviors among US youth: Prevalence and association with psychosocial adjustment. *Journal of the American Medical Association, 285,* 2094–2100. https://doi.org/10.1001/jama.285.16.2094.

Nishina, A., & Juvonen, J. (2005). Daily reports of witnessing and experiencing peer harassment in middle school. *Child Development, 76,* 435–450. https://doi.org/10.1111/j.1467-8624.2005.00855.x.

Olweus, D. (1993). *Bullying at school.* Malden: Blackwell.

Olweus, D. (2010). Understanding and researching bullying: Some critical issues. In S. R. Jimerson, S. M. Swearer, & D. L. Espelage (Eds.), *Handbook of bullying in schools: An international perspective* (pp. 9–34). New York: Routledge.

Olweus, D., Limber, S. P., Flerx, V. C., Mullin, N., Riese, J., & Snyder, M. (2007). *Olweus bullying prevention program: Schoolwide guide.* Center City: Hazelden.

Paquette, J. A., & Underwood, M. K. (1999). Gender differences in young adolescents' experiences of peer victimization: Social and physical aggression. *Merrill-Palmer Quarterly, 45,* 242–266.

Pouwels, J. L., Lansu, T. A. M., & Cillessen, A. H. N. (2018). A developmental perspective on popularity and the group process of bullying. *Aggression and Violent Behavior, 43,* 64–70. https://doi.org/10.1016/j.avb.2018.10.003.

Prinstein, M. J., Boergers, J., & Vernberg, E. M. (2001). Overt and relational aggression in adolescents: Social-psychological adjustment of aggressors and victims. *Journal of Clinical Child Psychology, 30,* 479–491. https://doi.org/10.1207/S15374424JCCP3004_05.

Rivers, I., Poteat, V. P., Noret, N., & Ashurst, N. (2009). Observing bullying at school: The mental health implications of witness status. *School Psychology Quarterly, 24,* 211–223. https://doi.org/10.1037/a0018164.

Rosen, L., Scott, S., & DeOrnellas, K. (2017). An overview of school bullying. In L. Rosen, S. Scott, & K. DeOrnellas (Eds.), *Bullying in the school: Perspectives from across campus* (pp. 1–22). New York: Palgrave MacMillan Higher Education.

Ross, S. W., Lund, E. M., Sabey, C. & Charlton, C. (2017). Students' perspectives on bullying. In L. Rosen, S. Scott, & K. DeOrnellas (Eds.), *Bullying in the school: Perspectives from across campus.* (pp. 23–48). New York: Palgrave MacMillan Higher Education.

Salmivalli, C. (1999). Participant role approach to school bullying: Implications for interventions. *Journal of Adolescence, 22,* 453–459. https://doi.org/10.1006/jado.1999.0239.

Salmivalli, C. (2010). Bullying and the peer group: A review. *Aggression and Violent Behavior, 15,* 112–120. https://doi.org/10.1016/j.avb.2009.08.00.

Salmivalli, C., Lagerspetz, K., Björkqvist, K., Österman, K., & Kaukialnen, A. (1996). Bullying as a group process: Participant roles and their relations to social status within the group. *Aggressive Behavior, 22,* 1–15.

Salmivalli, C., & Voeten, M. (2004). Connections between attitudes, group norms, and behaviour in bullying situations. *International Journal of Behavioral Development, 28,* 246–258. https://doi.org/10.1080/01650250344000488.

Schwartz, D., Gorman, A. H., Nakamoto, J., & Toblin, R. L. (2005). Victimization in the peer group and children's academic functioning. *Journal of Educational Psychology, 97,* 425–435. https://doi.org/10.1037/0022-0663.97.3.425.

Sigurdson, J. F., Wallander, J., & Sund, A. M. (2014). Is involvement in school bullying associated with general health and psychosocial adjustment outcomes in adulthood? *Child Abuse and Neglect, 38,* 1607–1617. https://doi.org/10.1016/j.chiabu.2014.06.001.

Smith, H., Polenik, K., Nakasita, S., & Jones, A. P. (2012). Profiling social, emotional and behavioural difficulties of children involved in direct and indirect bullying behaviours. *Emotional and Behavioural Difficulties, 17,* 243–257. https://doi.org/10.1080/13632752.2012.704315.

Smokowski, P., & Evans, C. (2019). *Bullying and victimization across the lifespan: Playground politics and power.* New York: Springer Nature.

Storch, E. A., Brassard, M. R., & Masia-Warner, C. (2003). The relationship of peer victimization to social anxiety and loneliness in adolescence. *Child Study Journal, 33,* 1–18. https://doi.org/10.1016/j.adolescence.2004.03.003.

Storch, E. A., & Masia-Warner, C. (2004). The relationship of peer victimization to social anxiety and loneliness in adolescent females. *Journal of Adolescence, 27,* 351–362. https://doi.org/10.1016/j.adolescence.2004.03.003.

Sullivan, T. N., Farrell, A. D., & Kliewer, W. (2006). Peer victimization in early adolescence: Association between physical and relational victimization and drug use, aggression, and delinquent behaviors among urban middle school students. *Development and Psychopathology, 18,* 119–137. https://doi.org/10.1017/S095457940606007X.

Sutton, J., & Smith, P. K. (1999). Bullying as a group process: An adaptation of the participant role approach. *Aggressive Behavior, 25,* 97–111. https://doi.org/10.1002/(sici)1098-2337.

Swearer, S. M., Espelage, D. L., Koenig, B., Berry, B., Collins, A., & Lembeck, P. (2012). A socio-ecological model for bullying prevention and intervention in early adolescence. In S. R. Jimerson, A. B. Nickerson, M. J. Mayer, & M. J. Furlong (Eds.), *Handbook of school violence and school safety: International research and practice, second edition* (2nd ed., pp. 333–356). New York: Routledge.

Underwood, M. K. (2003). *Social aggression among girls.* New York: Guilford.

Underwood, M. K. (2011). Aggression. In M. K. Underwood & L. H. Rosen (Eds.), *Social development* (pp. 207–234). New York: Guilford.

van den Berg, P., Wertheim, E. H., Thompson, J. K., & Paxton, S. J. (2002). Development of body image, eating disturbance, and general psychological functioning in adolescent females: A replication using covariance structure modeling in an Australian sample. *International Journal of Eating Disorders, 32,* 46–51. https://doi.org/10.1002/eat.10030.

Volk, A. A., Dane, A. V., & Marini, Z. A. (2014). What is bullying? A theoretical redefinition. *Developmental Review, 34,* 327–343. https://doi.org/10.1016/j.dr.2014.09.001.

Werth, J. M., Nickerson, A. B., Aloe, A. M., & Swearer, S. M. (2015). Bullying victimization and the social and emotional maladjustment of bystanders: A propensity score analysis. *Journal of School Psychology, 53,* 295–308. https://doi.org/10.1016/j.jsp.2015.05.004.

2

The Vantage Point of a Bully

Lara Mayeux and Molly O'Mealey

Decades of research attest to the importance of understanding the underlying causes, peer group dynamics, and adjustment problems associated with bullying in the peer group (e.g., Juvonen & Graham, 2014). The effects of victimization on children and adolescents who become the targets of a bully's wrath can be severe and long-lasting, and bullying itself is associated with a host of maladaptive behavioral and psychosocial outcomes (Rodkin, Espelage, & Hanish, 2015). Recent research has identified multiple participant roles in the peer group dynamics of bullying (e.g., Salmivalli, Lagerspetz, Björkqvist, Österman, & Kaukiainen, 1996); in this chapter, we focus on the bullies themselves.

A bully repeatedly and intentionally harms another person who is less strong or less powerful (Olweus, 1994). Bullying is best conceptualized as a type of proactive, unprovoked aggression that has some kind of instrumental goal or hostile intent (Salmivalli, 2010) and, rather than being applied indiscriminately, is typically focused on a small number

L. Mayeux (✉) · M. O'Mealey
University of Oklahoma, Norman, OK, USA
e-mail: lmayeux@ou.edu

of specific peers (e.g., Card & Hodges, 2006). Bullying can take many forms: It can be verbal, physical, or relational, and it can take place online or offline. While research traditionally focused on verbal and physical bullying, such as insults, name-calling, hitting, or slapping (e.g., Olweus, 1978), subsequent research has expanded the definition of bullying to include relational forms of aggression, which involve threats or harm to relationships (such as friendships or romantic relationships), peer acceptance, and social inclusion (Crick & Grotpeter, 1995). Similarly, while most studies of bullying focus on harm that occurs face-to-face or "in real life," a large and growing body of research highlights the harm associated with bullying that occurs via text message, social media, or other online or digital modalities (*cyberbullying*; Wright, 2018).

Estimates of the number of children and teens involved in bullying perpetration vary widely. A large multinational study found that about 11% of adolescents reported moderate to frequent involvement in offline bullying (Craig & Harel, 2004), whereas a more recent meta-analysis found the estimate to be considerably higher (about 35%; Modecki, Minchin, Harbaugh, Guerra, & Runions, 2014). Estimates of the prevalence of online or "cyber" bullying are typically lower (about 16% in the Modecki et al., 2014 meta-analysis). Further, these multiple forms of bullying often overlap. For example, adolescents who bully peers in person are likely to engage in cyberbullying as well (Kwan & Skoric, 2013; Pabian & Vandebosch, 2016). A study of German adolescents found that about half of the bullies identified in their sample used multiple forms of bullying (e.g., physical and relational; Scheithauer, Hayer, Petermann, & Jugert, 2006).

Bullying represents a dyadic relationship, clearly influenced by individual, family, and other factors, but embedded in the peer ecology (Pepler et al., 2006). As such, it both influences, and is influenced by, the behaviors and norms of the peer group. Rodkin and colleagues described bullying as an "asymmetric power relationship" between two peers that "unfolds over time and that potentially entangles others, such as bystanders" (Rodkin et al., 2015, p. 317). There are thus two important reciprocal influence processes at play. One is at the dyadic level, in which the bully and his or her victim shape each other's behavioral and psychosocial functioning over time. There is abundant evidence of the negative effects that bullies have on their victims (see Schwartz and colleagues, this volume). Less understood are the ways in which the victim's behaviors, either in general or in response to the bully's acts of aggression, influence the bully.

The other reciprocal influence process is at the broader level of the peer group, in which the bully's behavior affects peer group functioning while also being shaped by group norms (Rodkin et al., 2015). Most traditional or "offline" bullying occurs in the presence of peers (Hawkins, Pepler, & Craig, 2001), which puts witnesses in the position of having to decide how (and if) to respond. Further, because bullying is one way that peer groups reinforce social norms (Juvonen & Galván, 2008), peer group norms often support bullying behavior. Adolescents who are friends with each other often aggress against similar targets, suggesting another powerful source of peer group support for bullying (Card & Hodges, 2006). A recent meta-analysis found that peer influence-related variables, including peer reinforcement and associating with deviant peer networks, is the strongest contextual predictor of bullying behavior (Cook, Williams, Guerra, Kim, & Sadek, 2010).

Furthermore, bullying is affected by the overall school climate, including how much students feel their teachers and administrators care about their education and well-being (Espelage & Swearer, 2009). Bullying behavior is also linked to the level of aggression in the classroom, which can set a normative culture that supports bullying (Salmivalli & Voeten, 2004). Bullies also affect these elements of the peer ecology in a reciprocal fashion. For example, in schools where bullying is prevalent, students report feeling unsafe in poorly monitored spaces (Vaillancourt et al., 2010) and have poor perceptions of school safety and school climate that can negatively affect student behavior (Kasen, Berenson, Cohen, & Johnson, 2004).

Because it takes place in the digital world, cyberbullying operates somewhat differently from offline bullying, in terms of its effects on the peer ecology. In some instances, such as bullying via social media, the bully can choose to aggress against a victim in a very visible way. In these cases, the harm to victims can be amplified because the audience, and thus the reach, of the bullying is potentially infinite (Smith & Slonje,

2010). However, if the bully uses less public channels of communication, such as text or private messaging, it is not necessarily visible to other peers. Regardless of the method, digital bullies can aggress anonymously, minimizing the impact to themselves. Unlike traditional bullies, who see the effect of their actions, cyberbullies cannot witness the outcome of their bullying. As a result, unsurprisingly, cyberbullies typically underestimate the effect their bullying has on their victims (Campbell, Slee, Spears, Butler, & Kift, 2013).

As research on digital bullying is still emerging, we know little about the ways in which cyberbullying is embedded in the broader peer group. As with offline bullying, the effects of cyber victimization can be significant and multifaceted, ranging from depression and anxiety to substance use (Elgar et al., 2014). Similar to more traditional bullying, there is some evidence that cyberbullying behavior is influenced by perceived group norms about online aggression (Hinduja & Patchin, 2013; Sasson & Mesch, 2017). However, the extent to which cyberbullying involves enduring bully-victim relationships or affects peer group norms is unknown.

The Motivation to Bully

Early conceptualizations of bullies portrayed them as lacking in social intelligence or social skill (Crick & Dodge, 1994, 1999), but more recently, this view has been challenged. For example, bullies often score higher than their peers on perspective-taking tasks (Sutton, Smith, & Swettenham, 1999), and several studies have shown them to have good theory of mind skills (Smith, 2017). Despite common beliefs to the contrary, bullies do not lack empathy (Gini, 2006). In particular, it has been argued that bullies who use relational forms of aggression, which can involve the manipulation of individuals or entire peer groups, need strong social skills to be effective (Putallaz et al., 2007). Thus, rather than supporting a characterization of all bullies as oafish and unaware of the effects of their behavior on others, the extant literature suggests that bullies can be high in social and emotional intelligence (Peeters, Cillessen, & Scholte, 2010).

This conclusion begs a crucial question: If bullies understand the harm they do to their victims, why do they continue to bully? There are almost as many answers to this question as there are researchers studying it. Bullying has been viewed through the lenses of psychopathology (e.g., Golmaryami et al., 2016), parenting and family functioning (Nocentini et al., 2019), evolutionary psychology (Volk, Camilleri, Dane, & Marini, 2012), and social-ecological systems (Swearer Napolitano, Espelage, Vaillancourt, & Hymel, 2010), among many others. These differing perspectives have given us a rich understanding of the attitudes and motivations behind bullying behavior. Below, we summarize three key issues that play a role in bullying: social power, dating opportunities, and pro-bullying cognitive patterns.

Social Power

Researchers who study peer relations have identified multiple forms of peer status in middle-to-late childhood and adolescence (Rubin et al., 2015). One type of peer status is *social preference*, which is an indicator of peer acceptance and being well-liked by peers. Another is *popularity*, or social visibility and prestige, which is a measure of social power in the peer group (Mayeux, Houser, & Dyches, 2011). Though some youth are both well-liked and popular, social preference and popularity are distinct forms of status (e.g., Cillessen & Borch, 2006). A related construct is *coolness*, which is associated with having certain characteristics that are seen as desirable by peers (Bellmore, Villarreal, & Ho, 2011), and is more closely aligned with popularity than with social preference. Finally, some researchers have directly measured the peer group's perceptions of who has power (Vaillancourt, Hymel, & McDougall, 2003).

Bullies often have significant social power in the peer group. Bullying is correlated with popularity in both childhood and adolescence, and the association becomes stronger as children get older (Caravita & Cillessen, 2011; Caravita, Di Blasio, & Salmivalli, 2009). There is also a strong correlation between peer-nominated bullying and direct measures of power (Vaillancourt et al., 2003). Similarly, in a longitudinal study of middle school students, bullying in one school semester was associated with positive changes in cool status over time (Juvonen, Graham, & Schuster, 2003), suggesting that bullying predicts increased social status. Although there is currently very little research investigating the peer status of cyberbullies, a small number of studies have found positive links between popularity and digital bullying, particularly for girls (Badaly, Kelly, Schwartz, & Dabney-Lieras, 2013; Wright, 2014).

High-status bullies seem to be aware of the power their aggression affords them, and they behave in ways that perpetuate their own dominance. They tend to choose victims who are generally low in power and marginalized by the peer group (Hodges & Perry, 1999; Pellegrini, 1995) or who are submissive (Schwartz et al., 1998). In established bully-victim dyads that are recognized by the peer group, the bullies are seen by peers as having higher peer status than their victims (Rodkin, Hanish, Wang, & Logis, 2014). Furthermore, bullying incidents often take place in front of peers (Hawkins et al., 2001), which allows bullies to display their dominance to the peer group.

The distinction between being liked and being powerful is an important one, because the pattern of correlations between bullying and peer status suggest that some bullies may be willing to forego being liked in order to be popular. Bullies are typically not well-liked by peers (Caravita et al., 2009; Pellegrini, Bartini, & Brooks, 1999), particularly in childhood (Cook et al., 2010). Even popular bullies are more likely to be disliked by peers than are non-bullies (deBruyn, Cillessen, & Wissink, 2009). However, they often have reciprocated friendships, sometimes with other bullies (Pellegrini et al., 1999) and do not have trouble making friends (Nansel et al., 2001). They also report similar frequency of positive peer interactions compared to peers who are not involved in bullying at all (Andreou, Vlachou, & Didaskalou, 2005). Taken together, these findings suggest that some bullies enjoy significant social power in the peer group, and, while they may not be broadly well-liked, they do have friends. Given that many bullies enjoy social power and positive experiences with peers, they may perceive significant positive reinforcement for their aggressive behavior and feel little need to change it.

A final note regarding developmental trends is relevant. A recent meta-analysis indicates that while childhood bullies are often disliked or rejected, adolescent bullies are more likely to be well-accepted or popular (Cook et al., 2010). This is consistent with studies that have found negative correlations between aggression and peer acceptance in childhood, but non-significant or positive correlations between aggression and peer acceptance in adolescence (e.g., Cillessen & Mayeux, 2004). The function of aggressive behavior in the peer group undergoes a shift at the transition to adolescence, in part due to intensifying cross-sex peer interactions and competition for opposite-sex attention (Pellegrini & Long, 2003). This shift benefits bullies, in terms of their social power, their likeability among peers, and their potential as romantic partners.

Dating Opportunities

Bullying affords increased opportunities for dating. Evolutionary psychological perspectives argue that aggression plays a crucial role in sexual competition in adolescence. Boys who express physical dominance through aggression are more attractive to potential romantic partners (Volk et al., 2012). Mate value in adolescent girls is maximized by the use of indirect aggression that denigrates romantic rivals (Vaillancourt & Krems, 2018). Consistent with this view, physical aggression predicts dating behavior in sixth-grade boys (Pellegrini & Bartini, 2001), and relational aggression predicts dating in 11–14-year-olds of both genders, even controlling for attractiveness and popularity (Arnocky & Vaillancourt, 2012). Relational aggression has also been shown to predict increases in dating popularity over time for girls (Pellegrini & Long, 2003). Adolescent girls who are higher in overt physical and verbal forms of aggression are also more likely to report that they had a romantic partner than less aggressive girls (Miller et al., 2009).

Beyond links to aggressive behavior, romantic opportunities are associated with actual bullying as well. Bullies start dating at a younger age, engage in a wider variety of dating activities with their partners, and spend more non-school time with their dating partners than non-bullies (Connolly, Pepler, Craig, & Taradash, 2000). Physical bullying is associated with having more dating partners for boys, and relational bullying predicts more dating partners for girls (Dane, Marini, Volk,

& Vaillancourt, 2017). Bullying is also correlated with increased sexual opportunities. In one study of adolescents, a composite score reflecting physical, verbal, relational, sexual, and cyber forms of bullying was associated with a 1.5–2-fold increase in likelihood of having had sex (Volk et al., 2015). Dane and colleagues also found physical bullying to be linked to having had more sexual partners for adolescent boys (Dane et al., 2017).

Therefore, bullying may serve a valuable function for boys and girls in adolescence, when romantic and sexual interests are intensifying and opportunities for cross-sex interactions are more frequent (Bukowski, Sippola, & Newcomb, 2000). Bullies' aggressive behavior gets attention from others (Wilton & Campbell, 2011), allows them to engage in more effective competition for opposite-sex attention (Volk et al., 2012) and can increase their dating and sexual opportunities. These are powerful and high-impact benefits for adolescents: romantic relationships fulfill interpersonal needs for belonging, allow adolescents to explore their emerging identities as romantic and sexual beings, and can increase their social standing among peers (Connolly & McIsaac, 2011).

Pro-bullying Cognitive Patterns

Bullies have attitudes and cognitive biases that promote and sustain their bullying behavior toward peers. Bullies tend to have positive attitudes toward bullying behavior, even endorsing statements like "bullying may be fun sometimes" (Golmaryami et al., 2016; Pellegrini et al., 1999; van Goethem, Scholte, & Wiers, 2010). Bullies are also more likely to endorse retaliatory attitudes involving aggression, such as "it's okay to hit someone if they hit me first" (O'Brennan, Bradshaw, & Sawyer, 2009). There is some evidence that cyberbullies have similarly aggressogenic attitudes (Elledge et al., 2013). For example, one study of adolescent cyberbullies found that they underestimate the impact of their online aggression (Campbell et al., 2013).

Bullies also have self-views that maintain their aggressive behavior. A classic study by Björkqvist and colleagues showed that adolescent bullies view themselves as dominant and wish to be even more dominant

(Björkqvist, Ekman, & Lagerspetz, 1982). They have high self-efficacy for engaging in aggression (Andreou et al., 2005) and endorse goals related to the attainment of social status (Caravita & Cillessen, 2011; Sijtsema, Veenstra, Lindenberg, & Salmivalli, 2009).

Finally, studies have documented that while bullies do not lack empathy, their empathy does not inspire them to act in compassionate ways (Gini, Pozzoli, & Hauser, 2011). Bullies feel good about their harmful behaviors (Wilton & Campbell, 2011) and are able to morally disengage from their harmful behavior toward others (Gini, Pozzoli, & Hymel, 2014). Moral disengagement is the term given to several cognitive processes, such as blaming or dehumanizing the victim, that allow an individual to commit harmful acts against others while distancing themselves from guilt or self-recrimination. Moral disengagement can also allow bullies to reframe their aggression in a way that justifies it or makes it seem less harmful to the victim (Bandura, 2002). In one study, fourth- and eighth-grade bullies were more likely than victims or outsiders to evaluate a prototypical bullying scenario in terms of benefits to the bully rather than harm to the victim. The bullies in this study also tended to attribute feelings of pride to the hypothetical bully (Menesini et al., 2003). Moral disengagement processes that begin in the childhood or early adolescent years may intensify, becoming more automatic with time (Bandura, 2002). This might be one reason why young bullies are at increased risk of further delinquency and criminality as they get older (Hymel, Rocke-Henderson, & Bonanno, 2005).

Differences by Sex, Age, Race/Ethnicity, and Socioeconomic Status

Sex Differences

In general, boys engage in more bullying than girls do, including cyberbullying (Wang, Iannotti, & Nansel, 2009). Boys are more likely to self-report and are also identified by peers more often as bullies, both in childhood (e.g., Gini, 2006) and in adolescence (e.g., Caravita &

Cillessen, 2011; Espelage, Bosworth, & Simon, 2000). This sex difference holds even in studies that measure more stereotypically "female" behaviors, such as relational bullying (Scheithauer et al., 2006; Solberg & Olweus, 2003, but see also Wang et al., 2009, who found that girls were more likely than boys to be relational bullies). It is worth noting that sex differences obtained using observational methods are smaller in magnitude than those found in self- and peer-report studies (e.g., Craig & Pepler, 1997), suggesting that gender stereotypes and other biases may create overestimates of true sex differences. For example, peers in particular may subscribe to the belief that "girls manipulate and boys fight" (Björkqvist, Lagerspetz, & Kaukiainen, 1992, p. 117), and their nominations or ratings of peers may reflect those gender stereotypes. Similarly, boys and girls may be biased in their reporting of their own aggression, especially when the language used in self-report measures is gendered (e.g., boys may not think of their conversations about others as "gossip," since gossip is stereotypically feminine).

Developmental Differences

In terms of age differences, studies suggest that bullying, including cyberbullying, becomes more prevalent at the transition to adolescence (Pellegrini & Long, 2002), peaking in middle school and declining across the high school years (Nansel et al., 2001; Olweus, 1993). During the early adolescent years, peer status concerns become more salient (LaFontana & Cillessen, 2010), and romantic interests intensify (Connolly & McIsaac, 2011), which likely contribute to adolescents' increased aggression as peers compete for social status and romantic attention. It has also been shown that bullying increases after school transitions and then declines (Pellegrini & Long, 2002), suggesting that there is some renegotiation of the status hierarchy as adolescents begin middle school. Bullying is an effective means of establishing dominance over peers in a new, larger school context; once those dominance relationships have been established, adolescents can dial back their levels of aggression (Pellegrini & Long, 2002).

Racial/Ethnic Differences

Studies addressing racial and ethnic differences in bullying perpetration yield inconsistent findings. In one large-scale study, Hispanic youth reported slightly higher rates of bullying compared to White and Black youth (Nansel et al., 2001). Other studies of racially and ethnically diverse schools find that Black students are more likely to be bullies than Hispanic students (Juvonen et al., 2003; Peskin, Tortolero, & Markham, 2006). For example, a study of verbal and relational bullying in racially diverse middle schools found that Black students were more likely to engage in bullying compared to students of other race/ethnicities (Espelage, Hong, Kim, & Nan, 2018). Another study of a large, diverse, nationally representative sample found that Black adolescents were more involved in physical, verbal, and cyberbullying compared to White and Hispanic youth (Wang et al., 2009). However, other studies find no differences by race or ethnicity (e.g., Seals & Young, 2003). Given the limited evidence, it is difficult to draw conclusions about racial and ethnic differences in bullying.

Socioeconomic Differences

A number of socioeconomic factors have been identified as risk factors for bullying. Family hardship such as financial difficulties and family instability are risk factors (Copeland, Wolke, Angold, & Costello, 2013), as is being a part of a single-parent family (Jansen, Veenstra, Ormel, Verhulst, & Reijneveld, 2011). Adolescents who report spending the most time without adults present are more likely to bully others, as are those who expressed concerns about the safety of their neighborhood (Espelage et al., 2000). While these and other family-related factors (such as parental conflict or authoritarian parenting) have been shown to correlate with bullying perpetration, causal links have not been established (Cook et al., 2010). Further, these studies have typically focused on physical and verbal bullying. It is unclear whether these factors also increase risk for relational bullying and cyberbullying.

Effects on Adjustment

Bullies often have friends, are embedded within social networks, and have considerable social power among their peers (Caravita et al., 2009; Pellegrini et al., 1999). Thus, while some bullies are generally disliked by peers, they often enjoy the benefits of having social status and prominence in the peer group (Juvonen et al., 2003). At the same time, bullying is associated with significant risk of other forms of maladjustment. Compared to their non-bullying peers, bullies experience poorer adjustment outcomes and are at risk for a variety of mental and physical health risks. For example, bullying is associated with both internalizing and externalizing problems. Furthermore, there are developmental patterns evident in these risks. Bullies are more likely than their peers to exhibit externalizing behaviors such as getting into fights or being disruptive in school, and they report more expressions of anger (e.g., Golmaryami et al., 2016). These associations are often stronger in childhood than adolescence (Cook et al., 2010; Kumpulainen et al., 1998), suggesting a possible role for delayed emotion- or self-regulatory processes in bullies. Bullying is also linked to internalizing distress, such as anxiety (Baldry, 2004), depression (Espelage & Swearer, 2009) and psychosomatic symptoms (Gini & Pozzoli, 2009), but these links are stronger in adolescence than childhood (Cook et al., 2010). This age-related pattern may be due to greater social cognitive skills among adolescents compared to children; perhaps adolescent bullies become more aware of their general disliking by peers (deBruyn et al., 2009). Bullying perpetration is associated with higher risk of suicidal ideation (Hinduja & Patchin, 2010) and with poorer academic adjustment (Nansel et al., 2001; Nansel, Haynie, & Simons-Morton, 2003).

Bullying is also linked to health-risk-taking behaviors and harmful relationship patterns. For example, adolescent bullies are at increased risk of smoking, alcohol use, and drug use (Espelage & Swearer, 2009; Nansel et al., 2001). They also report more sexual risk-taking, such as casual sex and sex under the influence of drugs and alcohol (Holt, Matjasko, Espelage, Reid, & Koenig, 2013). Adolescent bullies are more likely to report engaging in physical and relational forms of dating aggression with romantic partners (Pepler et al., 2006), and they report lower romantic relationship quality (Connolly et al., 2000). Finally, bullying early in middle school predicts sexual harassment perpetration two years later for boys (Espelage, Basile, Rue, & Hamburger, 2015).

Longer-term longitudinal studies suggest that bullying predicts continued externalizing problems. Bullies are at higher risk of later delinquency and criminality, particularly if the bullying behavior emerges in early to middle childhood (Bender & Lösel, 2011; Olweus, 1993). The mechanism by which bullying is linked to long-term problem behaviors may lie in personality features. For example, being a bully is linked to callous-unemotional traits (e.g., a lack of empathy, guilt, or remorse after harming others; Golmaryami et al., 2016; Viding, Simmonds, Petrides, & Frederickson, 2009) and psychopathy (Fanti & Kimonis, 2012). In support of this pattern, bullying is also associated with an adult diagnosis of antisocial personality disorder (Copeland et al., 2013).

Emerging research suggests that perpetrating cyberbullying is associated with similar outcomes as more traditional forms of bullying. Cyberbullying is associated with depression (Wang, Nansel, & Iannotti, 2011), and uniquely predicts symptoms of depression and suicidal thoughts over and above engaging in physical, verbal, or relational bullying (Bonanno & Hymel, 2013). Cyberbullies, compared with peers not involved in cyberbullying as bullies or victims, report more internalizing, externalizing, and relationship problems (Campbell et al., 2013). Thus, digital and online forms of bullying clearly confer psychosocial risk, and the extant literature suggests that cyberbullies may face more internalizing problems than externalizing behaviors.

Implications for Prevention and Intervention

Bullying prevention and intervention has become a key focus of school resources in countries all over the world (e.g., Ttofi & Farrington, 2011). Anti-bullying curricula, training, and implementation can cost individual school districts thousands of dollars and many hours of staff time. Thus, evidence-based programs that take into account the group dynamics of bullies, victims, bystanders, and other bully roles, as well as the roles of school staff and other elements of the school ecology, are crucial in order for prevention and intervention to be effective.

From the perspective of the bullies themselves, preventing and intervening in bullying perpetration is difficult due to several converging factors. First, bullies often have significant social power, feel connected to peers, and are not lonely (e.g., Vaillancourt et al., 2003). Given how important peer status becomes at the transition to adolescence (LaFontana & Cillessen, 2010), convincing youth to stop engaging in a behavior that brings them considerable social prestige is a tall order, at least for those bullies who enjoy positive relationships with peers. The fact that bullying is also associated with dating opportunities compounds this issue (Dane et al., 2017). Second, bullies report that bullying others makes them feel good (Wilton & Campbell, 2011), and their cognitive biases support harmful behavior directed at others (van Goethem et al., 2010). Youth who derive positive feelings from bullying others, however short-lived the feelings may be, experience a powerful form of reinforcement for their harmful behavior. Finally, bullies are able to cognitively distance themselves from the harm they do their peers (Gini et al., 2014), greatly reducing any realistic, negative feedback from victims that might lead to positive change. Taken together, the social and emotional rewards for bullying, coupled with the moral disengagement that prevents bullies from having to face the extent of the harm they do their victims, support the development of a pattern of behavior that is difficult to interrupt.

Based on these findings, prevention and intervention programs that focus on ecological supports for bullying, such as the peer group and school climate, may be more effective than programs that focus on bullies (Vaillancourt et al., 2003). Convincing bullies to be kinder when being unkind is working just fine may be a losing battle. But creating a school environment that empowers the peer group to stand up to bullies may be more effective, especially if "standing up" means removing social reinforcers like power, peer status, and positive attention (see Fredrick and colleagues, this volume).

Conclusions and Future Directions for Research

Bullying is a pattern of targeted, chronic aggressive behavior toward peers of less power (Olweus, 1994). It creates long-term problems for both victim and perpetrator and both affects, and is affected, by the overall peer ecology in harmful ways (Rodkin et al., 2015). Bullies are reinforced for their harmful behavior via social, emotional, and cognitive rewards, and thus intervention efforts present significant challenges (e.g., Cook et al., 2010). Despite enormous advances in our understanding of more traditional verbal, physical, and relational bullying, the study of digital and cyberbullying is still developing. As the means by which children and adolescents communicate with each other change, so too must our research questions.

A major emerging issue for researchers is how bullying will continue to be affected by social media usage. With about 85% of American teenagers using some form of social media, understanding the potential harms associated with its use is crucial (Lenhart et al., 2011). Models such as the *transformation framework*, which views peer interactions through seven paradigms that coincide with social media usage—availability, publicness, permanence, visualness, cue absence, asynchonicty, and quantifiability—are proving useful in capturing the fundamental differences between traditional and cyberbullying (Nesi, Choukas-Bradley, & Prinstein, 2018). Negative face-to-face interactions that were once brief or temporary are now continuous, as bullies can take to a constantly available platform that victims cannot escape. Additionally, bullies can establish a vast social media presence through a larger "follower" platform, placing interactions on an amplified stage with a larger audience and more opportunities for bullying to occur (Sticca & Perren, 2013). Though we are better understanding the differences between traditional and cyberbullying, we as yet have only a basic understanding of how those differences might play out in terms of social and emotional outcomes for bullies.

For example, the anonymity of the bully has been shown to be a key factor in cyberbullying, but there is also research indicating that online selves are connected to offline selves, and therefore rarely anonymous (Wynn & Katz, 1997). In a study by Mishna, Saini, and Solomon (2009), students reported that most of their online bullying took place within their own social groups and relationships, rather than targeting more marginalized peers. Importantly, cyberbullying by a known peer is perceived as more harmful than cyberbullying by an unknown person (Whittaker & Kowalski, 2015). Thus, the identifiableness of known individuals on social media might mean that online bullying is even more hurtful than we realize, because the aggression is more directly personal and intentional. Teasing apart the causes and outcomes associated with these various configurations of online bullies and victims is an important goal.

Finally, a consistent trend in social media is that users are becoming younger and younger. Upwards of 73% of 8- to 18-year-olds use a social network site for half an hour per day or more (Lenhart, Ling, Campbell, & Purcell, 2010; Rideout, Foehr, & Roberts, 2010). These statistics will likely only increase as social media become more ubiquitous and families view mobile devices as a way to keep in touch and monitor child safety (Devitt & Roker, 2009). However, at the same time social media users are becoming younger, parents are further and further removed from cyber communication norms (Mishna et al., 2009), meaning that children are increasingly likely to engage with peers in online spaces that are unmonitored by parents or other safe adults. The effects of this mismatch on cyberbullying behavior is an important avenue for future research.

References

Andreou, E., Vlachou, A., & Didaskalou, E. (2005). The roles of self-efficacy, peer interactions and attitudes in bully-victim incidents: Implications for intervention policy-practices. *School Psychology International, 26,* 545–562. https://doi.org/10.1177/0143034305060789.

Arnocky, S., & Vaillancourt, T. (2012). A multi-informant longitudinal study on the relationship between aggression, peer victimization, and dating status in adolescence. *Evolutionary Psychology, 10,* 253–270. https://doi.org/10.1177/147470491201000207.

Badaly, D., Kelly, B. M., Schwartz, D., & Dabney-Lieras, K. (2013). Longitudinal associations of electronic aggression and victimization with social standing during adolescence. *Journal of Youth and Adolescence, 42,* 891–904. https://doi.org/10.1007/s10964-012-9787-2.

Baldry, A. C. (2004). The impact of direct and indirect bullying on the mental and physical health of Italian youngsters. *Aggressive Behavior, 30,* 343–355. https://doi.org/10.1002/ab.20043.

Bandura, A. (2002). Selective moral disengagement in the exercise of moral agency. *Journal of Moral Education, 31,* 101–119. https://doi.org/10.1080/0305724022014322.

Bellmore, A., Villarreal, V. M., & Ho, A. Y. (2011). Staying cool across the first year of middle school. *Journal of Youth and Adolescence, 40,* 776–785. https://doi.org/10.1007/s10964-010-9590-x.

Bender, D., & Lösel, F. (2011). Bullying at school as a predictor of delinquency, violence and other anti-social behaviour in adulthood. *Criminal Behaviour and Mental Health, 21,* 99–106. https://doi.org/10.1002/cbm.799.

Björkqvist, K., Ekman, K., & Lagerspetz, K. (1982). Bullies and victims: Their ego picture, ideal ego picture and normative ego picture. *Scandinavian Journal of Psychology, 23,* 307–313. https://doi.org/10.1111/j.1467-9450.1982.tb00445.x.

Björkqvist, K., Lagerspetz, K. M., & Kaukiainen, A. (1992). Do girls manipulate and boys fight? Developmental trends in regard to direct and indirect aggression. *Aggressive Behavior, 18,* 117–127. https://doi.org/10.1002/1098-2337(1992)18:2%3c117:AID-AB2480180205%3e3.0.CO;2-3.

Bonanno, R. A., & Hymel, S. (2013). Cyber bullying and internalizing difficulties: Above and beyond the impact of traditional forms of bullying. *Journal of Youth and Adolescence, 42,* 685–697. https://doi.org/10.1007/s10964-013-9937-1.

Bukowski, W. M., Sippola, L. K., & Newcomb, A. F. (2000). Variations in patterns of attraction of same- and other-sex peers during early adolescence. *Developmental Psychology, 36,* 147–154. https://doi.org/10.1037/0012-1649.36.2.147.

Campbell, M. A., Slee, P. T., Spears, B., Butler, D., & Kift, S. (2013). Do cyberbullies suffer too? Cyberbullies' perceptions of the harm they cause to others and to their own mental health. *School Psychology International, 34,* 613–629. https://doi.org/10.1177/0143034313479698.

Caravita, S. C. S., & Cillessen, A. H. N. (2011). Agentic or communal? Associations between interpersonal goals, popularity, and bullying in middle childhood and early adolescence. *Social Development, 21,* 376–395. https://doi.org/10.1111/j.1467-9507.2011.00632.x.

Caravita, S. C. S., Di Blasio, P., & Salmivalli, C. (2009). Unique and interactive effects of empathy and social status on involvement in bullying. *Social Development, 18,* 140–163. https://doi.org/10.1111/j.1467-9507.2008.00465.x.

Card, N. A., & Hodges, E. V. (2006). Shared targets for aggression by early adolescent friends. *Developmental Psychology, 42,* 1327–1338. https://doi.org/10.1037/0012-1649.42.6.1327.

Cillessen, A. H., & Borch, C. (2006). Developmental trajectories of adolescent popularity: A growth curve modelling analysis. *Journal of Adolescence, 29,* 935–959. https://doi.org/10.1016/j.adolescence.2006.05.005.

Cillessen, A. H., & Mayeux, L. (2004). From censure to reinforcement: Developmental changes in the association between aggression and social status. *Child Development, 75,* 147–163. https://doi.org/10.1111/j.1467-8624.2004.00660.x.

Connolly, J., & McIsaac, C. (2011). Romantic relationships in adolescence. In M. K. Underwood & L. H. Rosen (Eds.), *Social development: Relationships in infancy, childhood, and adolescence* (pp. 180–203). New York: Guilford Press.

Connolly, J., Pepler, D., Craig, W., & Taradash, A. (2000). Dating experiences of bullies in early adolescence. *Child Maltreatment, 5,* 299–310. https://doi.org/10.1177/1077559500005004002.

Cook, C. R., Williams, K. R., Guerra, N. G., Kim, T. E., & Sadek, S. (2010). Predictors of bullying and victimization in childhood and adolescence: A meta-analytic investigation. *School Psychology, 25,* 65–83. https://doi.org/10.1037/a0020149.

Copeland, W. E., Wolke, D., Angold, A., & Costello, E. J. (2013). Adult psychiatric outcomes of bullying and being bullied by peers in childhood and adolescence. *JAMA Psychiatry, 70,* 419–426. https://doi.org/10.1001/jamapsychiatry.2013.504.

Craig, W. M., & Harel, Y. (2004). Bullying, physical fighting and victimization. In C. Currie, C. Roberts, A. Morgan, R. Smith, W. Settertobulte, O. Samdal, et al. (Eds.), *Young people's health in context: International report from the HBSC 2001/02 survey. WHO policy series: Health policy for children and adolescents* (pp. 134–144). Copenhagen: WHO Regional Office for Europe.

Craig, W., & Pepler, D. J. (1997). Observations of bullying and victimization in the schoolyard. *Canadian Journal of School Psychology, 13,* 41–60. https://doi.org/10.1177/082957359801300205.

Crick, N. R., & Dodge, K. A. (1994). A review and reformulation of social information-processing mechanisms in children's social adjustment. *Psychological Bulletin, 115,* 74–101. https://doi.org/10.1037/0033-2909.115.1.74.

Crick, N. R., & Dodge, K. A. (1999). 'Superiority' is in the eye of the beholder: A comment on Sutton, Smith, and Swettenham. *Social Development, 8,* 128–131. https://doi.org/10.1111/1467-9507.00084.

Crick, N. R., & Grotpeter, J. K. (1995). Relational aggression, gender, and social-psychological adjustment. *Child Development, 66,* 710–722. https://doi.org/10.1111/j.1467-8624.1995.tb00900.x.

Dane, A. V., Marini, Z. A., Volk, A. A., & Vaillancourt, T. (2017). Physical and relational bullying and victimization: Differential relations with adolescent dating and sexual behavior. *Aggressive Behavior, 43,* 111–122. https://doi.org/10.1002/ab.21667.

deBruyn, E. H., Cillessen, A. H., & Wissink, I. B. (2009). Associations of peer acceptance and perceived popularity with bullying and victimization in early adolescence. *The Journal of Early Adolescence, 30,* 543–566. https://doi.org/10.1177/0272431609340517.

Devitt, K., & Roker, D. (2009). The role of mobile phones in family communication. *Children and Society, 23,* 189–202. https://doi.org/10.1111/j.1099-0860.2008.00166.x.

Elgar, F. J., Napoletano, A., Saul, G., Dirks, M. A., Craig, W. M., Poteat, P. V. …, Koenig, B. W. (2014). Cyberbullying victimization and mental health in adolescents and the moderating role of family dinners. *JAMA Pediatrics, 168,* 1015–1022. https://doi.org/10.1001/jamapediatrics.2014.1223.

Elledge, L. C., Williford, A., Boulton, A. J., DePaolis, K. J., Little, T. D., & Salmivalli, C. (2013). Individual and contextual predictors of cyberbullying: The influence of children's provictim attitudes and teachers' ability to intervene. *Journal of Youth and Adolescence, 42,* 698–710. https://doi.org/10.1007/s10964-013-9920-x.

Espelage, D. L., Basile, K. C., Rue, D. L., & Hamburger, M. E. (2015). Longitudinal associations among bullying, homophobic teasing, and sexual violence perpetration among middle school students. *Journal of Interpersonal Violence, 30,* 2541–2561. https://doi.org/10.1177/0886260514553113.

Espelage, D. L., Bosworth, K., & Simon, T. R. (2000). Examining the social context of bullying behaviors in early adolescence. *Journal of Counseling & Development, 78,* 326–333. https://doi.org/10.1002/j.1556-6676.2000.tb01914.x.

Espelage, D. L., Hong, J. S., Kim, D. H., & Nan, L. (2018). Empathy, attitude towards bullying, theory-of-mind, and non-physical forms of bully perpetration and victimization among US middle school students. *Child & Youth Care Forum, 47,* 45–60. https://doi.org/10.1007/s10566-017-9416-z.

Espelage, D. L., & Swearer, S. M. (2009). Contributions of three social theories to understanding bullying perpetration and victimization among school-aged youth. In M. J. Harris (Ed.), *Bullying, rejection, and peer victimization: A social cognitive neuroscience perspective* (pp. 151–170). New York: Springer.

Fanti, K. A., & Kimonis, E. R. (2012). Bullying and victimization: The role of conduct problems and psychopathic traits. *Journal of Research on Adolescence, 22,* 617–631. https://doi.org/10.1111/j.1532-7795.2012.00809.x.

Gini, G. (2006). Social cognition and moral cognition in bullying: What's wrong? *Aggressive Behavior, 32,* 528–539. https://doi.org/10.1002/ab.20153.

Gini, G., & Pozzoli, T. (2009). Association between bullying and psychosomatic problems: A meta-analysis. *Pediatrics, 123,* 1059–1065. https://doi.org/10.1542/peds.2008-1215.

Gini, G., Pozzoli, T., & Hauser, M. (2011). Bullies have enhanced moral competence to judge relative to victims, but lack moral compassion. *Personality and Individual Differences, 50,* 603–608. https://doi.org/10.1016/j.paid.2010.12.002.

Gini, G., Pozzoli, T., & Hymel, S. (2014). Moral disengagement among children and youth: A meta-analytic review of links to aggressive behavior. *Aggressive Behavior, 40,* 56–68. https://doi.org/10.1002/ab.21502.

Golmaryami, F. N., Frick, P. J., Hemphill, S. A., Kahn, R. E., Crapanzano, A. M., & Terranova, A. M. (2016). The social, behavioral, and emotional correlates of bullying and victimization in a school-based sample. *Journal of Abnormal Child Psychology, 44,* 381–391. https://doi.org/10.1007/s10802-015-9994-x.

Hawkins, D. L., Pepler, D. J., & Craig, W. M. (2001). Naturalistic observations of peer interventions in bullying. *Social Development, 10,* 512–527. https://doi.org/10.1111/1467-9507.00178.

Hinduja, S., & Patchin, J. W. (2010). Bullying, cyberbullying, and suicide. *Archives of Suicide Research, 14,* 206–221. https://doi.org/10.1080/13811118.2010.494133.

Hinduja, S., & Patchin, J. W. (2013). Social influences on cyberbullying behaviors among middle and high school students. *Journal of Youth and Adolescence, 42,* 711–722. https://doi.org/10.1007/s10964-012-9902-4.

Hodges, E. V., & Perry, D. G. (1999). Personal and interpersonal antecedents and consequences of victimization by peers. *Journal of Personality and Social Psychology, 76,* 677. https://doi.org/10.1037//0022-3514.76. 4.677&%23xB7.
Holt, M. K., Matjasko, J. L., Espelage, D., Reid, G., & Koenig, B. (2013). Sexual risk taking and bullying among adolescents. *Pediatrics, 132,* e1481–e1487. https://doi.org/10.1542/peds.2013-0401.
Hymel, S., Rocke-Henderson, N., & Bonanno, R. A. (2005). Moral disengagement: A framework for understanding bullying among adolescents. *Journal of Social Sciences, 8,* 1–11.
Jansen, D. E., Veenstra, R., Ormel, J., Verhulst, F. C., & Reijneveld, S. A. (2011). Early risk factors for being a bully, victim, or bully/victim in late elementary and early secondary education. The longitudinal TRAILS study. *BMC Public Health, 11,* 440. https://doi.org/10.1186/1471-2458-11-440.
Juvonen, J., & Galván, A. (2008). Peer influence in involuntary social groups: Lessons from research on bullying. In M. J. Prinstein & K. A. Dodge (Eds.), *Understanding peer influence in children and adolescents* (pp. 225–244). New York: Guilford Press.
Juvonen, J., & Graham, S. (2014). Bullying in schools: The power of bullies and the plight of victims. *Annual Review of Psychology, 65,* 159–185. https://doi.org/10.1146/annurev-psych-010213-115030.
Juvonen, J., Graham, S., & Schuster, M. A. (2003). Bullying among young adolescents: The strong, the weak, and the troubled. *Pediatrics-English Edition, 112,* 1231–1237. https://doi.org/10.1542/peds.112.6.1231.
Kasen, S., Berenson, K., Cohen, P., & Johnson, J. G. (2004). The effects of school climate on changes in aggressive and other behaviors related to bullying. In D. L. Espelage, & S. M. Swearer (Eds.), *Bullying in American schools: A social-ecological perspective on prevention and intervention* (pp. 187–210). Mahwah: Lawrence Erlbaum Associates Publishers.
Kumpulainen, K., Räsänen, E., Henttonen, I., Almqvist, F., Kresanov, K., Linna, S. ..., Tamminen, T. (1998). Bullying and psychiatric symptoms among elementary school-age children. *Child Abuse & Neglect, 22*(7), 705–717. https://doi.org/10.1016/S0145-2134(98)00049-0.
Kwan, G. C. E., & Skoric, M. M. (2013). Facebook bullying: An extension of battles in school. *Computers in Human Behavior, 29,* 16–25. https://doi.org/10.1016/j.chb.2012.07.014.
LaFontana, K. M., & Cillessen, A. H. (2010). Developmental changes in the priority of perceived status in childhood and adolescence. *Social Development, 19,* 130–147. https://doi.org/10.1111/j.1467-9507.2008.00522.x.

Lenhart, A., Ling, R., Campbell, S., & Purcell, K. (2010). Teens and mobile phones: Text messaging explodes as teens embrace it as the centerpiece of their communication strategies with friends. *Pew Internet & American Life Project.* https://www.pewinternet.org/2010/04/20/teens-and-mobile-phones/.

Lenhart, A., Madden, M., Smith, A., Purcell, K., Zickuhr, K., & Rainie, L. (2011). Teens, kindness and cruelty on social network sites: How American teens navigate the new world of digital Citizenship. *Pew Internet & American Life Project.* https://www.pewinternet.org/2011/11/09/teens-kindness-and-cruelty-on-social-network-sites/.

Mayeux, L., Houser, J. J., & Dyches, K. D. (2011). Social acceptance and popularity: Two distinct forms of peer status. In A. H. N. Cillessen, D. Schwartz, & L. Mayeux (Eds.), *Popularity in the peer system* (pp. 79–102). New York: Guilford Press.

Menesini, E., Sanchez, V., Fonzi, A., Ortega, R., Costabile, A., & Lo Feudo, G. (2003). Moral emotions and bullying: A cross-national comparison of differences between bullies, victims and outsiders. *Aggressive Behavior, 29,* 515–530. https://doi.org/10.1002/ab.10060.

Miller, S., Lansford, J. E., Costanzo, P., Malone, P. S., Golonka, M., & Killeya-Jones, L. A. (2009). Early adolescent romantic partner status, peer standing, and problem behaviors. *The Journal of Early Adolescence, 29,* 839–861. https://doi.org/10.1177/0272431609332665.

Mishna, F., Saini, M., & Solomon, S. (2009). Ongoing and online: Children and youth's perceptions of cyber bullying. *Children and Youth Services Review, 31,* 1222–1228. https://doi.org/10.1016/j.childyouth.2009.05.004.

Modecki, K. L., Minchin, J., Harbaugh, A. G., Guerra, N. G., & Runions, K. C. (2014). Bullying prevalence across contexts: A meta-analysis measuring cyber and traditional bullying. *Journal of Adolescent Health, 55,* 602–611. https://doi.org/10.1016/j.jadohealth.2014.06.007.

Nansel, T. R., Haynie, D. L., & Simons-Morton, B. (2003). The association of bullying and victimization with middle school adjustment. *Journal of Applied School Psychology, 19,* 45–61. https://doi.org/10.1300/J008v19n02_04.

Nansel, T. R., Overpeck, M., Pilla, R. S., Ruan, W. J., Simons-Morton, B., & Scheidt, P. (2001). Bullying behaviors among US youth: Prevalence and association with psychosocial adjustment. *JAMA: Journal of the American Medical Association, 285,* 2094–2100. https://doi.org/10.1001/jama.285.16.2094.

Nesi, J., Choukas-Bradley, S., & Prinstein, M. J. (2018). Transformation of adolescent peer relations in the social media context: Part 1—A theoretical framework and application to dyadic peer relationships. *Clinical Child and Family Psychology Review, 21,* 267–294. https://doi.org/10.1007/s10 567-018-0261-x.

Nocentini, A., Fiorentini, G., Di Paola, L., & Menesini, E. (2019). Parents, family characteristics and bullying behavior: A systematic review. *Aggression and Violent Behavior, 45,* 41–50. https://doi.org/10.1016/j.avb.2018. 07.010.

O'Brennan, L. M., Bradshaw, C. P., & Sawyer, A. L. (2009). Examining development differences in the social-emotional problems among frequent bullies, victims, and bully/victims. *Psychology in the Schools, 46,* 100–115. https://doi.org/10.1002/pits.20357.

Olweus, D. (1978). *Aggression in the schools: Bullies and whipping boys.* Washington: Hemisphere.

Olweus, D. (1993). Bully/victim problems among schoolchildren: Long-term consequences and an effective intervention program. In S. Hodgins (Ed.), *Mental disorder and crime* (pp. 317–349). Newbury Park: Sage.

Olweus D. (1994). Bullying at School. In Huesmann L.R. (Ed.), *Aggressive behavior.* Springer. https://doi.org/10.1007/978-1-4757-9116-7_5.

Pabian, S., & Vandebosch, H. (2016). Developmental trajectories of (cyber)bullying perpetration and social intelligence during early adolescence. *The Journal of Early Adolescence, 36,* 145–170. https://doi.org/10.1177/027 2431614556891.

Peeters, M., Cillessen, A. H., & Scholte, R. H. (2010). Clueless or powerful? Identifying subtypes of bullies in adolescence. *Journal of Youth and Adolescence, 39,* 1041–1052. https://doi.org/10.1007/s10964-009-9478-9.

Pellegrini, A. D. (1995). A longitudinal study of boys' rough-and-tumble play and dominance during early adolescence. *Journal of Applied Developmental Psychology, 16,* 77–93. https://doi.org/10.1016/0193-3973(95)90017-9.

Pellegrini, A. D., & Bartini, M. (2001). Dominance in early adolescent boys: Affiliative and aggressive dimensions and possible functions. *Merrill-Palmer Quarterly, 47,* 142–163. https://doi.org/10.1353/mpq.2001.0004.

Pellegrini, A. D., Bartini, M., & Brooks, F. (1999). School bullies, victims, and aggressive victims: Factors relating to group affiliation and victimization in early adolescence. *Journal of Educational Psychology, 91,* 216–224. https://doi.org/10.1037/0022-0663.91.2.216.

Pellegrini, A. D., & Long, J. D. (2002). A longitudinal study of bullying, dominance, and victimization during the transition from primary school through secondary school. *British Journal of Developmental Psychology, 20,* 259–280. https://doi.org/10.1348/026151002166442.

Pellegrini, A. D., & Long, J. D. (2003). A sexual selection theory longitudinal analysis of sexual segregation and integration in early adolescence. *Journal of Experimental Child Psychology, 85,* 257–278. https://doi.org/10.1016/S0022-0965(03)00060-2.

Pepler, D. J., Craig, W. M., Connolly, J. A., Yuile, A., McMaster, L., & Jiang, D. (2006). A developmental perspective on bullying. *Aggressive Behavior, 32,* 376–384. https://doi.org/10.1002/ab.20136.

Peskin, M. F., Tortolero, S. R., & Markham, C. M. (2006). Bullying and victimization among Black and Hispanic adolescents. *Adolescence, 41,* 467–484.

Putallaz, M., Grimes, C. L., Foster, K. J., Kupersmidt, J. B., Coie, J. D., & Dearing, K. (2007). Overt and relational aggression and victimization: Multiple perspectives within the school setting. *Journal of School Psychology, 45,* 523–547. https://doi.org/10.1016/j.jsp.2007.05.003.

Rideout, V. J., Foehr, U. G., & Roberts, D. F. (2010). *Generation M 2: Media in the Lives of 8-to 18-Year-Olds.* Henry J. Kaiser Family Foundation. https://files.eric.ed.gov/fulltext/ED527859.pdf.

Rodkin, P. C., Espelage, D. L., & Hanish, L. D. (2015). A relational framework for understanding bullying: Developmental antecedents and outcomes. *American Psychologist, 70,* 311–321. https://doi.org/10.1037/a0038658.

Rodkin, P. C., Hanish, L. D., Wang, S., & Logis, H. A. (2014). Why the bully/victim relationship is so pernicious: A gendered perspective on power and animosity among bullies and their victims. *Development and Psychopathology, 26,* 689–704. https://doi.org/10.1017/S0954579414000327.

Rubin, K. H., Bukowski, W. M., & Bowker, J. C. (2015). Children in peer groups. In *Handbook of Child Psychology and Developmental Science* (pp. 1–48). https://doi.org/10.1002/9781118963418.childpsy405.

Salmivalli, C. (2010). Bullying and the peer group: A review. *Aggression and Violent Behavior, 15,* 112–120. https://doi.org/10.1016/j.avb.2009.08.007.

Salmivalli, C., Lagerspetz, K., Björkqvist, K., Österman, K., & Kaukiainen, A. (1996). Bullying as a group process: Participant roles and their relations to social status within the group. *Aggressive Behavior, 22,* 1–15. https://doi.org/10.1002/(SICI)1098-2337(1996)22:1%3c1::AID-AB1%3e3.0.CO;2-T.

Salmivalli, C., & Voeten, M. (2004). Connections between attitudes, group norms, and behaviour in bullying situations. *International Journal of Behavioral Development, 28,* 246–258. https://doi.org/10.1080/01650250344000488.

Sasson, H., & Mesch, G. (2017). The role of parental mediation and peer norms on the likelihood of cyberbullying. *The Journal of Genetic Psychology, 178,* 15–27. https://doi.org/10.1080/00221325.2016.1195330.

Scheithauer, H., Hayer, T., Petermann, F., & Jugert, G. (2006). Physical, verbal, and relational forms of bullying among German students: Age trends, gender differences, and correlates. *Aggressive Behavior, 32,* 261–275. https://doi.org/10.1002/ab.20128.

Schwartz, D., Dodge, K. A., Coie, J. D., Hubbard, J. A., Cillessen, A. H., Lemerise, E. A., et al. (1998). Social-cognitive and behavioral correlates of aggression and victimization in boys' play groups. *Journal of Abnormal Child Psychology, 26,* 431–440. https://doi.org/10.1023/A:1022695601088.

Seals, D., & Young, J. (2003). Bullying and victimization: Prevalence and relationship to gender, grade level, ethnicity, self-esteem, and depression. *Adolescence, 38,* 735–747.

Sijtsema, J. J., Veenstra, R., Lindenberg, S., & Salmivalli, C. (2009). Empirical test of bullies' status goals: Assessing direct goals, aggression, and prestige. *Aggressive Behavior, 35,* 57–67. https://doi.org/10.1002/ab.20282.

Smith, P. K. (2017). Bullying and theory of mind: A review. *Current Psychiatry Reviews, 13,* 90–95. https://doi.org/10.2174/1573400513666170502123214.

Smith, P. K., & Slonje, R. (2010). Cyberbullying: The nature and extent of a new kind of bullying, in and out of school. In S. Jimerson, S. Swearer, & D. Espelage (Eds.), *The international handbook of school bullying* (pp. 249–262). New York: Routledge.

Solberg, M. E., & Olweus, D. (2003). Prevalence estimation of school bullying with the Olweus bully/victim questionnaire. *Aggressive Behavior, 29,* 239–268. https://doi.org/10.1002/ab.10047.

Sticca, F., & Perren, S. (2013). Is cyberbullying worse than traditional bullying? Examining the differential roles of medium, publicity, and anonymity for the perceived severity of bullying. *Journal of Youth and Adolescence, 42,* 739–750. https://doi.org/10.1007/s10964-012-9867-3.

Sutton, J., Smith, P. K., & Swettenham, J. (1999). Social cognition and bullying: Social inadequacy or skilled manipulation? *British Journal of Developmental Psychology, 17,* 435–450. https://doi.org/10.1348/026151099165384.

Swearer Napolitano, S. M., Espelage, D. L., Vaillancourt, T., & Hymel, S. (2010). What can be done about school bullying? Linking research to educational practice. *Educational Researcher, 39*, 38–47. https://doi.org/10.3102/0013189X09357622.

Ttofi, M. M., & Farrington, D. P. (2011). Effectiveness of school-based programs to reduce bullying: A systematic and meta-analytic review. *Journal of Experimental Criminology, 7*, 27–56. https://doi.org/10.1007/s11292-010-9109-1.

Vaillancourt, T., Brittain, H., Bennett, L., Arnocky, S., McDougall, P., Hymel, …, Cunningham, L. (2010). Places to avoid: Population-based study of student reports of unsafe and high bullying areas at school. *Canadian Journal of School Psychology, 25*, 40–54. https://doi.org/10.1177/0829573509358686.

Vaillancourt, T., Hymel, S., & McDougall, P. (2003). Bullying is power: Implications for school-based intervention strategies. *Journal of Applied School Psychology, 19*, 157–176. https://doi.org/10.1300/J008v19n02_10.

Vaillancourt, T., & Krems, J. (2018). An evolutionary psychological perspective of indirect aggression in girls and women. In S. Coyne & J. Ostrov (Eds.), *The development of relational aggression* (pp. 111–126). Oxford: Oxford University Press.

van Goethem, A. A. J., Scholte, R. H. J., & Wiers, R. W. (2010). Explicit- and implicit bullying attitudes in relation to bullying behavior. *Journal of Abnormal Child Psychology, 38*, 829–842. https://doi.org/10.1007/s10802-010-9405-2.

Viding, E., Simmonds, E., Petrides, K. V., & Frederickson, N. (2009). The contribution of callous-unemotional traits and conduct problems to bullying in early adolescence. *Journal of Child Psychology and Psychiatry, 50*, 471–481. https://doi.org/10.1111/j.1469-7610.2008.02012.x.

Volk, A. A., Camilleri, J. A., Dane, A. V., & Marini, Z. A. (2012). Is adolescent bullying an evolutionary adaptation? *Aggressive Behavior, 38*, 222–238. https://doi.org/10.1002/ab.21418.

Volk, A. A., Dane, A. V., Marini, Z. A., & Vaillancourt, T. (2015). Adolescent bullying, dating, and mating: Testing an evolutionary hypothesis. *Evolutionary Psychology, 13*, 1–11. https://doi.org/10.1177/1474704915613909.

Wang, J., Iannotti, R. J., & Nansel, T. R. (2009). School bullying among adolescents in the United States: Physical, verbal, relational, and cyber. *Journal of Adolescent Health, 45*, 368–375. https://doi.org/10.1016/j.jadohealth.2009.03.021.

Wang, J., Nansel, T. R., & Iannotti, R. J. (2011). Cyber and traditional bullying: Differential association with depression. *Journal of Adolescent Health, 48,* 415–417. https://doi.org/10.1016/j.jadohealth.2010.07.012.

Whittaker, E., & Kowalski, R. M. (2015). Cyberbullying via social media. *Journal of School Violence, 14,* 11–29. https://doi.org/10.1080/15388220. 2014.949377.

Wilton, C., & Campbell, M. A. (2011). An exploration of the reasons why adolescents engage in traditional and cyberbullying. *Journal of Educational Sciences and Psychology, 63,* 101–109.

Wright, M. F. (2014). Predictors of anonymous cyber aggression: The role of adolescents' beliefs about anonymity, aggression, and the permanency of digital content. *Cyberpsychology, Behavior, and Social Networking, 17,* 431–438. https://doi.org/10.1089/cyber.2013.0457.

Wright, M. F. (2018). Youths and cyberbullying: Description, theories, and recommendations. In V. C. Bryan, A. T. Musgrove & J. R. Powers (Eds.), *Handbook of research on human development in the digital age* (pp. 364–384). IGI Publishing. https://doi.org/10.4018/978-1-5225-2838-8.ch016.

Wynn, E., & Katz, J. E. (1997). Hyperbole over cyberspace: Self-presentation and social boundaries in Internet home pages and discourse. *The Information Society, 13,* 297–327. https://doi.org/10.1080/019722497129043.

3

The Vantage Points of Assistants and Reinforcers

Claire P. Monks and Sarah E. O'Toole

The current chapter focusses on the roles of assistants and reinforcers in bullying. Within this chapter we will outline the nature and extent of these roles, exploring some of the risk factors, including individual and contextual factors. We will conclude with implications for prevention and intervention work as well as proposals for future research directions.

Observational studies have noted that bullying rarely occurs in a social vacuum; other children are frequently present. Craig and Pepler (1998) reported that peers were present in around 85% of bullying episodes. Children also report witnessing bullying with some frequency; Cappadocia, Pepler, Cummings, and Craig (2012) found that most children reported witnessing bullying behaviors at least once during a three-week interval (ranging from 26% for physical bullying to 62% for verbal

C. P. Monks (✉)
University of Greenwich, Institute for Lifecourse Development, School of Human Sciences, London, UK
e-mail: c.p.monks@gre.ac.uk

S. E. O'Toole
University of College London, London, UK

© The Author(s) 2020
L. Rosen et al. (eds.), *Bullies, Victims, and Bystanders*,
https://doi.org/10.1007/978-3-030-52939-0_3

bullying and 67% for social bullying). Furthermore, O'Connell, Pepler, and Craig (1999) noted that peers may display different bystanding behaviors during episodes of bullying; taking active or passive bystanding roles. They found that reinforcement of bullying occurred 54% of the time, and 21% of the time peers joined in with bullying.

It is now widely recognized that bullying, rather than being a dyadic interaction between a bully and a victim, is a group process and this peer-dynamic may influence the continuation of the behaviors of those involved (Salmivalli, 2010a). The seminal work of Christina Salmivalli (Salmivalli, Lagerspetz, Björkqvist, Österman, & Kaukiainen, 1996) explored the group nature of bullying, identifying six participant roles in bullying. Two of the more peripheral roles are those of the assistant and reinforcer. These roles have had less focus within the research literature than other roles, such as the bully, victim, or defender, but have been identified as playing an influential role in the peer-dynamics that may affect the motivation and continuation of bullying. Thus, although they have been less frequently studied, the roles of assistant and reinforcer may be vital ones on which to focus our attention when considering the development of intervention and prevention programs focused on school bullying.

Definition

The roles of assistant and reinforcer are often viewed as being pro-bullying. Specifically, the assistant role refers to an individual who does not initiate bullying but joins in when someone else (the ringleader bully) has started it (Salmivalli, 2010a). Reinforcers are individuals who are present during bullying episodes and may display varied behaviors. These behaviors may be more active or passive. Reinforcing can describe an individual simply being present during an episode of bullying (passive bystanding). Being present and not responding negatively to bullying may be seen by the bully as condoning or supporting their behavior. Reinforcing behaviors may also involve more active bystanding, such as laughing or actively encouraging the bully, but not actively joining in with the bullying, as this would be considered as the behavior of an assistant. What these reinforcing behaviors have in common is that they may be seen as providing a social reward (either through an audience or through active encouragement), which may reinforce the aggressive actions of the bully (Salmivalli, 2010a).

It is important to note that in comparison to the other roles, assistant and reinforcer have been relatively understudied. Furthermore, many studies examining the assistant and reinforcer roles have not looked at these roles individually. Assistant and reinforcer roles are highly intercorrelated (e.g., $r = 0.68$) (Pouwels, Salmivalli et al., 2018b). Thus, sometimes they are merged together into a broader role such as "followers." Goossens, Olthof, and Dekker (2006) collapsed assistant and reinforcer behaviors into one "follower" role which they found was highly correlated to the bully role (rs between 0.90 and 0.93). Other times, assistant and reinforcer are considered within a broader pro-bullying role and are analyzed in combination with bullies (e.g., Pouwels, Lansu, & Cillessen, 2018a).

Prevalence of the Role

Salmivalli et al.'s (1996) initial study of the participant roles with pupils during early adolescence identified 6.8% of pupils taking the role of assistant and 19.5% as reinforcers. Although percentages vary by the method employed to assign individuals to "roles" (Goossens et al., 2006), research has indicated that there are age-related differences in the display of reinforcing and assisting during childhood and adolescence.

Limited research has focused on the participant roles during early childhood. Research by Belacchi and Farina (Belacchi & Farina, 2010, 2012; Farina & Belacchi, 2014) reported on teacher-rated behavior of three- to six-year-olds. Although they obtained reports of each participant role, reinforcer and assistant were merged into a group with bullies, named "Hostile" for analysis. Preschool educators in Finland reported that preschoolers (3–6-years-old) behaved in ways that reinforced or assisted others' aggression (Repo & Sajaniemi, 2015), although other studies have suggested that these "roles" are less apparent during the early years. Monks et al. (Monks & Smith, 2010; Monks, Smith, &

Swettenham, 2003) found that children aged 4–6 years were unlikely to be reported by teachers or peers as behaving as assistants or reinforcers. In addition, there was a lack of consistency in who was identified as behaving in these ways. Similarly, Camodeca, Caravita, and Coppola (2015) noted that the roles were highly inter-correlated during early childhood, suggesting reinforcer and assistant are not well distinguished at this point in development.

These age-related changes in follower roles may reflect individual as well as social factors. Young children typically hold a more inclusive concept of bullying that includes any act of unjustified aggression (Monks & Smith, 2006; Smith, Madsen, & Moody, 2006). The identification of peripheral bullying roles may consequently reflect the development of a more sophisticated understanding of bullying.

The social structures of classroom peer groups also change with development. During early childhood, peer groups tend not to have such a strong hierarchical structure as social prominence is often temporary due to the fact children typically engage in dyadic relationships and either aggress directly or escape social relationships that are unfavorably asymmetric (Schäfer, Korn, Brodbeck, Wolke, & Schulz, 2005). In later childhood and adolescence, there is an increase in reciprocal behaviors that extend beyond a dyad, resulting in the formation of more complex peer clusters (Cairns & Cairns, 1991). These more complex peer relations are more likely to be hierarchically structured, which may result in more group based bullying roles being identifiable. It is possible that children are displaying some assisting or reinforcing behaviors during early childhood, but are doing so inconsistently, and perhaps in tandem with other behaviors such as aggression. Huitsing and Monks (2018) argue that although victimization during the early school years differs from bullying later on, there are still some group processes in play, which may support continued victimization and develop into the more stable group dynamics that are observed during middle childhood and adolescence.

Looking at later childhood and adolescence, it appears that there are age-trends in the data in relation to the relative prevalence rates of reinforcer and assistant roles. Salmivalli, Lappalainen, and Lagerspetz (1998) found that assistants were more common with age, increasing from 6.3 to 12.6% from grade 6 (age 12–13 years) to grade 8 (age 14–15 years), but there was little change in the proportion of reinforcers over the two-year interval (17.3–16.2%). These age-related trends have also been found in other studies—for example, Pouwels, Lansu, and Cillessen (2016) reported more "followers" (assistants and reinforcers) in their secondary school aged pupils (mean age 16 years old) than Goossens et al. (2006) identified in primary aged children (mean age 9 years-old) (24% vs 16%) using similar methods. A more recent study by Pouwels, van Noorden, Lansu, and Cillessen (2018c) examined these age-trends in the participant roles cross-sectionally among a group aged between 8 and 18 years. They reported that the proportion assigned to a pro-bullying role (bully or follower—assistant/reinforcer) increased from 30% among 8–12-year-olds to 34% among 12–14-year-olds to 35% among 14–18-year-olds. It has been suggested that these age-related trends may be linked to motivations for involvement in bullying. The theory of antisocial behavior (Moffitt, 1993) suggests that there is an increase in the attractiveness of antisocial behavior by peers during adolescence, which we discuss in more detail later.

In addition to age, gender differences in follower roles have been found. There is a consistent body of evidence that has indicated that boys are more frequently assigned to the roles of reinforcer and assistant than girls (Demaray, Summers, Jenkins, & Becker, 2014; Salmivalli et al., 1996, 1998). Gender differences in the prevalence of follower roles may reflect differing socialization processes of boys and girls. Girls tend to be more empathic and prosocial than boys, and the use of aggressive behavior by girls is often less accepted than by boys (Eagly & Wood, 1991; Ickes, Gesn, & Graham, 2000).

More recently, research has explored gender differences in pro-bullying roles in cyberbullying situations. In line with traditional bullying literature, boys between 8 and 12 years-old were more likely to be assigned to the role of cyber-assistant and less likely to be assigned to the role of cyber-defender (Quirk & Campbell, 2014). Interestingly, there were no differences found in the prevalence of cyberbullying roles for girls. However, a study of older adolescents between 14 and 19 years-old failed to find gender or age related differences in cyber-assistant or cyber-reinforcer roles (Song & Oh, 2018). Traditional bullying and cyberbullying roles may therefore show different age and gender patterns.

Greater research attention needs to be directed toward demographic comparisons of cyber-assistants and cyber-reinforcers.

Understanding of cultural differences across follower roles is limited. Comparisons of prior research across different countries indicate that the prevalence of follower roles may be similar. For instance, in samples of Canadian children between 5 and 12 years-old, children assisted or reinforced the bully between 21 and 32% of the time (Atlas & Pepler, 1998; O'Connell et al., 1999). Similarly, in a sample of 573 Finnish children between 11 and 12 years-old, 26% reported assisting or reinforcing bullying (Salmivalli et al., 1996). In a sample of Dutch 16-year-old adolescents, 24% were categorized as followers of the bully (Pouwels et al., 2016). However, these studies did not directly examine ethnicity and focused on Western countries.

Attitudes/Motivations

In contrast to the research focused on motivations for aggressive or defending behavior, there has been less focus on why children may assist an aggressor or reinforce the aggression of others. However, if these children's behaviors are implicated in the maintenance of bullying then it is vital to understand their motivations to behave in ways that may encourage or support continued bullying in order for interventions to appropriately address these (Salmivalli, 2010a). It is likely that there are varied and perhaps changing motivations for assisting or reinforcer behavior, dependent on the child's age, existing status, and friendship opportunities within their peer group. Research has suggested that two important motivations for engaging in "follower" behaviors include the fear of victimization (Bierman, 2004) and a need to fit in (Garandeau & Cillessen, 2006).

Generally, children tend to rate bullying behavior negatively (Menesini et al., 1997) and this includes individuals who are identified as followers. Pouwels, Lansu, and Cillessen (2017) noted that followers were equally as negative as victims and defenders in their evaluations of hypothetical incidents of bullying. However, the authors argue that given that followers support aggression, it is unlikely that this accurately reflects their true opinions. Rather, this may reflect social desirability in responses. When asked to rate real peers, followers appear to rate other aggressive peers positively, and research has consistently found that reinforcers and assistants form friendships with other followers or bullies (Witvliet et al., 2010). Bullies are often high in perceived popularity (Prinstein & Cillessen, 2003). Garandeau and Cillessen (2006) have suggested that given the perceived status of bullies, children may assist or reinforce out of a need to belong to a group. Additionally, it has been found that assistants place a higher value on the tangible and status rewards achieved by aggression than children in other participant roles (Andreou & Metallidou, 2004). Furthermore, when asked why they do not stand up to the bully, children frequently report that they are scared or worried that they may become the next victim (Cappodocia et al., 2012). Thus, children may also assist or reinforce the bully's behavior out of fear of victimization (Bierman, 2004).

A recent paper by Pouwels, Lansu, et al. (2018a) explained potential motivations for follower behavior from the viewpoint of Hawley's resource control theory (Hawley, 2015) and Moffitt's (1993) developmental taxonomy of antisocial behavior. Resource control theory argues that individuals behave strategically in order to gain and maintain resources and dominance in the peer group. Hawley (2015) indicates that the most successful strategy includes both prosocial and coercive control—that she terms "bistrategic control." Thus, individuals may be behaving aggressively (e.g., assistants) or indirectly by supporting/condoning aggression (e.g., reinforcers) in a strategy to enhance or maintain their status within the peer group.

Moffitt's (1993) theory of antisocial behavior also focuses on the perceived "benefits" of antisocial and aggressive behavior, with a particular focus on adolescence. Moffitt argues that during adolescence, antisocial behaviors are viewed more positively by young people—perhaps as they are viewed as more "grown-up" and mature behaviors—and so are considered as being more attractive, and thus more strongly related to peer-status. This may account for the increase in follower type behaviors during adolescence. Research indicates that the role of reinforcer or assistant is associated with relatively high levels of peer-status, which appears to increase from childhood into adolescence. During childhood (4–6 years-old), bullies, reinforcers, and assistants are as popular as defenders. However, by later adolescence (14–18 years-old), bullies and their followers are more popular than defenders among both same- and opposite-gender peers (Pouwels, van Noorden, et al., 2018c). Research has indicated that although they may be individually disliked by peers, young people who take a pro-bullying role (bully, reinforcer, assistant) demonstrate a high level of popularity within the peer group as a whole (Pouwels et al., 2016). In addition, social status at 9–14 years-old predicted bullying roles at 16–17 years-old (Pouwels, van Noorden, et al., 2018c). Adolescents who showed a stable level of popularity were more likely to be identified as bullies or followers. Assistant and reinforcer roles may thus be more strongly associated with social status in later adolescence, and this association with high status may act as a motivating factor for young people to take these pro-bullying roles.

The research on motivations to join in or support bullying suggests that young people may choose to behave as assistants or reinforcers as a means of protecting themselves from victimization (Bierman, 2004) or enhancing their social status by aligning themselves with the bully (Garandeau & Cillessen, 2006). This understanding of young people's motivations for assisting or reinforcing bullying may provide important insights for intervention and prevention programs. In particular, it may be useful to help children and young people to find other ways of enhancing their peer-status that do not involve supporting bullying. In addition, the promotion of a culture within the school which does not support bullying and in which vulnerable, isolated children are supported may decrease the levels of pupils aligning themselves with the bullies.

Individual Differences

While there is an extensive literature on individual characteristics associated with ringleader bully and victim roles, less is known about the individual difference factors associated with the assistant and reinforcer roles. Behavioral and personality characteristics have been linked to pro-bullying behavior. In line with research on bullies, followers demonstrate higher levels of aggression and its associated characteristics, including conduct problems (aggressive and antisocial behavior), callous-unemotional traits (limited empathy, lack of guilt, and shallow affect), and positive expectation of aggression leading to reward (Crapanzano, Frick, Childs, & Terranova, 2011). According to their peers, bullies and their followers (16 years-old) were uncooperative and also less likely to help others, but more likely to be leaders and be humorous (Pouwels et al., 2016). In addition, followers aged 8–10 years-old have been found to be less friendly toward victims and show greater emotional instability compared to defenders (Tani, Greenman, Schneider, & Fregoso, 2003).

Assistants and reinforcers may consequently endorse bullying because they are aggressive, perceive aggression as resulting in reward, and have a lack of empathy for victims. It has been noted that bystanders to bullying, including followers, were less likely to have been a bully before (Oh & Hazler, 2009), suggesting that these children may show a less extreme aggressive profile than bullies. However, this study considered bystanders as a group, which included both assistants and reinforcers as well as outsiders and defenders. Thus, these results may be influenced by the more prosocial role of the defender. However, other research has indicated that followers are less aggressive than bullies (Pouwels et al., 2016). Further, the majority of adolescents identified as bullies/followers showed decreasing trajectories of aggression between 9–14 and 16–17 years-old (Pouwels, van Noorden, et al., 2018c). This indicates that externalizing behavior is more strongly associated with bullying behavior in childhood than adolescence. This decrease in aggression may reflect developmental changes in the nature of aggression; children who engaged in high levels of aggression and fighting in middle childhood, may use other types of aggression, such as relational aggression, in adolescence.

Followers may be less powerful and visible within the peer group and show less extreme negative behavior in comparison to bullies. The lower levels of aggression demonstrated by assistants and reinforcers may account for their lower position in the peer hierarchy than bullies. Due to their close proximity to bullies in the peer hierarchy, followers may pose a threat to bullies' status (Prinstein & Cillessen, 2003). Thus, bullies may demonstrate higher levels of negative and aggressive behavior than assistants and reinforcers in order to defend their central position in the peer group.

There may also be individual differences in the social-cognitive skills of bullies and followers. Ringleader bullies may require greater social-cognitive skills than their followers as they are required to initiate bullying and lead followers (Sutton, Smith, & Swettenham, 1999). Sutton et al. (1999) found that among 7–10-year-olds, followers had poorer social-cognitive scores than bullies. However, follower behaviors (as well as bullying) were significantly and positively related to cognitive aspects of social cognition, which involve the ability to understand someone else's perspective. This indicates that children involved in bullying, either as the instigators or followers demonstrate some perspective taking skills.

Social-cognitive skills may be less central to bullying behavior in the preschool period because bullying is less socially sophisticated during this period. Other research has found that social competence is negatively associated with pro-bullying roles including follower behaviors in children between 2 and 6 years-old (Camodeca et al., 2015). Older children (10 year-olds) who are involved in assisting the bully showed lower self-efficacy for assertion and self-regulatory skills (Andreou & Metallidou, 2004). Though, social skills, including empathy and cooperation, as well as self-regulation were negatively correlated with assisting behavior in adolescents 11–14 years-old (Jenkins, Demaray, Fredrick, & Summers, 2016). These findings suggest that assistants and reinforcers in middle childhood and adolescence may have some developed perspective taking skills, but may also have lower levels of empathy and self-regulation, which may place them at risk of behaving more aggressively.

Furthermore, although reinforcers and assistants do not necessarily view victims more negatively than do other children in anti-bullying roles (Pouwels et al., 2017), it has been suggested that they may be more likely to downplay the negative effects of bullying. As a result, they may feel justified in not taking an anti-bullying stance (Gini, 2006; Jenkins et al., 2016). Followers between 8 and 11 years old reported significantly higher levels of moral disengagement (e.g., distancing oneself from ethical standards of behavior) than children who were not involved in bullying (Gini, 2006). Pozzoli, Gini, and Vieno (2012) also found a positive relation between moral disengagement and pro-bullying behaviors during later childhood. A study that assessed the tendency for 14–19-year-olds to engage in negative or positive bystander behavior (assisting, reinforcing, not involved, defending) revealed that experience of perpetration, high moral disengagement, low empathy, high antisocial conformity, close relationship with the perpetrator, and low perceived control lead to a greater likelihood of assisting bullying (Song & Oh, 2018). Bystanders with high moral disengagement engaged in low defending behavior regardless of the presence of other bystanders.

Through moral disengagement individuals can minimize their perceptions of the negative effect of their actions or the harm caused to the victim. Moral disengagement may allow followers to consider their pro-bullying behavior as acceptable by enabling them to view bullying as being for a moral purpose (moral justification) or seeing it as acceptable in contrast to worse behavior (advantageous comparison). Moral disengagement can also result in the victim being dehumanized or seen as responsible for provoking the aggression. Thus, moral disengagement may allow followers to protect themselves from negative feelings, such as guilt or shame, which are usually associated with bullying (Bandura, 1999, 2002). In turn, this may facilitate the continuation of their pro-bullying behavior. Indeed, adolescents (11–17 years-old) who frequently assisted with bullying were less likely to negative feelings regarding bullying (Wachs, 2012).

When looking at cyberbullying, research has indicated findings that are similar to those reported for offline bullying. In the limited research examining the behavior of individuals who observe cyberbullying, cyberbullying bystander behavior has also been found to be related to moral disengagement (DeSmet et al., 2016). Thus, similar mechanisms of moral disengagement may mean that individuals who witness traditional or cyberbullying may not intervene and may in fact join in or reinforce the behavior of the perpetrator.

The Ecological System

Since the work of Bronfenbrenner (1986), it has long been acknowledged that a child's development is not only influenced by individual-level factors, but also by the child's immediate and broader social contexts. The social-ecological framework (Espelage & Swearer, 2011; Hong & Espelage, 2012) suggests that bystander behavior is an ecological phenomena in which contextual variables, including school and classroom climate, play an important role. Research has noted that individual behavior in relation to bullying can be influenced by the social norms and levels of behavior displayed by friendship groups, the class, and the entire school.

Friendship Groups

Children inclined toward bullying, either as bullies, reinforcers, or assistants, have larger friendship networks; networks that they formed together (Hutton, Salmivalli, & Lagerspetz, 2006). Children who adopt complementary participant roles in bullying situations typically belong to the same friendship groups, resulting in pro-bullying friendship clusters (Salmivalli, Huttunen, & Lagerspetz, 1997), suggesting that children who bully others select peers who hold similar pro-bullying attitudes to themselves to form friendship groups. In addition, children who have been rejected by their peers may seek out a deviant peer group with whom to socialize as this may be the only option open to them (Miller-Johnson, Coie, Maumary-Gremaud, Lochman, & Terry, 1999). Despite links to delinquent behavior, deviant peer groups may provide social status, camaraderie, a sense of belonging, and reinforcement of self-worth. Children may side with the bully in the hopes that they will gain favor with the bully, and ultimately be accepted into the bully's social network. Children who are rejected by the peer group are at greater risk of being victimized (Bierman, 2004). Thus, as noted earlier, one motivation for socially rejected children to support the bully could be as a form of self-protection. Reinforcing the bullying of another peer, reduces the chances of becoming the victim yourself.

The greater the extent to which a child's peer network bullies others or assists or reinforces bullying, the more the child themselves will engage in this behavior (Salmivalli et al., 1997). Therefore, pro-bullying friendship groups may socialize and reinforce bullying behavior. Adolescents (11–19 years-old) who reported greater negative peer pressure and whose friendship groups endorsed higher levels of delinquent behavior, reported higher assisting and reinforcing behavior (Evans & Smokowski, 2017). Peer clusters share similar bullying-related attitudes, social cognitions, and behaviors (Espelage, Holt, & Henkel, 2003; Witvliet et al., 2010). Indeed, bullies and their followers show similar aggressive social cognitions that support participation in bullying (Andreou & Metallidou, 2004). Further, Oh and Hazler (2009) reported that a closer peer relationship with the bully resulted in more assisting and reinforcing behavior.

A pro-bullying network has its own set of norms regarding acceptable and unacceptable behavior that guides members' decisions and behavior. For example, in friendship networks of 8–13-year-olds, the more similar group members were to one another in a pro-bullying network, the greater the extent to which they directly assisted the bully (Duffy & Nesdale, 2009). It has also been argued that children's participant roles may become a self-fulfilling prophecy (Salmivalli, 1999). When a child adopts a particular participant role they may face challenges in changing their role: the friendship group punishes behavior that contradicts children's roles and rewards behaviors in accordance with the role. Children's self-concept may also be intertwined with their participant role; they may define themselves by their role and believe they are incapable of behaving in another way.

Classroom

Bystander behavior including levels of reinforcing and assisting has been found to vary across classrooms (Atria, Strohmeier, & Spiel, 2007; Salmivalli et al., 2011). This may reflect classroom context, which includes teacher–student and student–student interactions (Zedan, 2010). It is known that children with a stronger genetic predisposition for aggressive behavior show higher levels of aggression toward others, which is especially true when classroom norms favor aggression (Brendgen, Girard, Vitaro, Dionne, & Boivin, 2015). Classrooms that support a culture of bullying encourage students to adopt pro-bullying roles. Children in classes where there are higher levels of pro-bullying behaviors, tend to experience more frequent bullying (Salmivalli et al., 2011; Thornberg & Wänström, 2018). A study of 104 classrooms of 10–13 year-olds in 63 public schools located across Sweden found students in classes with more boys and a less authoritative classroom climate had higher levels of pro-bullying roles (Thornberg, Wänström, & Jungert, 2018). Boys were more inclined to reinforce bullying when they belonged to classrooms with a less authoritative climate. Furthermore, research has indicated that teacher behavior influences pro-bullying behavior. Choi and Cho (2012) found that students 8–18 years-old were more likely to be classed as assistants if they received low levels of teacher support. Further, it has been argued that the behavior of assistants and reinforcers provides the bully with social rewards which may appear to legitimize or even value their aggression (e.g., Salmivalli et al., 1996). Thus, these behaviors have been identified as being important within the peer context in encouraging the initiation and maintenance of the behavior of bullies.

Sentse, Veenstra, Kiuru, and Salmivalli (2015) examined the relation between reported attitudes toward bullying and classroom levels of bullying as predictors of pro-bullying behavior such as assisting and reinforcing. They found that classroom levels of bullying were predictive of later pro-bullying behavior by children over and above pro-bullying perceptions. They argue that children in classrooms where there are high pro-bullying norms may feel that their behavior is legitimized and may lead to social rewards. Classrooms in which popular students engage frequently in bullying results in a culture more accepting of bullying (Dijkstra, Lindenberg, & Veenstra, 2008), suggesting that the norms set by popular students are more influential than norms of averagely popular students. This is in line with research which has found that classroom peer ecologies characterized by strong status hierarchies promote bullying (Wolke, Woods, & Samara, 2009). Children in pro-bullying roles have been found to be more popular (Pouwels, van Noorden, et al., 2018c), which may relate to the higher prevalence of bullying in such classrooms via bullies' exacerbated social influence on the peer group.

Classroom bullying climate may become particularly important during pre-adolescence. The relationship between classroom norms and bullying was stronger for older children (11–12 years-old) compared to younger children (9–11 years-old) (Salmivalli & Voeten, 2004). This may reflect the more central role of the peer group as children move into adolescence (Salmivalli & Voeten, 2004). Pro-bullying peer groups may become more cemented in adolescence and the relationship between pro-bullying attitudes and behavior may be exacerbated. Further research is needed to confirm this hypothesis, which takes into account changing classroom contexts from childhood to adolescence. Although younger children typically remain in the same class throughout the school day, adolescent learning contexts tend to be more varied. Adolescent peer groups often change throughout the school day and include individuals within and outside the classroom. A greater understanding of the role of classroom context would be gained if research took into account informal peer group influences (Espelage, Low, & Jimerson, 2014), where adolescents may be exposed to both anti- and pro-bullying climates.

The School

The climate of the school also plays a role in promoting assisting and reinforcing behavior. School climate refers to the shared beliefs, values, and attitudes that shape interactions between students, teachers, and school staff, and that sets the parameters of norms and acceptable behavior within the school (Bradshaw, Waasdorp, Debnam, & Johnson, 2014). A positive school climate characterized by an anti-bullying stance, intervening in bullying, authoritative climate (e.g., high level of structure and support) and high school connectedness is linked to lower bullying behavior, including assisting and reinforcing (Ahmed, 2008; Cornell & Huang, 2016; Denny et al., 2014; Fink, Patalay, Sharpe, & Wolpert, 2018). Further, school environments in which the aggressive behavior of bullies is inextricably linked to passivity of victims, in which school staff are often not aware of the bullying, and in which other children are not sure how to intervene, promote a culture of bullying (Charach, Pepler, & Ziegler, 1995). Viewing the school as a dangerous environment (which may be as a result of aggression or bullying in school) results in students feeling unsafe and promotes negative bystander behavior as a way of avoiding victimization (Bierman, 2004). Added to this, environments where there is a high level of aggressive behavior are those where negative bystander behavior may be the norm. Bystanders may imitate the aggression they witness in the school environment and assist and reinforce the bully.

The evidence reviewed above indicates that school climates that promote a culture of bullying do so by creating an environment in which bullying is not prevented (e.g., Charach et al., 1995). However, this research has often failed to consider the specific impact of school climate on the role of assistants and reinforcers. Further, there has been limited research that has considered school level-organization factors such as differences between private and public schools, rural and urban schools, single and mixed sex schools. It has been posited that mixed-sex environments may be beneficial for boys due to lower aggression (Fabes, Martin, Hanish, Galligan, & Pahlke, 2015). Single-sex schooling may increase gender stereotypes, which for boys in boys-only schools may exacerbate aggressive behaviors (Lee, Marks, & Byrd, 1994). Indeed, students (12–19 years-old) in girls-only schools reported significantly less bullying, whereas students in boys-only schools reported more bullying (Denny et al., 2014). Although differences in relation to assisting and reinforcing bullying were not examined, it would be hypothesized that increased levels of reinforcing and assisting would accompany elevated levels of bullying.

Online Peer Group

The majority of studies to date have focused on the role of the peer context in traditional bullying situations, neglecting the role that the peer group may play in online environments in relation to cyberbullying. Emerging evidence has suggested that the peer context may also play an important role in online pro-bullying behavior. For instance, peer group norms have been found to influence bystander behavior in cyberbullying as well as traditional bullying (Bastiaensens et al., 2015; Patterson, Allan, & Cross, 2015). Children are more likely to actively assist and support cyberbullies due to peer pressure if other bystanders show an accepting attitude toward cyberbullying (Bastiaensens et al., 2016). Bystanders with a close relationship with the bully were less likely to assist or reinforce cyberbullying if other bystanders were present than if they were absent, suggesting that even those children who have positive relationships with the bully and may be more inclined toward pro-bullying behavior may moderate their behavior in the presence of others (Song & Oh, 2018).

Effects on Adjustment

As with other areas of research, there has been comparatively little research examining the effects of bullying exposure on the adjustment of reinforcers and assistants. However, it has been noted that observing bullying can have negative effects on the mental health of young people. Rivers, Poteat, Noret, and Ashurst (2009) found that witnesses to school bullying (which included reinforcers and assistants, but also defenders) had elevated mental health risks. Similarly, in a study that also did not differentiate between the different roles of those who witnessed bullying, Callaghan, Kelly, and Molcho (2019) noted that individuals who witnessed bullying, but were neither a bully nor a victim, were at higher risk for a number of negative outcomes including an increased risk for psychological and somatic symptoms and low life satisfaction compared with those who did not report observing bullying.

Rivers et al. (2009) suggest several possible reasons for this increased risk of negative outcomes for the witnesses of bullying, which may also be relevant for those who take a pro-bullying stance. As noted earlier, individuals who observe bullying may join in or act in a reinforcing manner out of a concern with "fitting in" or worry about being the next target (Bierman, 2004; Garandeau & Cillessen, 2006). Thus, children and young people may be supporting the behavior of the bully as a way of trying to protect themselves from being victimized. These motivations may actually lead them to feel anxious given their potentially precarious position. Further research is needed to explore the experiences of individuals who take on the roles of reinforcer and assistant specifically. Currently, these roles are often examined within the broader context of individuals who are present and witness bullying but are not themselves bullies or victims. However, the behavior displayed by this broad group of individuals may vary considerably and may include prosocial as well as antisocial responses. This is problematic as little research differentiates these roles beyond identifying them as witnessing bullying, but clearly the role taken can have an influence on the impact witnessing bullying may have on observers.

Implications for Prevention and Intervention

It has been argued that bullying cannot be fully understood without consideration of the classroom context, where bullying participant roles develop and contribute to maintaining or preventing bullying (Salmivalli, 2010a). Applying the participant roles approach to interventions leads to the assumption that the most effective means of intervening against bullying will be directed toward the whole group and not just bullies and victims (Salmivalli, 1999). As reviewed earlier, bystander behavior influences bullying behavior and thus may be central to preventing bullying (Polanin, Espelage, & Pigott, 2012; see also Fredrick, Jenkins, & Dexter, this volume). The potential of bystanders to prevent bullying is great as these children represent the vast majority of participants and without the supporting role of assistants and reinforcers, bullies may be less confident in their bullying. Indeed, classrooms characterized by higher levels of reinforcing were found to have higher levels of bullying (Salmivalli et al., 2011). Bullying is greater in classrooms where bullying is socially rewarded; that is, bullying is reinforced and victimized children are rarely defended.

Targeting children who are bystanders to bullying is thought to be essential to the prevention of bullying (Hawkins, Pepler, & Craig, 2001; Oh & Hazler, 2009) and may be a more effective approach than trying to change the behavior of the bully (Frey, Hirschstein, Edstrom, & Snell, 2009; Kärnä et al., 2011). The behavior of bullies may be more entrenched. They display higher levels of aggression than reinforcers and assistants and their behavior may therefore be more challenging to change directly (Oh & Hazler, 2009). But, through changing the behavior of followers, the bully's behavior may also be influenced (Salmivalli, 1999). By removing their supporters and audience, it is likely that bullying will become less socially rewarding for them. Added to this, taking into account the participant roles that children adopt in interventions may also be necessary as attitudes toward how to address bullying may vary across the different roles (Camodeca & Goossens, 2007). Bullies and their followers were less supportive of assertiveness as a means to address bullying than defenders, outsiders, and those not involved. Despite followers being a part of the bullying situation, they can also be an effective part of its solution. On the one hand, assistants and reinforcers understand that bullying is wrong and wish to stop it, but on the other hand, they strive to secure their own status and safety within the peer group (Salmivalli, 2014).

Based on the participant roles approach, Salmivalli (1999) has suggested a bullying intervention that considers the different participant roles. She suggested that interventions should involve three facets to change the participant roles children adopt: (1) general awareness raising about participant roles; (2) self-reflection; and (3) assertiveness training. Introducing students to the different participant roles and encouraging them to reflect upon their behavior may increase their understanding of how their behavior may encourage bullying even if they did not mean to do so. Commitment to new behaviors that discourage bullying through discussion or role-play is carried out. Increasing students' assertiveness in resisting peer pressure may reduce their motivation to join in and support bullying, even if that is what other students in the class expect. Research has indicated that many pupils feel that they could join in with bullying. A survey of 2437 adolescents 11–14 years-old revealed that nearly a quarter of students felt that they could join in bullying situations (assisting) (Unnever & Cornell, 2008). Thus, encouraging children to reflect on the impact of assisting and reinforcing behavior and to resist the peer pressure to assist or reinforce bullying may reduce pro-bullying behavior.

A meta-analysis of school-based bystander intervention programs (e.g., Creating a Peaceful School Learning Environment, Expect Respect, KiVa, Steps to Respect) concluded that it is possible to change responses to bullying and increase defending behavior (Polanin et al., 2012). These programs, which focused on bystander behavior, increased bystander intervention (Polanin et al., 2012) and decreased student's tendency to reinforce bullying (Kärnä et al., 2011). Based on the participant role approach, the KiVa anti-bullying intervention (consisting of student lessons, online anti-bullying games, school-based KiVa teams tackling identified cases of bullying) has been found to reduce bullying behavior via its influence on bystander behavior (Saarento & Salmivalli, 2015). As a result of the intervention, levels of reinforcing decreased, which was associated with a decrease in bullying and victimization. The KiVa intervention influenced students' perceptions of how their peers responded to bullying (Saarento & Salmivalli, 2015). Students perceived their peers to be engaging in more defending of victims in their class, which in turn led to a reduction in their own engagement in pro-bullying behaviors.

Peer support programs have also been developed to tackle bullying with consideration of the participant roles. Peer support programs involve training volunteer students in active listening, empathy, and problem-solving skills in order to provide them with the skill set to work with the peer group to manage peer conflict and support peers to relate to each other in a more constructive manner (Cowie & Wallace, 2000). Peer support programs can also play a central role in altering participant roles (Smith, 2004). These approaches may support children moving from the role of assistant/reinforcer to defender by challenging their attitudes toward bullying and providing them with the skills and confidence to challenge bullying (Price & Jones, 2001; Smith, 2004).

There have been mixed results regarding the effectiveness of peer support programs. A peer counseling approach adopted in Finnish schools with 13–15 year-olds involved a one-week intervention in which eight peer counselors were trained to promote good relationships between students and social responsibility and to encourage a safe school atmosphere (Salmivalli, 2010b). The intervention involved peer-led discussion, newsletters, classroom announcements on the topic of bullying, and activities such as creating anti-bullying posters. This intervention led to a decline in self-reported bullying, but not peer-reported or observed bullying. Whereas a befriending intervention that aimed to increase students' bystander responsibilities, encouraging them to enact more defending behaviors rather than pro-bullying behaviors, adopted in Italian middle schools resulted in a decrease in negative behaviors and attitudes toward victims (Menesini, Codecasa, Benelli, & Cowie, 2003).

School-based anti-bullying interventions that aim to address students' bullying-related attitudes and group norms, including bystander behaviors, have also been generalized to cyberbullying. Offline bystanders often maintain this role in an online environment and consequently the techniques utilized to reduce traditional bullying may be utilized to address cyberbullying (Pearce et al., 2011). The NoTrap! Cyberbullying intervention for adolescents was developed to prevent both traditional bullying and cyberbullying (Palladino et al., 2016). The intervention consists of two phases. The first phase is led by adults and the second phase is led by students who act as peer educators both online and offline. Peer educators work to enhance awareness and provide support to those involved in bullying and promote cooperation among peers (encouraging peers to develop empathy and problem-solving skills). An evaluation of this intervention with 14–15 year-old Italian students found no significant difference in either bullying or cyberbullying immediately following the intervention. However, six months later, students who participated in the intervention showed lower levels of bullying and cyberbullying. This is likely to capture those in peripheral bullying roles (e.g., assistants and reinforcers), but the direct impact on these students was not examined.

Future Issues

We concur with Salmivalli (2010b) and others that working on changing the pro-bullying behaviors and attitudes of bystanders is an important focus for intervention programs. As research suggests that assistants and reinforcers play a role in providing social rewards to the bully by being seen to approve of their aggressive behavior, it is important that intervention programs work with children and young people who take these follower roles with the aim of decreasing the perceived rewards of bullying. We argue that it would therefore be useful to examine the effects of intervention and prevention programs on children's bystander behaviors. Research has often failed to explore the impact of interventions on the role of assistant and reinforcer; however, by changing their behaviors intervention programs may remove the audience or support for the bully's behavior, which it has been argued would then result in a reduction of bullying behavior.

In addition, a potentially useful line of research would involve examining the development of the peer-dynamics that support bullying across early to middle childhood. Research with preschoolers indicates that the more peripheral roles of assistant and reinforcer may be less apparent during this period of development, but that by middle childhood they are identifiable and are displayed by individuals with some stability. By further understanding the development of these pro-bullying behaviors and attitudes we may be well placed to develop prevention programs to work with young children. It has been argued that interventions appear to be more effective with younger children than during adolescence (Jimenez-Barbero, Ruiz-Hernández, Llor-Zaragoza, Pérez-García, & Llor-Estebana, 2016), thus it is imperative that we develop age-appropriate prevention/intervention programs to address the behavior of children early on.

In addition, we suggest that research needs to further investigate the characteristics of children who are involved in bullying as assistants and reinforcers. Identifying individual characteristics associated with the roles of assistants and reinforcers will highlight whether followers and bullies have similar or contrasting individual characteristics and will inform efforts to identify children at risk of adopting these negative bystander roles as well as prevention and intervention efforts. Added to this, the role of classroom and school contexts in the promotion of pro-bullying behavior provides important insights for intervention programs and requires further investigation (Charach et al., 1995; Salmivalli et al., 2011; Thornberg & Wänström, 2018), including understanding the impact of stable and unstable classroom contexts and type of school (e.g., same- or mixed-sex). It is important to understand the social motivating factors which play a role in children taking pro-bullying roles in order that these motivations are minimized. The limited amount of research which has focused on motivations for assisting and reinforcing suggests varied motivations, with some individuals taking these roles in order to gain favor with the bully and avoid victimization themselves and others strategically aligning themselves with the bully in order to enhance their peer-status (Bierman, 2004; Garandeau & Cillessen, 2006). It also appears that there may be important age-related differences for the adoption of these pro-bullying behaviors. For example, it appears that pro-bullying behaviors may be more strongly associated with peer-status within adolescence (Moffitt, 1993). Thus, it is vital when designing anti-bullying programs that the age of participants is considered in order that we understand why individuals may be taking these particular roles in bullying.

From the research reviewed in the current chapter, there is clear evidence that follower behaviors such as those of reinforcer and assistant play an important role in the bullies' motivations to engage in bullying, but also in their continuation of these behaviors. The perceived social rewards of bullying conveyed through these follower behaviors are an important focus for intervention and prevention programs. There is promising evidence that indicates that considering the participant roles has a positive impact on reducing bullying; in particular, tackling the roles of reinforcer and assistant can be a way of decreasing the social rewards gained from bullying. Thus, it is clear that furthering our understanding of these follower roles is vital for us to develop more effective anti-bullying programs. Furthermore, by understanding the age-related changes and motivations for taking these roles, we can further tailor age-appropriate interventions to support anti-bullying work with children and adolescents within school contexts.

References

Ahmed, E. (2008). 'Stop it, that's enough': Bystander intervention and its relationship to school connectedness and shame management. *Vulnerable Children and Youth Studies, 3,* 203–213. https://doi.org/10.1080/17450120802002548.

Andreou, E., & Metallidou, P. (2004). The relationship of academic and social cognition to behaviour in bullying situations among Greek primary school children. *Educational Psychology, 24,* 27–41. https://doi.org/10.1080/0144341032000146421.

Atlas, R. S., & Pepler, D. J. (1998). Observations of bullying in the classroom. *The Journal of Educational Research, 92,* 86–99. https://doi.org/10.1080/00220679809597580.

Atria, M., Strohmeier, D., & Spiel, C. (2007). The relevance of the school class as social unit for the prevalence of bullying and victimization. *European Journal of Developmental Psychology, 4,* 372–387. https://doi.org/10.1080/17405620701554560.

Bandura, A. (1999). Moral disengagement in the perpetration of inhumanities. *Personality and Social Psychology Review, 3,* 193–209. https://doi.org/10.1207/s15327957pspr0303_3.

Bandura, A. (2002). Selective moral disengagement in the exercise of moral agency. *Journal of Moral Education, 31,* 101–119. https://doi.org/10.1080/0305724022014322.

Bastiaensens, S., Pabian, S., Vandebosch, H., Poels, K., Van Cleemput, K., DeSmet, A., & De Bourdeaudhuij, I. (2016). From normative influence to social pressure: How relevant others affect whether bystanders join in cyberbullying. *Social Development, 25,* 193–211. https://doi.org/10.1111/sode.12134.

Bastiaensens, S., Vandebosch, H., Poels, K., Van Cleemput, K., DeSmet, A., & De Bourdeaudhuij, I. (2015). 'Can I afford to help?' How affordances of communication modalities guide bystanders' helping intentions towards harassment on social network sites. *Behaviour & Information Technology, 34,* 425–435. https://doi.org/10.1080/0144929x.2014.983979.

Belacchi, C., & Farina, E. (2010). Prosocial/hostile roles and emotion comprehension in preschoolers. *Aggressive Behavior, 36,* 371–389. https://doi.org/10.1002/ab.20361.

Belacchi, C., & Farina, E. (2012). Feeling and thinking of others: Affective and cognitive empathy and emotion comprehension in prosocial/hostile

preschoolers. *Aggressive Behavior, 38,* 150–165. https://doi.org/10.1002/ab.
21415.
Bierman, K. L. (2004). *Peer rejection.* New York: Guilford.
Bradshaw, C. P., Waasdorp, T. E., Debnam, K. J., & Johnson, S. L. (2014).
Measuring school climate in high schools: A focus on safety, engagement,
and the environment. *Journal of School Health, 84,* 593–604. https://doi.
org/10.1111/josh.12186.
Brendgen, M., Girard, A., Vitaro, F., Dionne, G., & Boivin, M. (2015).
Gene-environment correlation linking aggression and peer victimization: Do
classroom behavioral norms matter? *Journal of Abnormal Child Psychology,
43,* 19–31. https://doi.org/10.1007/s10802-013-9807-z.
Bronfenbrenner, U. (1986). Ecology of the family as a context for human development. *Developmental Psychology, 22,* 521–530. https://doi.org/10.1037/
0012-1649.22.6.723.
Cairns, R. B., & Cairns, B. D. (1991). Social cognition and social networks:
A developmental perspective. In D. J. Pepler & K. H. Rubin (Eds.), *The
development and treatment of childhood aggression* (pp. 411–448). Hillsdale:
Lawrence Erlbaum Associates Inc.
Callaghan, M., Kelly, C., & Molcho, M. (2019). Bullying and bystander
behaviour and health outcomes among adolescents in Ireland. *Journal
of Epidemiology and Community Health, 73,* 416–421. https://doi.org/10.
1136/jech-2018-211350.
Camodeca, M., Caravita, S. C., & Coppola, G. (2015). Bullying in preschool:
The associations between participant roles, social competence, and social
preference. *Aggressive Behavior, 41,* 310–321. https://doi.org/10.1002/ab.
21541.
Camodeca, M., & Goossens, F. A. (2007). Children's opinions on effective strategies to cope with bullying: The importance of bullying role and
perspective. *Educational Research, 47,* 93–105. https://doi.org/10.1080/001
3188042000337587.
Cappadocia, M. C., Pepler, D., Cummings, J. G., & Craig, W. (2012). Individual motivations and characteristics associated with bystander intervention
during bullying episodes among children and youth. *Canadian Journal
of School Psychology, 27,* 201–216. https://doi.org/10.1177/082957351245
0567.
Charach, A., Pepler, D. J., & Ziegler, S. (1995). Bullying at school: A Canadian
perspective. *Education Canada, 35,* 12–18.
Choi, S., & Cho, Y. I. (2012). Influence of psychological and social factors on
bystanders' roles in school bullying among Korean-American students in the

United States. *School Psychology International, 34,* 67–81. https://doi.org/10.1177/0143034311430406.

Cornell, D., & Huang, F. (2016). Authoritative school climate and high school student risk behavior: A cross-sectional multi-level analysis of student self-reports. *Journal of Youth and Adolescence, 45,* 2246–2259. https://doi.org/10.1007/s10964-016-0424-3.

Cowie, H., & Wallace, P. (2000). *Peer support in action.* London: Sage.

Craig, W. M., & Pepler, D. J. (1998). Observations of bullying and victimization in the school yard. *Canadian Journal of School Psychology, 13,* 41–59. https://doi.org/10.1177/082957359801300205.

Crapanzano, A. M., Frick, P. J., Childs, K., & Terranova, A. M. (2011). Gender differences in the assessment, stability, and correlates to bullying roles in middle school children. *Behavioral Science Law, 29,* 677–694. https://doi.org/10.1002/bsl.1000.

Demaray, M. K., Summers, K. H., Jenkins, L. N., & Becker, L. D. (2014). The bullying participant behaviors questionnaire (BPBQ): Establishing a reliable and valid measure. *Journal of School Violence, 15,* 158–188. https://doi.org/10.1080/15388220.2014.964801.

Denny, S., Peterson, E. R., Stuart, J., Utter, J., Bullen, P., Fleming, T. …, Milfont, T. (2014). Bystander intervention, bullying, and victimization: A multilevel analysis of New Zealand high schools. *Journal of School Violence, 14,* 245–272. https://doi.org/10.1080/15388220.2014.910470.

DeSmet, A., Bastiaensens, S., Van Cleemput, K., Poels, K., Vandebosch, H., Cardon, G., & De Bourdeaudhuij, I. (2016). Deciding whether to look after them, to like it, or leave it: A multidimensional analysis of predictors of positive and negative bystander behavior in cyberbullying among adolescents. *Computers in Human Behaviour, 57,* 398–415. https://doi.org/10.1016/j.chb.2015.12.051.

Dijkstra, J. K., Lindenberg, S., & Veenstra, R. (2008). Beyond the class norm: Bullying behavior of popular adolescents and its relation to peer acceptance and rejection. *Journal of Abnormal Child Psychology, 36,* 1289–1299. https://doi.org/10.1007/s10802-008-9251-7.

Duffy, A. L., & Nesdale, D. (2009). Peer groups, social identity, and children's bullying behavior. *Social Development, 18,* 121–139. https://doi.org/10.1111/j.1467-9507.2008.00484.x.

Eagly, A. H., & Wood, W. (1991). Explaining sex differences in social behavior: A meta-analytic perspective. *Personality and Social Psychology Bulletin, 17,* 306–315. https://doi.org/10.1177/0146167291173011.

Espelage, D. L., Holt, M. K., & Henkel, R. R. (2003). Examination of peer-group contextual effects on aggression during early adolescence. *Child Development, 74,* 205–220. https://doi.org/10.1111/1467-8624.00531.
Espelage, D. L., Low, S. K., & Jimerson, S. R. (2014). Understanding school climate, aggression, peer victimization, and bully perpetration: Contemporary science, practice, and policy. *School Psychology Quarterly, 29,* 233–237. https://doi.org/10.1037/spq0000090.
Espelage, D. L., & Swearer, S. M. (2011). *Bullying in North American schools* (2nd ed.). New York: Routledge.
Evans, C. B., & Smokowski, P. R. (2017). Negative bystander behavior in bullying dynamics: Assessing the impact of social capital deprivation and anti-social capital. *Child Psychiatry and Human Development, 48,* 120–135. https://doi.org/10.1007/s10578-016-0657-0.
Fabes, R. A., Martin, C. L., Hanish, L. D., Galligan, K., & Pahlke, E. (2015). Gender-segregated schooling: A problem disguised as a solution. *Educational Policy, 29,* 431–447. https://doi.org/10.1177/0895904813492382.
Farina, E., & Belacchi, C. (2014). The relationship between emotional competence and hostile/prosocial behavior in Albanian preschoolers: An exploratory study. *School Psychology International, 35,* 475–484. https://doi.org/10.1177/0143034313511011.
Fink, E., Patalay, P., Sharpe, H., & Wolpert, M. (2018). Child- and school-level predictors of children's bullying behavior: A multilevel analysis in 648 primary schools. *Journal of Educational Psychology, 110,* 17–26. https://doi.org/10.1037/edu0000204.
Frey, K. S., Hirschstein, M. K., Edstrom, L. V., & Snell, J. L. (2009). Observed reductions in school bullying, nonbullying aggression, and destructive bystander behavior: A longitudinal evaluation. *Journal of Educational Psychology, 101,* 466–481. https://doi.org/10.1037/a0013839.
Garandeau, C. F., & Cillessen, A. H. N. (2006). From indirect aggression to invisible aggression: A conceptual view on bullying and peer group manipulation. *Aggression and Violent Behavior, 11,* 612–625. https://doi.org/10.1016/j.avb.2005.08.005.
Gini, G. (2006). Social cognition and moral cognition in bullying: What's wrong? *Aggressive Behavior, 32,* 528–539. https://doi.org/10.1002/ab.20153.
Goossens, F. A., Olthof, T., & Dekker, P. H. (2006). New participant role scales: Comparison between various criteria for assigning roles and indications for their validity. *Aggressive Behavior, 32,* 343–357. https://doi.org/10.1002/ab.20133.

Hawley, P. H. (2015). Social dominance in childhood and its evolutionary underpinnings: Why it matters and what we can do. *Pediatrics, 135,* S31–38. https://doi.org/10.1542/peds.2014-3549D.

Hawkins, L., Pepler, D., & Craig, W. (2001). Naturalistic observations of peer interventions in bullying among elementary school children. *Social Development, 10,* 512–527. https://doi.org/10.1111/1467-9507.00178.

Hong, J. S., & Espelage, D. L. (2012). A review of research on bullying and peer victimization in school: An ecological system analysis. *Aggression and Violent Behavior, 17,* 311–322. https://doi.org/10.1016/j.avb.2012.03.003.

Huitsing, G., & Monks, C. P. (2018). Who victimizes whom and who defends whom? A multivariate social network analysis of victimization, aggression, and defending in early childhood. *Aggressive Behavior, 44,* 394–405. https://doi.org/10.1002/ab.21760.

Hutton, A., Salmivalli, C., & Lagerspetz, K. (2006). Friendship networks and bullying in schools. *Annals of the New York Academy of Sciences, 794,* 355–359. https://doi.org/10.1111/j.1749-6632.1996.tb32541.x.

Ickes, W., Gesn, P. R., & Graham, T. (2000). Gender differences in empathic accuracy: Differential ability or differential motivation? *Personal Relationships, 7,* 95–109. https://doi.org/10.1111/j.1475-6811.2000.tb00006.x.

Jenkins, L. N., Demaray, M. K., Fredrick, S. S., & Summers, K. H. (2016). Associations among middle school students' bullying roles and social skills. *Journal of School Violence, 15,* 259–278. https://doi.org/10.1080/15388220.2014.986675.

Jimenez-Barbero, J. A., Ruiz-Hernández, J. A., Llor-Zaragoza, L., Pérez-García, M., & Llor-Estebana, B. (2016). Effectiveness of anti-bullying school programs: A meta-analysis. *Children and Youth Services Review, 61,* 165–175. https://doi.org/10.1016/j.childyouth.2015.12.015.

Kärnä, A., Voeten, M., Little, T. D., Poskiparta, E., Kaljonen, A., & Salmivalli, C. (2011). A large-scale evaluation of the KiVa anti-bullying program: Grades 4–6. *Child Development, 82,* 311–330. https://doi.org/10.1111/j.1467-8624.2010.01557.x.

Lee, V. E., Marks, H. M., & Byrd, T. (1994). Sexism in single-sex and coeducational independent secondary school classrooms. *Sociology of Education, 67,* 92–120. https://doi.org/10.2307/2112699.

Menesini, E., Codecasa, E., Benelli, B., & Cowie, H. (2003). Enhancing children's responsibility to take action against bullying: Evaluation of a befriending intervention in Italian middle schools. *Aggressive Behavior, 29,* 1–14. https://doi.org/10.1002/ab.80012.

Menesini, E., Eslea, M., Smith, P. K., Genta, M. L., Giannetti, E., Fonzi, A., & Costabile, A. (1997). Cross-national comparison of children's attitudes towards bully/victim problems in school. *Aggressive Behavior, 23*, 245–257. https://doi.org/10.1002/(SICI)1098-2337(1997)23: 4%3c245:AID-AB3%3e3.0.CO;2-J

Miller-Johnson, S., Coie, J. D., Maumary-Gremaud, A., Lochman, J., & Terry, R. (1999). Relationship between childhood peer rejection and aggression and adolescent delinquency severity and type among African American youth. *Journal of Emotional Behavioural Disorders, 7*, 137–146. https://doi.org/10.1177/106342669900700302.

Moffitt, T. E. (1993). Adolescence-limited and life-course-persistent antisocial behavior: A developmental taxonomy. *Psychological Review, 100*, 674–701. https://doi.org/10.1037/0033-295X.100.4.674.

Monks, C. P., & Smith, P. K. (2006). Definitions of bullying: Age differences in understanding of the term and the role of experience. *British Journal of Developmental Psychology, 24*, 801–821. https://doi.org/10.1348/026151005 X82352.

Monks, C. P., & Smith, P. K. (2010). Peer, self and teacher nominations of participant roles taken in victimisation by five- and eight-year-olds. *Journal of Aggression, Conflict and Peace Research, 2*, 4–14. https://doi.org/10.5042/jacpr.2010.0532.

Monks, C. P., Smith, P. K., & Swettenham, J. (2003). Aggressors, victims, and defenders in preschool: Peer, self-, and teacher reports. *Merrill-Palmer Quarterly, 49*, 453–469. https://doi.org/10.1353/mpq.2003.0024.

O'Connell, P., Pepler, D., & Craig, W. (1999). Peer involvement in bullying: Insights and challenges for intervention. *Journal of Adolescence, 22*, 437–452. https://doi.org/10.1006/jado.1999.0238.

Oh, I., & Hazler, R. J. (2009). Contributions of personal and situational factors to bystander reactions to school bullying. *School Psychology International, 30*, 291–310. https://doi.org/10.1177/0143034309106499.

Palladino, B. E., Nocentini, A., & Menesini, E. (2016). Evidence-based intervention against bullying and cyberbullying: Evaluation of the NoTrap! program in two independent trials. *Aggressive Behavior, 42*, 194–206. https://doi.org/10.1002/ab.21636.

Patterson, L. J., Allan, A., & Cross, D. (2015). Adolescent bystanders' perspectives of aggression in the online versus school environments. *Journal of Adolescence, 49*, 60–67. https://doi.org/10.1016/j.adolescence.2016.02.003.

Pearce, N., Cross, D., Monks, H., Waters, S., & Falconer, S. (2011). Current evidence of best practice in whole-school bullying intervention and its potential to inform cyberbullying interventions. *Australian Journal of Guidance and Counselling, 21,* 1–21. https://doi.org/10.1375/ajgc.21.1.1.

Polanin, J. R., Espelage, D. L., & Pigott, T. D. (2012). A meta-analysis of school-based bullying prevention programs' effects on bystander intervention behavior. *School Psychology Review, 41,* 47–65.

Pouwels, J. L., Lansu, T. A. M., & Cillessen, A. H. N. (2016). Participant roles of bullying in adolescence: Status characteristics, social behavior, and assignment criteria. *Aggressive Behavior, 42,* 239–253. https://doi.org/10.1002/ab.21614.

Pouwels, J. L., Lansu, T. A. M., & Cillessen, A. H. N. (2017). Adolescents' explicit and implicit evaluations of hypothetical and actual peers with different bullying participant roles. *Journal of Experimental Child Psychology, 159,* 219–241. https://doi.org/10.1016/j.jecp.2017.02.008.

Pouwels, J. L., Lansu, T. A. M., & Cillessen, A. H. N. (2018a). A developmental perspective on popularity and the group process of bullying. *Aggression and Violent Behavior, 43,* 64–70. https://doi.org/10.1016/j.avb.2018.10.003.

Pouwels, J. L., Salmivalli, C., Saarento, S., van den Berg, Y. H. M., Lansu, T. A. M., & Cillessen, A. H. N. (2018b). Predicting adolescents' bullying participation from developmental trajectories of social status and behavior. *Child Development, 89,* 1157–1176. https://doi.org/10.1111/cdev.12794.

Pouwels, J. L., van Noorden, T. H. J., Lansu, T. A. M., & Cillessen, A. H. N. (2018c). The participant roles of bullying in different grades: Prevalence and social status profiles. *Social Development, 27,* 732–747. https://doi.org/10.1111/sode.12294.

Pozzoli, T., Gini, G., & Vieno, A. (2012). Individual and class moral disengagement in bullying among elementary school children. *Aggressive Behavior, 38,* 378–388. https://doi.org/10.1002/ab.21442.

Price, S., & Jones, R. A. (2001). Reflections on anti-bullying peer counselling in a comprehensive school. *Educational Psychology in Practice, 17,* 35–40. https://doi.org/10.1080/02667360124466.

Prinstein, M. J., & Cillessen, A. H. N. (2003). Forms and functions of adolescent peer aggression associated with high levels of peer status. *Merrill-Palmer Quarterly, 49,* 310–342. https://doi.org/10.1353/mpq.2003.0015.

Quirk, R., & Campbell, M. (2014). On standby? A comparison of online and offline witnesses to bullying and their bystander behaviour. *Educational Psychology, 35,* 430–448. https://doi.org/10.1080/01443410.2014.893556.

Repo, L., & Sajaniemi, N. (2015). Prevention of bullying in early educational settings: Pedagogical and organisational factors related to bullying. *European*

Early Childhood Education Research Journal, 23, 461–475. https://doi.org/ 10.1080/1350293X.2015.1087150.
Rivers, I., Poteat, V. P., Noret, N., & Ashurst, N. (2009). Observing bullying at school: The mental health implications of witness status. *School Psychology Quarterly, 24,* 211–223. https://doi.org/10.1037/a0018164.
Saarento, S., & Salmivalli, C. (2015). The role of classroom peer ecology and bystanders' responses in bullying. *Child Development Perspectives, 9,* 201–205. https://doi.org/10.1111/cdep.12140.
Salmivalli, C. (1999). Participant role approach to school bullying: Implications for interventions. *Journal of Adolescence, 22,* 453–459. https://doi.org/ 10.1006/jado.1999.0239.
Salmivalli, C. (2010a). Bullying and the peer group: A review. *Aggression and Violent Behavior, 15,* 112–120. https://doi.org/10.1016/j.avb.2009.08.007.
Salmivalli, C. (2010b). Peer-led intervention campaign against school bullying: Who considered it useful, who benefited? *Educational Research, 43,* 263–278. https://doi.org/10.1080/00131880110081035.
Salmivalli, C. (2014). Participant roles in bullying: How can peer bystanders be utilized in interventions? *Theory into Practice, 53,* 286–292. https://doi. org/10.1080/00405841.2014.947222.
Salmivalli, C., Huttunen, A., & Lagerspetz, K. M. J. (1997). Peer networks and bullying in schools. *Scandinavian Journal of Psychology, 38,* 305–312. https://doi.org/10.1111/1467-9450.00040.
Salmivalli, C., Lagerspetz, K., Björkqvist, K., Österman, K., & Kaukiainen, A. (1996). Bullying as a group process: Participant roles and their relations to social status within the group. *Aggressive Behavior, 22,* 1–15. https://doi.org/ 10.1002/(SICI)1098-2337.
Salmivalli, C., Lappalainen, M., & Lagerspetz, K. M. J. (1998). Stability and change of behavior in connection with bullying in schools: A two-year follow-up. *Aggressive Behavior, 24,* 205–218. https://doi.org/10.1002/(SIC I)1098-2337.
Salmivalli, C., & Voeten, M. (2004). Connections between attitudes, group norms, and behaviour in bullying situations. *International Journal of Behavioral Development, 28,* 246–258. https://doi.org/10.1080/016502503440 00488.
Salmivalli, C., Voeten, M., & Poskiparta, E. (2011). Bystanders matter: Associations between reinforcing, defending, and the frequency of bullying behavior in classrooms. *Journal of Clinical Child & Adolescent Psychology, 40,* 668–676. https://doi.org/10.1080/15374416.2011.597090.

Schäfer, M., Korn, S., Brodbeck, F. C., Wolke, D., & Schulz, H. (2005). Bullying roles in changing contexts: The stability of victim and bully roles from primary to secondary school. *International Journal of Behavioural Development, 29,* 323–335. https://doi.org/10.1080/01650250544000107.

Sentse, M., Veenstra, R., Kiuru, N., & Salmivalli, C. (2015). A longitudinal multilevel study of individual characteristics and classroom norms in explaining bullying behaviors. *Journal of Abnormal Child Psychology, 43,* 943–955. https://doi.org/10.1007/s10802-014-9949-7.

Smith, P. K. (2004). Bullying: Recent developments. *Child and Adolescent Mental Health, 9,* 98–103. https://doi.org/10.1111/j.1475-3588.2004.00089.x.

Smith, P. K., Madsen, K. C., & Moody, J. C. (2006). What causes the age decline in reports of being bullied at school? Towards a developmental analysis of risks of being bullied. *Educational Research, 41,* 267–285. https://doi.org/10.1080/0013188990410303.

Song, J., & Oh, I. (2018). Factors influencing bystanders' behavioral reactions in cyberbullying situations. *Computers in Human Behavior, 78,* 273–282. https://doi.org/10.1016/j.chb.2017.10.008.

Sutton, J., Smith, P. K., & Swettenham, J. (1999). Social cognition and bullying: Social inadequacy or skilled manipulation? *British Journal of Developmental Psychology, 17,* 435–450. https://doi.org/10.1348/026151099165384.

Tani, F., Greenman, P. S., Schneider, B. H., & Fregoso, M. (2003). Bullying and the big five: A study of childhood personality and participant roles in bullying incidents. *School Psychology International, 24,* 131–146. https://doi.org/10.1177/0143034303024002001.

Thornberg, R., & Wänström, L. (2018). Bullying and its association with altruism toward victims, blaming the victims, and classroom prevalence of bystander behaviors: A multilevel analysis. *Social Psychology of Education, 21,* 1133–1151. https://doi.org/10.1007/s11218-018-9457-7.

Thornberg, R., Wänström, L., & Jungert, T. (2018). Authoritative classroom climate and its relations to bullying victimization and bystander behaviors. *School Psychology International, 39,* 663–680. https://doi.org/10.1177/0143034318809762.

Unnever, J. D., & Cornell, D. G. (2008). The culture of bullying in middle school. *Journal of School Violence, 2,* 5–27. https://doi.org/10.1300/J202v02n02_02.

Wachs, S. (2012). Moral disengagement and emotional and social difficulties in bullying and cyberbullying: Differences by participant role. *Emotional and*

Behavioural Difficulties, 17, 347–360. https://doi.org/10.1080/13632752.
2012.704318.
Witvliet, M., Olthof, T., Hoeksma, J. B., Goossens, F. A., Smits, M. S. I., & Koot, H. M. (2010). Peer group affiliation of children: the role of perceived popularity, likeability, and behavioral similarity in bullying. *Social Development, 19*, 285–303. https://doi.org/10.1111/j.1467-9507.2009.005 44.x.
Wolke, D., Woods, S., & Samara, M. (2009). Who escapes or remains a victim of bullying in primary school? *British Journal of Developmental Psychology, 27*, 835–851. https://doi.org/10.1348/026151008X383003.
Zedan, R. (2010). New dimensions in the classroom climate. *Learning Environments Research, 13*, 75–88. https://doi.org/10.1007/s10984-009-9068-5.

4

The Outsider Vantage Point

Greg R. Machek, Jaynee L. Bohart, Ashlyn M. Kincaid, and Emily A. Hattouni

Introduction: An Ecological Perspective

In the last three decades, a relatively large body of research has been devoted to understanding the personal characteristics of students and their possible interaction with more general ecological factors (Bronfenbrenner, 1979) to help explain beliefs and behaviors surrounding bullying in schools (Pozzoli, Gini, & Vieno, 2012). This research has been motivated by the agreed upon notion that peer aggression is an inherently social phenomena and incidents of bullying rarely occur without the knowledge of others in their social environment. For example, Craig, Pepler, and Atlas (2000) utilized naturalistic observations via video cameras and microphones on 34 first through sixth graders. These students were observed in both the classroom and

---

G. R. Machek (✉)
Department of Psychology, University of Montana, Missoula, MT, USA
e-mail: greg.machek@mso.umt.edu

J. L. Bohart · A. M. Kincaid · E. A. Hattouni
University of Montana, Missoula, MT, USA

© The Author(s) 2020
L. Rosen et al. (eds.), *Bullies, Victims, and Bystanders*,
https://doi.org/10.1007/978-3-030-52939-0_4

playground settings, and researchers found that peers were involved (i.e., aggressing, observing, interacting with the bully and/or victim, or intervening) in 79% of observed playground instances and 85% of classroom-based incidents of aggression.

This chapter will introduce the reader to the definition of the outsider role, provide information on its prevalence, and detail the individual and ecological characteristics that help explain why a large proportion of students tend toward this participant disposition. Understanding such characteristics can inform interventions that attempt to make students more likely to become active agents against school bullying. We primarily focus on traits that are relevant to outsiders within face-to-face encounters, as opposed to online or cyberbullying, due to the bulk of research having been done in this area. Additionally, we highlight two published anti-bullying curricula that specifically aim to sway bystanders toward active defending.

Definition and Prevalence of the Outsider Role

Defining Outsiders

Outsiders are a subset of bystanders who are usually privy to the existence of bullying yet take on passive tendencies, such as not getting involved and wittingly avoiding the situation (Salmivalli, Lagerspetz, Björkqvist, Österman, & Kaukiainen, 1996). Importantly, outsiders differ from other "bystanders" who opt to take on more active roles, such as defenders, reinforcers, and assistants (Ettekal, Kochenderfer-Ladd, & Ladd, 2015; Gini, Albiero, Benelli, & Altoè, 2008; Obermann, 2011; see also Fredrick, Jenkins, & Dexter, this volume; Monks & O'Toole, this volume). Jeffrey, Miller, and Linn (2001) suggest that all students are motivated to adopt bullying roles in order to protect themselves from victimization. However, evidence indicates that outsiders may be less self-reliant and less adept at problem-solving (Pozzoli & Gini, 2010) as well as less able to cope independently with victimization compared to defenders (Pronk, Goossens, Olthof, de Mey, & Willemen,

2013). As a result of self-preservation and certain skill deficits, outsiders rely on physical and emotional avoidance strategies when faced with bullying situations, and some evidence indicates that outsiders cope with bullying situations by mentally and emotionally distancing themselves from victims (Pozzoli & Gini, 2010).

Operationalization of the different participant roles has most commonly been achieved through the use of the Participant Role Questionnaire (PRQ)[1] (Demaray, Summers, Jenkins, & Becker, 2016; Salmivalli et al., 1996). In its original use, the PRQ consisted of 48 items describing behaviors that students are likely to engage in when bullying occurs (Salmivalli et al., 1996). These researchers looked at 573 sixth graders in Finland and found that 87% of the pupils were able to be assigned a particular participant role, such as bullies, reinforcers of the bully, assistants to the bully, defenders of the victim, and outsiders.

Prevalence

In Salmivalli and colleagues' (1996) original PRQ research, the largest single group was that of the outsiders, which comprised 23.7% of their total sample (11.7% assigned as victims; 8.2% as bullies; 19.5% as reinforcers; 6.8% as assistants; 17.3% as defenders; and 12.7% having no role). Subsequent research has shown relatively similar rates for outsiders, though occasionally lower. For example, Sutton and Smith (1999) found that outsiders comprised only 11.9% of their sample, a much smaller percentage than found by Salmivalli et al. (1996). However, this research included a slightly younger sample (7–10 years of age), and a shortened PRS scale that made use of an interview technique to gather data. Utilizing an older, Dutch high school-aged sample, Pouwels, Lansu, and Cillessen (2016) also used a shortened version of the PRQ, as well as the

---

[1] It should be noted that the PRQ has also been referred to as the Participant Roles Scale (PRS; e.g., Crapanzano, Frick, Childs, & Terranova, 2011; Goossens, Olthof, & Dekker, 2006; Lucas-Molina, Williamson, Pulido, & Calderón, 2014; Sutton & Smith, 1999) and that other derivatives of the scale have been created over the years, such as versions with slightly modified content, shortened, translated into various languages, and/or which have employed methodological changes (see Demaray et al., 2016; Goossens et al., 2006; Lucas-Molina et al., 2014).

same cutoff criteria for roles as Salmivalli et al. (1996) on 1638 students. This peer-report method evidenced a similar distribution of the outsider role as Salmivalli et al. (1996) at 24.1% of the overall sample. Additionally, Hara (2002) looked at 100 12–14 year-old students in Japan and found that 29.6% took on the outsider role. Overall, these selected studies, from differing age ranges and countries, suggest a prevalence rate in the 12–30% range for outsiders.

Despite the variation in distribution across different research samples, the outsider role consistently ranks as the most common role, particularly when researchers use the PRQ (Salmivalli et al., 1996) or its numerous derivatives. There is evidence that this holds true across developmental levels as well. For example, in a study sampling 238 3rd through 12th graders, the group defined as outsiders turned out to be the relatively largest group in all grade levels collected: 17.2% in 3rd through 6th graders, 17.6% in 7th through 9th graders, and 14.9% in 10th through 12th graders (Choi & Cho, 2012).

Factors Affecting Distribution of Role Categorization

Methodological Considerations. Methodological differences, such as peer versus self-report strategies, can affect role distribution. For example, Nickerson and Mele-Taylor (2014) used a self-report version of the Bullying Participant Roles Survey (BPRS), a derivative of the PRQ, and discovered the following role grouping: defenders = 51.5%; victims = 18.3%; bullies = 14.9%; and outsiders = 9.9%. In the BPRS, assistant and reinforcer behaviors are collapsed into the general bully category due to an inability of factor analytic techniques to validly separate these roles (see Lucas-Molina et al., 2014 for a thorough review). Their self-report distribution, when compared to Salmivalli et al. (1996), shows a lower number of outsiders and those in the general aggressive role. One explanation offered by the authors is that social desirability effects (Edwards, 1953) are at play in self-report measures and favor a subset of children who would like to cast themselves in a particularly positive light as defenders. This may result in a redistribution of students' endorsements away from the outsider category.

Other methodological reasons for different prevalence rates include how cutoffs for role categorization are set, such as whether to categorize participants based on an absolute percentage of peer endorsement or on relative, dimensional values compared to other peers within the same school or classroom (Pouwels et al., 2016). Generalizability across cultures and the range used in Likert response categories have also been offered as factors to consider (Demaray et al., 2016).

Gender. Gender differences within the outsider role have most often favored girls (e.g., Goossens et al., 2006; Pronk, Olthof, & Goossens, 2016; Salmivalli et al., 1996; Salmivalli, Huttunen, & Lagerspetz, 1997), with some exceptions (Nickerson, Mele, & Princiotta, 2008). For example, Salmivalli and colleagues' (1996) sample showed a 40.2–7.3% differential, significantly in favor of girls, while boys had a higher representation in the more aggressive roles. Pouwels and colleagues' (2016) older Dutch sample also showed a significant difference in the gender distribution, with girls comprising 55% of the outsider role. One reason for gender differences could simply be due to the fact that aggressive behavior is more glorified and accepted among boys (Salmivalli et al., 1996).

Early Indicators of the Role

A relatively small amount of research has been dedicated to participant role traits in very young children; however, what has been done gives insight into the possible characterological origins of the role. For example, Belacchi and Farina (2010) investigated the differences in emotional understanding of pre-school students (mean age 4 years, 10 months) assigned different participant roles. In this sample of pre-schoolers, the outsider role was negatively correlated with emotional understanding, suggesting they may have had more difficulty with skills such as recognition of facial expressions of emotion and understanding desire-based emotions. Camodeca and Coppola (2018) also found an overall tendency for outsiders in a pre-school sample to be emotionally dysregulated, suggesting that shying away from conflict is related to their levels of anxiety, frustration, and distress in such situations. These authors also found the teachers' behaviors and relationships with the preschools were important considerations because even the outsiders that were more emotionally stable did not help victims if they had conflictual relationships with their teachers.

Stability of the Role

Overall, bullying participant roles have shown moderate consistency over time (Salmivalli, Lappalainen, & Lagerspetz, 1998), though a number of factors may influence this stability, such as reporting method, gender, peer ecology, and dispositional factors. Salmivalli and colleagues (1998) followed students from the sixth through eighth grades. In addition to finding moderate stability for all roles, they discovered that boys tended to be more stable in the outsider role than girls when considering peer nominations, but girls evidenced greater stability in the outsider role when considering self-nominations than boys. This study also showed that stability may be peer-influenced as it was greater for students that stayed with largely the same classmates over the study period. More recent research has replicated evidence of stability with a smaller Italian sample of 9–14 year-olds (Mazzone, Camodeca, & Salmivalli, 2016) by showing a significant correlation between outsider ratings approximately 10 months apart. This study also found that low guilt and high shame increased the predictability of staying in the outsider role.

Other research has shown that the stability of the outsider role is related to the stability of a student's general aggressive tendencies. For example, Pouwels and colleagues (2018) found that adolescents that form the outsider group are overrepresented in a "low aggression stable" cluster, suggesting that these students consistently do not show aggressive tendencies across childhood and early adolescence.

Adjustment

Research has shown that direct involvement in bullying affects the various participants in a number of ways. Moore and colleagues (2017) conducted a meta-analysis of 165 studies which revealed that being bullied was associated with internalizing symptoms, poorer physical health, substance abuse, and suicidality. Additional research has shown that victimization is associated with greater alcohol use in high school students and more difficulty making friends (Nansel, Overpeck, & Pilla, 2007). On the other hand, engaging in bullying has been positively associated with fighting, alcohol use, smoking, lower academic achievement, worse perceptions of school climate, lower quality peer relationships, and increased loneliness (Nansel et al., 2007). As for individuals that concurrently bully others and get bullied themselves, their role has been positively associated with fighting, smoking, lower academic achievement, poorer peer relations, and loneliness as well (Nansel et al., 2007).

However, few studies have investigated the impact on outsiders as defined in this chapter. Rivers, Poteat, Noret, and Ashurst (2009) conducted one of the only studies that endeavored to measure the effects of witnessing bullying above and beyond the effects of being involved as a main participant (bully or victim), though this was done through a statistical control method and not through the identification of an outsider subgroup. These authors found that witness status was correlated with mental health risk as measured by the Brief Symptom Inventory (BSI; Derogatis, 1994) after controlling for perpetrator and victim status. They also concluded that mental health risk was not driven by victimization history as witnesses with and without significant personal histories of victimization were equally likely to be affected by their experiences in observing peer aggression. Other research, though, does show that the witness' personal victimization history may be a factor in predicting the effects of witnessing aggression. For instance, Werth, Nickerson, Aloe, and Swearer (2015) found that bystanders who also had significant exposure as victims scored higher than bystanders without victim histories on a measure of social maladjustment, highlighting the need to consider the individual's past victimization exposure when determining the level of risk and needed support. Overall, adjustment outcomes in the outsider group is an important area for further research, particularly research that defines group membership in line with traditional participant role categorization.

Interpersonal and Situational Factors Related to Outsider Role

Despite the evidence of relative stability discussed above, it is also likely that students take on characteristics of multiple roles. For example, Gumpel, Zioni-Koren, and Bekerman (2014) followed 20 10th graders over an entire academic year in an ethnographic study aimed at discovering dispositional and situational factors related to participant roles. They noted that outsiders, along with assistants, defenders, and reinforcers, tend to manifest fluidity between roles depending on situational dynamics. Thus, it is of primary importance—in terms of interventions—to understand the intraindividual and situational factors that help predict outsider behavior, or conversely, may help predict why and when an outsider would choose to lend support to victimized peers instead of remaining on the sidelines.

Interpersonal Relationship Factors

Peer Pressure and Proximal Group Norms. Students who choose to engage in negative bystander behaviors (assist and reinforce the bully) tend to indicate high levels of perceived peer pressure to do so (Evans & Smokowski, 2017). Likewise, this can work in the opposite direction, as low levels of perceived peer pressure to intervene have been shown to be predictive of passive bystander behavior (Pozzoli et al., 2012). The latter study also demonstrated that the perceived norms of the classroom ecology predicted bystander behavior. Specifically, low levels of participant-perceived classroom attitudes regarding defending behavior were associated with higher levels of passive bystanding. This study also averaged all student nominations regarding defending and passive bystanding behavior within their classroom to come up with a "descriptive norm" for that setting that indicated how much each behavior was considered normative for the class. These classroom norms predicted bystander behavior; for example, if norms regarding defending were low, scores on passive bystanding were higher. These peer influences were stronger in middle schoolers than primary grade children, which is consistent with research on the salience of peer influence on behaviors in early adolescence (Brown, 2004). Results from Salmivalli and colleagues (1998), cited above, that showed more role stability for those students who stayed with their immediate peer group throughout the study lends further support for the idea that the immediate peer ecology compels characteristic participant role behaviors. Respondents' perceptions of their parents' expectations regarding intervening have also been shown to affect a student's willingness to get help or remain a bystander (Rigby & Johnson, 2006). Finally, very young children, such as kindergartners, may be less influenced by proximal norms if they are still struggling to understand others' emotions or do not yet understand or value social norms (Camodeca & Coppola, 2016).

Relationship with Victims. Social psychologists have noted that bystanders are more likely to intervene in situations in which the victim is considered an in-group member (Levine, Cassidy, Brazier, & Reicher, 2002). Researchers of school bullying have similarly investigated whether a bystander's relationship with the victim predicts if that person remains a passive outsider or gets involved, thus necessitating the need for school personnel to have a good understanding of the sociometric dynamics among their students (Oh & Hazler, 2009). Oh and Hazler (2009) suggest that bystanders consider their relationship to both the victim and the aggressor when making decisions about whether to intervene, and subsequent actions are likely an attempt to preserve a preexisting relationship status (Meter & Card, 2015). Thus, the closer the relationship a bystander has with a bully, the more likely they are to take on assistant or reinforcer behaviors. Conversely, a closer relationship with the victim predicts staying outside or defending behavior. Bellmore, Ting-Lan, You, and Hughes (2012) provide empirical evidence for this dynamic. They sought to understand factors that explain why some passive bystanders may act as defenders. The researchers provided bullying vignettes to

470 sixth graders and asked them to rate a number of ways in which they may or may not intervene as well as information on the relationship between the respondent and the victims and onlookers (e.g., classmate, friend, unknown). Their respondents were significantly more likely to suggest that they would help the victim (i.e., move away from traditional outsider behavior), particularly by confronting the bully or comforting the victim, if the victim was identified as a friend. Ma (2019) evidenced similar results when assessing 730 seventh graders in southern Taiwan, and this study evidenced an interaction by gender showing this relationship was strongest for females.

Social Status. Outsiders are often regarded by classmates in neutral or ambiguous terms. For example, Goossens and colleagues (2006) found that outsiders' social status tended toward being neglected as opposed to rejected, whereas aggressors tended to be controversial or more often actively rejected by peer nomination. Similarly, Salmivalli and colleagues (1996) looked at most and least liked peer nominations as they related to participant roles and found that outsiders were a little below average on both social acceptance and social rejection; compare this to high social acceptance and low social rejection for defenders (see also Fredrick, Jenkins, & Dexter, this volume; Lambe, Cioppa, Hong, & Craig, 2018 for comprehensive reviews of social traits that relate to defenders). The same theme surfaced in a study by Pouwels et al. (2016) that found that outsiders were neither particularly liked nor disliked. Although outsiders were "relatively" unpopular and withdrawn in this sample of 1638 Dutch adolescents, they were not as unpopular or withdrawn as victims. This is important because it has been found that peer rejection status predicts victimization. It may be that outsiders possess a degree of other non-behavioral traits, such as attractiveness, academic and athletic competence, and level of SES status, which have been shown to be protective of victimization, even in rejected youth (Knack, Vasilinka, Vaillancourt, Hymel, & McDougal, 2012).

Perceptions of Severity. There is some evidence that the severity of peer aggression can influence intentions to help. For example, Chen, Chang, and Cheng (2016) specifically examined the severity of peer harassment in hopes of helping to explain action or inaction among bystanders. Their small study of 24 seventh through ninth graders in southern Taiwan interviewed students high on either defender or outsider traits. Among other influential factors covered elsewhere in this chapter, the authors found that 70% of their participants felt that the severity of victimization could prompt them to act, particularly by informing teachers in cases of very serious aggression. It should be noted that severity perceptions are probably influenced by the type of aggression too, with physical aggression likely considered the most harmful by non-involved students (Chen, Cheng, & Ho, 2015).

Despite Chen and colleagues' (2016) results, other research suggests that outsiders do not consistently interpret victimization as severe. This is evident in bullying research that has invoked the "bystander effect" to help understand action and inaction in events with multiple witnesses (Bellmore et al., 2012; Jenkins & Nickerson, 2017; Ma, 2019; Menolascino & Jenkins, 2018). The term came to prominence through the research of Latané and Darley (1968), who monitored the occurrence and speed of participant responses to another person in health distress. The experimental conditions differed by the existence and/or amount of other witnesses, and the research revealed that the presence of additional bystanders substantially reduced help-seeking behavior. One of the authors' main conclusions was that the reduced action was caused by diffusion of responsibility, which was largely due to the participant looking for clues in the reactions of the other present witnesses. Latané and Darley (1970) subsequently presented an intervention model based on the bystander effect which puts forth five necessary steps of intervening in an emergency: (a) recognizing the event, (b) interpreting the event as an emergency, (c) accepting that it is a personal responsibility to do something, (d) having knowledge of what to do, and (e) actually intervening.

Jenkins and Nickerson (2017) specifically tested Latané and Darley's (1970) bystander intervention model relative to participant roles in situations of school bullying to understand if particular roles—as well as gender—predicted each step of the model. Unsurprisingly, defenders significantly predicted active behaviors in each of the five steps; however, outsiders only evidenced a significant negative correlation with actually intervening, which is understandable given their role. And although girls in this study tended to interpret incidents of peer harassment as more severe compared to boys, outsiders, as a whole, did not interpret the situations as particularly severe. This finding is consistent with a study by Pronk et al. (2016) that found that awareness of victim distress significantly predicted defender status, but not outsider status. It is possible that in some cases students may witness bullying so frequently that habituation results in some students not perceiving bullying as an emergency warranting intervention (Thornberg et al., 2012). Such normalization is likely to be more prevalent in schools that have high rates of aggressive interactions and a culture that does not consistently emphasize taking hurtful behavior seriously. Jenkins and Nickerson (2017) also found that outsiders did not feel that they should intervene, or perceive themselves as possessing ample knowledge about what to do, at least as compared to students who actually interceded.

Family Involvement

It has been noted that many anti-bullying programs focus solely on the school environment with little to no parent involvement (Grassetti et al., 2018). However, a child's home environment and family support have been shown to influence the participant roles they take on. Grassetti and colleagues (2018) looked at 106 fourth through sixth graders and compared peer-reported bystander behaviors with the type of advice parents gave their children about how to—or how to not—intervene during situations of bullying. They found that when caregivers told their children to stop the bully or to support the victim, bystander intervention was more likely. Conversely, when caregivers told their children to not get involved, bystander intervention was less likely. These results support a relationship between caregiver advice on bullying and students' behavior at school.

Developmental differences in attachment and empathy response have also been suggested to play a part in students adopting the participant role of an outsider. Nickerson et al. (2008) sought to determine the impact of attachment to mother, attachment to father, and empathy on self-reported participant roles. These researchers found that a higher level of empathy and attachment (especially with the mother) decreased the odds of a student identifying as an outsider. Similarly, Li, Chen, Chen, and Wu (2015), found that parental support increased the likelihood that a child would take on the defender role.

The above studies strongly suggest that intervention efforts should specifically target parents. Sending home informational booklets that contain the school's program aims would be a good start in encouraging caregivers to furnish appropriate advice on to their child regarding the need to intervene. Research has also shown that positive parenting is related to a child taking on the defender role (Valdés-Cuervo, Alcántar-Nieblas, Martínez-Ferrer, & Parra-Pérez, 2018). Positive parenting involves discipline focused on accountability, healthy family climates, and supportive environments. Parents should also be informed that giving emotional support to their children will help them cope with negative emotions, which prepares children to take on a defender role instead of an outsider role (Li et al., 2015).

Intraindividual Characteristics

Cognitive Processing Factors

Theory of Mind. Theory of mind perspectives focus on the ability of students to understand others' perspectives and emotional states, and it has been debated whether some aggressors possess and use these skills to their advantage when preying upon others (e.g., see Crick & Dodge, 1999; Sutton, Smith, & Swettenham, 1999a, 1999b; Sutton et al., 2001). More specifically, do some bullies leverage intact theory of mind skills to better understand how to inflict harm while minimizing detection by others (Sutton et al., 1999a)? Although this debate has largely centered on understanding aggressor behavior, the construct also has importance in understanding the behavior of other participants. For example, Sutton and colleagues (1999a) suggested that further examination of emotion recognition and understanding might illuminate the relationship between social cognition and outsider behaviors. At this point, the research is decidedly mixed on the issue. When applying theory of mind attributes to the different roles, Gini (2006) found that bullies and defenders were quite capable of understanding the thoughts, beliefs, and intentions of others whereas victims struggled to do so, and outsiders were somewhere in between the other roles. Other researchers have found that outsider behavior is actually predicted by a child's relatively lower ability in understanding others' mental states, but that it is unrelated to being able to understand emotional states (Sutton et al., 1999c). Conversely, Belacchi and Farina (2010) found that outsider behavior was associated with a poorer understanding of emotions in others caused by desires, as well as poorer recognition of facial expressions. Given the inconclusiveness of the current research, definitive conclusions cannot be made regarding the relationship between theory of mind abilities and outsider tendencies without more research. It may be that the trait differs among outsiders, or that it interacts with gender or developmental level.

Social Information Processing. When examining social information processing (SIP; i.e., the mental process of assessing a social situation and deciding how to act) by bullying participant roles, Camodeca and Goossens (2005) found that outsiders processed social situations without a high likelihood of making hostile attributions. That is, outsiders do not tend to reflexively interpret the intentions of others' behaviors as hostile when they are not necessarily so. They also found that outsiders did not tend to be reactively (angrily retaliating toward perceived threats) or proactively (deliberate, cold-blooded, and goal-oriented harm toward others) aggressive. Moreover, an investigation of social-cognitive antecedents, such as distress awareness, transference of responsibility to intervene, and cost-reward analysis revealed no connection with outsiders (Pronk et al., 2016). Furthermore, Andreou and Metallidou (2004) examined children's expectations that aggression would result in rewards or suffering in addition to how much they valued each result and found no associations with outsider behavior. Therefore, it appears that outsider behavior is not readily explained by specific SIP deficits, such as those seen in more reactively and proactively aggressive children (Dodge, Lochman, Harnish, Bates, & Pettit, 1997), and that interventions for outsiders would not seem to be enhanced by a primary focus on their interpretation of others' behaviors and intentions as defined by the SIP model.

Perceptions of Responsibility and Blame

Outsiders have reported not intervening because the bullying situation did not directly involve them, they wanted to remain uninvolved, or they thought the victim deserved to be bullied (Cappadocia, Pepler, Cummings, & Craig, 2012). Additionally, outsider behavior has been negatively associated with feelings of personal responsibility for intervening (Pozzoli & Gini, 2010). For boys in particular, their willingness to intervene has been associated with the acceptance that intervening is their responsibility (Menolascino & Jenkins, 2018). However, students often employ justification techniques to avoid feeling responsible for intervening. Hara (2002) found that 76.7% of outsiders agreed that the bullying they witnessed was justified or deserved; 73.1% of the time outsiders blamed the victim, 11.5% of the time they denied that the bullying caused harm, and 15.4% of the time they gave other reasons why the bullying was acceptable.

Empathy

Related research suggests that both outsiders and defenders have high levels of empathy relative to other roles (Rieffe & Camodeca, 2016), though it is important to consider how "empathy" is defined. Studies have examined different dimensions of empathy, including one of its precursors—perspective taking—along with empathic responsiveness, concern, distress, and anger (Espelage, Green, & Polanin, 2012; Nickerson & Mele-Taylor, 2014; Nickerson et al., 2008; Pozzoli, Gini, & Thornberg, 2017). The findings from these studies generally suggest that low levels of empathetic factors are associated with a higher likelihood of outsider behavior.

It appears that most research on empathy specifically focuses on its (a) cognitive and (b) affective underpinnings (e.g., Haddock & Jimerson, 2017; Menolascino & Jenkins, 2018; Pöyhönen, Juvonen, & Salmivalli, 2010; Rieffe & Camodeca, 2016). Cognitive empathy has to do with a logical understanding of what victims endure, whereas affective empathy involves emotional sharing in the victims' suffering (Pöyhönen et al., 2010). There is evidence that the affective component of empathy, rather than the cognitive component, is particularly related to outsider behavior. Specifically, lower levels of affective empathy seem to differentiate outsiders from defenders (Bellmore et al., 2012; Haddock & Jimerson, 2017; Yang & Kim, 2017), whereas cognitive empathy has been found to be unrelated to outsider behavior (Menolascino & Jenkins, 2018; Pöyhönen et al., 2010). Even so, affective empathy has been found to be only marginally related to outsider behavior (Lucas-Molina, Pérez-Albéniz, Fonseca-Pedrero, & Giménez-Dasí, 2018), and some have suggested that empathic responses are necessary but not sufficient determinants of actual behavior (Obermann, 2011). Further, there may be a gender effect when considering affective and cognitive aspects of empathy: boys' willingness to intervene has been found to be associated with their affective empathy, whereas other factors have been found to predict girls' intervention efforts (Menolascino & Jenkins, 2018). Since girls are relatively stable in their levels of affective empathy, it may be necessary to focus more on increasing skills in boys (e.g., perspective taking) that lead to emotional sharing and subsequent helping. Empathic skills can be strengthened using a variety of activities as part of an intervention (e.g., role-playing, problem-solving games, storytelling, and teacher-led classroom discussions; Nickerson et al., 2008).

Emotional Reactions

Some students may be particularly influenced by the emotional reactions surrounding incidents of school bullying, and this may contribute to both joining and defending behavior. It may also help explain why many outsiders choose to stay uninvolved. While some students state that they do not try to stop bullying because it is exciting to watch, more students report negative feelings (e.g., fear, worry, concern) as the cause of their inaction (Thornberg et al., 2012). Researchers have found that fear and concerns for safety are particularly related to outsider behavior (Bellmore et al., 2012; Yang & Kim, 2017). Specifically, Cappadocia and colleagues (2012) found that 24% of outsiders reported being generally afraid of the situation, 15% reported concerns about getting in trouble for reporting, and 5% worried they would become the next target. Outsiders have also been found to worry about being ostracized or that they may face retaliation if they intervene in a situation (Chen et al., 2016). In addition, research shows that individuals who believe that they will not be bullied in the future actually intend to intervene more than individuals who evaluate their vulnerability more realistically (Chapin & Brayack, 2016). Such findings are supported by research that has found outsider behavior to positively predict sensitivity to punishment and negatively predict sensitivity to reward, whereas no such relationship has been seen in defenders (Pronk et al., 2015). These researchers similarly conclude that outsiders may not intervene because they are highly sensitive to possible repercussions but not to possible reinforcement for defending.

Personal History of Victimization

As stated earlier, student roles are somewhat stable and are predicted by their own past roles as well as their friends' current roles (Salmivalli et al., 1998). Additionally, students' past victimization experiences may also contribute to the roles they choose to adopt, prospectively. For example, Chapin and Brayack (2016) found that adolescents who experienced verbal, physical, and social bullying did not report intending to intervene more than adolescents without such histories. On the other hand, Rigby and Johnson (2006) found that adolescents with more extensive experience being bullies, but not victims, were associated with fewer intentions to intervene. However, Chapin and Brayack (2016) also found that despite their stated intentions, students who were bullied in the past were actually more likely to report having intervened in a bullying situation during a 30-day period. Even though adolescents did not believe their past histories impacted their intentions to intervene, their pasts actually were in fact associated with their future intervention efforts. Therefore, outsiders who occasionally intervene, or who intervene in more indirect and less noticeable ways, may do so because of past histories that include experiencing peer aggression firsthand.

Moral Disengagement

Additional research into the outsider role has focused on moral disengagement, or separating oneself from the morality involved in decision-making. Gini, Thornberg, and Pozzoli (2018) identified moral disengagement as a moderator between defending and passive bystander behaviors among adolescents. These researchers found that an individual's moral disengagement was negatively correlated to levels of moral distress when faced with a bullying scenario. Additionally, they found that the level of moral distress was negatively related to being a passive bystander. They concluded that individuals with higher levels of moral disengagement experience less moral distress, and are more likely to engage in passive bystander behavior, or in other words, be an outsider. Additionally, Haddock and Jimerson (2017) found that individuals in the outsider role, as rated by self-reports, had the highest levels of moral disengagement, and these levels were significantly higher than those of defenders, victim/defenders, and the comparison group. This suggests that outsiders may struggle to understand what is right and wrong in morally challenging situations. Similar findings were reported by Levasseur, Desbiens, and Bowen (2017) who found that students in the outsider and bully roles showed more disengagement from moral reasoning compared to students in the defender role.

Personality Characteristics

Noting that outsiders and defenders both espouse a certain level of anti-bullying attitudes, and that outsiders also sometimes defend victims (Pronk et al., 2016), researchers have sought to discern factors that nonetheless separate these two categories. For example, Pronk and colleagues (2015) looked at both Big Five personality traits, as well as the participants' ratings for sensitivity to punishment and rewards, in 591 Dutch fifth and sixth graders. Personality factors that were associated with outsider behavior in this study included being lower in extraversion and higher in impulse control, suggesting a higher tendency toward inhibition in potentially socially risky situations. Pronk and colleagues (2015) suggest that this adds to the behavioral inhibition in outsiders because they may be particularly afraid of retaliation from the bully, or they do not see the social value in standing up for the victim. Another study examining the Italian version of the Big Five personality traits in 134 Italian third and fourth graders found outsiders to be lower in extroversion and agreeableness, suggesting that outsiders are less prosocial compared to defenders (Tani, Greenman, Schneider, & Fregoso, 2003). These findings are consistent with research suggesting that outsiders evidence a low desire to be socially dominant or utilize coercive or prosocial strategies in aid of victims compared to defenders (Olthof, Goossens, Vermade, Aleva, & van der Muelen, 2011).

Researchers have also specifically compared the personality characteristics of outsiders to victims and have found similarities, though outsiders tend to be less extreme compared to victims (Pouwels et al., 2016). Specifically, outsiders and victims have been associated with elevated levels of withdrawn behavior and below-average levels of peer-valued characteristics (i.e., receiving attention from others, popularity, leadership abilities, attractiveness, and humor; Pouwels et al., 2016). Outsiders have also been found to be more conscientious and emotionally stable than victims (Tani et al., 2003). Additionally, Pouwels and colleagues (2016) found that outsiders tend to have more reciprocal friendships than victims. This is likely because outsiders are easier to interact with due to their lower levels of aggression and higher levels of prosocial behavior compared to victims (Pouwels et al., 2016).

Self-Esteem and Self-Concept

Both self-esteem (i.e., global self-regard; how one feels about oneself) and self-concept (i.e., what one believes about oneself, including who they are and their domain-specific strengths and weaknesses) have been shown to distinguish outsiders from other roles (Salmivalli, 1998). For example, high self-esteem was found to be related to defenders but not outsiders (Yang & Kim, 2017). As for outsiders' self-concepts, they appear to have average or above-average views of themselves behaviorally and family-wise (Salmivalli, 1998). In other words, outsiders generally believe that they act in socially acceptable ways and are close with their families. However, outsiders have also been found to view themselves as physically and socially inept compared to their peers, and it has been suggested that these self-perceived vulnerabilities may motivate outsiders to remain passive in bullying situations (Salmivalli, 1998).

Attitudes Toward Aggression

Outsiders' attitudes toward bullying appear to be quite mixed. Some evidence suggests that outsiders are against bullying or supportive of victims (Salmivalli & Voeten, 2004). However, other studies have found that attitudes about bullying are unrelated to outsider behavior (Espelage et al., 2012; Pozzoli & Gini, 2010) or that all bullying roles generally agree that bullying is bad and supporting victims is good (Pouwels et al., 2017; Rigby & Johnson, 2006). Furthermore, some researchers have even found that outsiders think positively about bullying and that it is simply a part of growing up (Yang & Kim, 2017). Given the aforementioned findings, it may be unsurprising that Haddock and Jimerson (2017) concluded that outsiders' attitudes toward bullying are much less definitive than defenders' clearly anti-bullying, pro-victim stance. Finally, attitudes are likely only part of the equation; some research shows that pro-victim attitudes generate greater feelings of responsibility to intervene, and that both factors together are negatively associated with outsider behavior (Pozzoli & Gini, 2012).

Social Skills

Social Competence. Social competence has been defined as the coordination of social skills that enable people to appropriately and positively interact with others to achieve their goals (Camodeca, Caravita, & Coppola 2015). Some research has demonstrated no association between outsiders and social skills (Andreou & Metallidou, 2004; Jenkins, Demaray, Frederick, & Summers, 2016), but other studies have found significant relationships. For example, according to observations of outsiders, they exhibit social competence deficits (Camodeca et al., 2015). However, when researchers have measured specific social skills (i.e., empathy, self-control, cooperation, and assertion) via self-reports, associations between social skills and outsiders have not been found (Jenkins et al., 2016).

Social Self-Efficacy and Preferred Means of Intervention

In addition to examining outsiders' social skills, researchers have also looked into their beliefs about their social skills. For example, evidence suggests that adolescents' beliefs about their competence and assertiveness in social situations can differentiate outsiders from defenders (Gini et al., 2008). Specifically, researchers have found that self-efficacy for intervention, or the belief that one could successfully identify and assist a victim, is negatively associated with outsider behavior (Gini et al., 2008; Thornberg & Jungert, 2013; Thornberg, Wänström, Hong, & Espelage, 2017). According to self-reports, outsiders reported fewer intentions to intervene when they were unsure of what to do or had doubts about whether intervening would help the victim (Cappadocia et al., 2012; Chen et al., 2016). Similarly, Evans and Smokowski (2015) proposed that students with high levels of optimism are more likely to intervene because they anticipate positive results from their actions. However, these researchers also found that intentions had little relationship to actual behaviors. These findings suggest that students in the outsider role do not reliably believe they have the skills, ability, or knowledge about how to effectively defend or intervene in a bullying situation.

Self-efficacy beliefs may also affect bullying participants' preferred intervention methods. In a study by Pronk and colleagues (2013), which sampled 761 Dutch 10–14 year-olds, outsiders and defenders were similarly high in self-efficacy and intent to intervene; however, when self-efficacy was divided into self-efficacy for direct intervention (e.g., telling a bully to stop) and indirect intervention (e.g., comforting a victim afterward being bullied), differences between the two roles emerged. Specifically, outsiders were found to be significantly less confident about directly intervening compared to defenders. In contrast, both roles were equally confident in their abilities to provide indirect intervention. Interestingly, such indirect means of supporting victims may be less noticeable to peers, thus possibly leading to an under-identification of some supportive behaviors by outsiders. Indirect strategies are also more likely to be favored by girls, perhaps because the nature of bullying in girls is generally more relational.

Implications for Prevention and Intervention

To this point, we hope that much of the information presented serves as an instructional map for intervention efforts. We have intentionally focused on research that directs the reader to many of the salient factors that delineate outsiders from more active assistants in curtailing bullying; understanding these factors can be informative in developing intervention strategies. For example, involving parents as influential agents, increasing perspective taking and empathic responding, especially in boys, and finding ways to increase self-efficacy beliefs regarding defending behavior could all be aspects of viable intervention approaches. In addition, there are a number of comprehensive intervention programs that have been designed—to some degree—to explicitly target and influence outsiders. These programs are built around the notion that outsiders can reinforce negative behavior with their silence, and that onlooker behavior may be easier to influence and change than the behavior of hardcore aggressors (Ahmed, 2008; Salmivalli, Kaukiainen, Kaistaniemi, & Lagerspetz, 1999). Two such programs are presented next.

Bully Prevention in Positive Behavioral Support (BP-PSB)—Stop. Walk. Talk

The Stop. Walk. Talk program (Ross & Horner, 2009) was created as a Tier 1 (universal) initiative for schools that employ a three-tiered positive behavior supports (PBIS or PBS) system. In three-tiered models, Tier 1 supports target all students, Tier 2 supports target a smaller subset of students with specific needs, and Tier 3 supports are intensive and individualized for students with the highest level of academic and/or behavioral needs. The Stop. Walk. Talk. program specifically targets outsiders by emphasizing, to all students, the importance of responding appropriately to bullying behavior using a three-step response system—*Stop. Walk. Talk.* This system does not include the typical outsider response of ignoring the behavior or avoiding intervening. Students are taught to respond to disrespectful behavior by first saying "stop" while also using an accompanying gesture to the same effect. If saying "stop" does not end the disrespectful actions or words, then students are taught to "walk" away from the situation. There is a chance that the disrespectful behavior could still continue and, in that instance, students are taught to "talk," or tell an adult what is happening. The idea behind BP-PBS is that by teaching students appropriate responses to bullying behavior, it will decrease the social reinforcement that fuels bullying behavior, such as the silent reinforcement that outsiders give when they do nothing. Results show that when BP-PBS has been implemented, there is a 21% increase in bystanders saying "stop," and an 11% increase in bystanders assisting the victim in moving away from the bullying situation. Bystanders were also less likely to reinforce bully behavior (17% decrease); for example, bystanders showed a decrease in the behaviors common in the reinforcer and assistant roles.

KiVa Anti-bullying Program

KiVa is another anti-bullying program designed to prevent inappropriate responses to bullying while simultaneously increasing appropriate responses (Salmivalli, 2010). The program aims to increase peer involvement by strengthening bystanders' sense of self-efficacy to intervene and support victims of bullying (Salmivalli, 2010). Within the curriculum, victims are asked to identify peers who could be allies and support them in getting away from bullying situations. The peers who are identified could be bystanders who need to be taught the skills needed to intervene and assist the victim (Williford et al., 2012). The KiVa program can also fit within a three-tiered support system and most of KiVa occurs at the Tier 1 level. For example, all students would take part in teacher-led anti-bullying lessons that focus on positive peer interactions, awareness of social pressures, awareness of what bullying looks like, and knowledge of what students, and specifically bystanders, can do to prevent or end bullying (Salmivalli, Kärnä, & Poskiparta, 2011). Tier 2 and 3 interventions would involve interventions specifically targeting bullies and victims that have not responded to Tier 1 supports. Bystanders could be utilized in Tier 2 and 3 interventions by being part of a team of peer supports for the victims of bullying (Salmivalli et al., 2011). Results of KiVa implementation in 117 intervention schools against 117 control schools have shown that the program reduces bullying reports and victimization (Kärnä et al., 2011).

Technology and Social Media

As mentioned at the beginning, the scope of this chapter prevents full exploration of outsider behavior as it pertains to cyberbullying. Nonetheless, this form of aggression is of primary importance as school-aged children are increasingly connected to an online environment. Therefore, we present a brief overview of current knowledge, relevant to the outsider role.

First, the potential number of outsiders involved in cyberbullying may be far greater than possible for traditional bullying because outsiders of cyberbullying do not have to be physically present during the incident. Specifically, passive bystanders can be created in a multitude of ways, such as by witnessing the bullying occur in real time online, being present with the perpetrator or victim when the act occurs, or afterward by witnessing the outcome (e.g., photo, email, text, video, etc.; Li, Smith, & Cross, 2012). According to data reported by Lenhart and colleagues (2011), 88% of teens who reported using social media said they witnessed cyber aggression at least once in a while and 90% reported ignoring the incidents, thus demonstrating the potential number of cyber-outsiders. Furthermore, Juvonen and Gross (2008) found that the vast majority (90%) of a sample of 1444 12–17 year-olds in their study did not tell adults about bullying they witnessed online.

There is a tendency, particularly for outsiders, to retain their role across offline and online environments and victims of cyberbullying often know their aggressors from school (Quirk & Campbell, 2015). However, other research supports role flexibility, too. After examining discussions from nine online focus groups involving 61 adolescents, DeSmet and colleagues (2014) concluded that bystanders of cyberbullying were fluid in the roles they assumed (e.g., would sometimes be defenders, outsiders, reinforcers, etc.) because all of the participants reported that their defending behavior would depend on context (i.e., victim characteristics, bully characteristics, and the social situation). Additionally, they found that some participants reported simultaneously supporting the bully (via comments or likes) and the victim (via comforting them in person).

Many factors contribute to adopting the outsider role in cyberbullying. DeSmet and colleagues (2014) reported that these determinants overlap with traditional forms of bullying. Specifically, passive cyber-outsider behavior was self-reported to be related to moral disengagement, low importance for supporting in-group members, low self-efficacy for defending, perceived acceptability of passivity, perceiving the victim as being unpopular, and whether the fairness of the situation was clear or ambiguous. Van Cleemput, Vandebosch, and Pabian (2014) also attempted to capture cyber-outsiders' reasons for remaining passive and found that 49% of participants reported it was none of their business, 31.8% worried that they would become victims too, 30.6% were unsure of how to help, 15.6% could not help, 13% attributed responsibility to the victim, and 11.4% reported other reasons.

Holfeld (2014) examined the effects of manipulating a hypothetical victim's reaction to cyberbullying (i.e., passive, active, or reactive) in an online blog format. The researcher analyzed the responses on this blog by about 1100 middle-school students. This study found that 67% of male and 54.5% of female outsiders attributed the cyberbullying to a victim characteristic (e.g., the victim's behavior, personality, sexuality). Furthermore, cyber-outsiders were more likely to attribute responsibility and blame for victimization to passive victims rather than active or retaliatory victims. Regarding cyber-outsiders' characteristics, Wachs (2012) found that this role is associated with feeling dissatisfied with school and unpopular. In another study, Van Cleemput and colleagues (2014) found cyber-outsiders to be older, lower in empathic concern, and less likely to have experienced traditional victimization themselves.

Future Issues

The outsider role is relatively understudied when compared to more active bullying roles, making it a fruitful group for study. Possibly the most important area for continued research regards the creation of intervention strategies that influence peer attitudes about bullying so that defending behavior becomes more normative and important in the immediate ecology (Pouwels et al., 2016). The primary goal of such a strategy is to change the behavior of the passive bystander. It has been suggested that this type of effort needs to be in addition to primary bullying prevention efforts, and must directly address attitudes related to prosocial tendencies by relaying strong and consistent messaging about the importance about intervening while providing abundant support from adults in the school environment (Polanin, Espelage, & Pigott, 2012). At the same time, as we increase the emphasis on pushing passive bystanders into more active, prosocial roles, we need to be aware that defending can have a psychosocial cost and future longitudinal research needs to more clearly examine the climate variables that can serve to moderate this potential negative impact (Lambe, Hudson, Craig, &

Pepler, 2017). Additionally, more research needs to be undertaken on the psychosocial outcomes related to witnessing bullying for passive bystanders without significant histories as victims or aggressors.

In terms of intrapersonal variables, more research on moral emotions, such as shame and guilt, is needed, particularly about how these play out longitudinally (developmentally) and how this development may be impacted by their dyadic relationship with contextual variables over time (Mazzone et al., 2016). This type of research could expose how some outsiders take on different roles over time, when possible role shifts happen, developmentally, and the determining factors at play. Related, although the participant role approach has been of great utility in helping understand student behavior in bullying situations, research has also shown a considerable overlap in student behavior across roles. Future research could endeavor to embrace this complexity instead of assigning each student to a static role identity only (Nickerson & Mele-Taylor, 2014).

Future research specific to cyberbullying should incorporate situational, social, and relational factors, such as on what platform the cyberbullying takes place (e.g., Facebook, Snapchat, Instagram, etc.) and whether victims are friends on, or offline, with the bystanders (Allison & Bussey, 2016; DeSmet et al., 2014). In addition, the motives behind cyberbullying are not well understood and may present a worthy endeavor for future investigators (Kowalski, Giumetti, Schroeder, & Lattanner, 2014). Moreover, as additional research is conducted, the field of cyberbullying must advance to integrate the salient situational, social, and intrapersonal factors into a comprehensive understanding of cyber-outsiders. These research findings must then be integrated into the overall intervention efforts within the schools to combat bullying in all formats.

References

Ahmed, E. (2008). 'Stop it, that's enough': Bystander intervention and its relationship to school connectedness and shame management. *Vulnerable Children and Youth Studies, 3,* 203–213. https://doi.org/10.1080/174501 20802002548.

Allison, K., & Bussey, K. (2016). Cyber-bystanding in context: A review of the literature on witnesses' responses to cyberbullying. *Children and Youth Services Review, 65,* 183–194. https://doi.org/10.1016/j.childyouth.2016.03.026.

Andreou, E., & Metallidou, P. (2004). The relationship of academic and social cognition to behaviour in bullying situations among Greek primary school children. *Educational Psychology, 24,* 27–41. https://doi.org/10.1080/0144341032000146421.

Belacchi, C., & Farina, E. (2010). Prosocial/hostile roles and emotion comprehension in preschoolers. *Aggressive Behavior, 36,* 371–389. https://doi.org/10.1002/ab.20361.

Bellmore, A., Ting-Lan, M., You, J., & Hughes, M. (2012). A two-method investigation of early adolescents' responses upon witnessing peer victimisation in school. *Journal of Adolescence, 35,* 1265–1276. https://doi.org/10.1016/j.adolescence.2012.04.012.

Bronfenbrenner, U. (1979). *The ecology of human development: Experiments by nature and design.* Cambridge: Harvard University Press.

Brown, B. B. (2004). Adolescents' relationships with peers. In R. M. Lerner & L. Steinburg (Eds.), *Handbook of adolescent psychology* (2nd ed., pp. 363–394). Hoboken: Wiley.

Camodeca, M., Caravita, S. C., & Coppola, G. (2015). Bullying in preschool: The association between participant roles, social competence, and social preference. *Aggressive Behavior, 41,* 310–321. https://doi.org/10.1002/ab.21541.

Camodeca, M., & Coppola, G. (2016). Bullying, empathic concern, and internalization of rules among preschool children: The role of emotion understanding. *International Journal of Behavioral Development, 40,* 459–465. https://doi.org/10.1177/016502.

Camodeca, M., & Coppola, G. (2018). Participant roles in preschool bullying: The impact of emotion regulation, social preference, and quality of the teacher-child relationship. *Social Development, 28,* 3–21. https://doi.org/10.1111/sode.12320.

Camodeca, M., & Goossens, F. A. (2005). Aggression, social cognitions, anger and sadness in bullies and victims. *Journal of Child Psychology and Psychiatry and Allied Disciplines, 46,* 186–197. https://doi.org/10.1111/j.1469-7610.2004.00347.x.

Cappadocia, M. C., Pepler, D., Cummings, J. G., & Craig, W. (2012). Individual motivations and characteristics associated with bystander intervention during bullying episodes among children and youth. *Canadian Journal of School Psychology, 27,* 201–216. https://doi.org/10.1177/082957351245 0567.

Chen, L. M., Chang, L. Y. C., & Cheng, Y. Y. (2016). Choosing to be a defender or an outsider in a school bullying incident: Determining factors and the defending process. *School Psychology International, 37,* 289–302. https://doi.org/10.1177/0143034316632282.

Chen, L. M., Cheng, W., & Ho, H. C. (2015). Perceived severity of school bullying in elementary schools based on participants' roles. *Educational Psychology, 35,* 484–496. https://doi.org/10.1080/01443410.2013.860220.

Chapin, J., & Brayack, M. (2016). What makes a bystander stand by? Adolescents and bullying. *Journal of School Violence, 15,* 424–437. https://doi.org/10.1080/15388220.2015.1079783.

Choi, S., & Cho, Y. I. (2012). Influence of psychological and social factors on bystanders' roles in school bullying among Korean-American students in the United States. *School Psychology International, 34,* 67–81. https://doi.org/10.1177/0143034311430406.

Craig, W., Pepler, D., & Atlas, R. S. (2000). Observations of bullying in the playground and in the classroom. *School Psychology International, 21,* 22–36. https://doi.org/10.1177/0143034300211002.

Crapanzano, A. M., Frick, P. J., Childs, K., & Terranova, A. M. (2011). Gender differences in the assessment, stability, and correlates to bullying roles in middle school children. *Behavioral Sciences & the Law, 29,* 677–694. https://doi.org/10.1002/bsl.1000.

Crick, N., & Dodge, K. A. (1999). 'Superiority' is in the eye of the beholder: A comment on Sutton, Smith, and Swettenham. *Social Development, 8,* 128–131. https://doi.org/10.1111/1467-9507.00084.

Demaray, M. K., Summers, K. H., Jenkins, L. N., & Becker, L. D. (2016). Bullying participant behaviors questionnaire (BPBQ): Establishing a reliable and valid measure. *Journal of School Violence, 15,* 158–188. https://doi.org/10.1080/15388220.2014.964801.

Derogatis, L. R. (1994). *Symptom checklist-90-R (SCL-90-R): Administration, scoring and procedures manual* (3rd ed.). National Computer Systems.

DeSmet, A., Veldeman, C., Poels, K., Bastiaensens, S., Van Cleemput, K., Vandebosch, H., & De Bourdeaudhuij, I. (2014). Determinants of self-reported bystander behavior in cyberbullying incidents amongst adolescents. *Cyberpsychology, Behavior, and Social Networking, 17,* 207–215. https://doi.org/10.1089/cyber.2013.0027.

Dodge, K. A., Lochman, J. E., Harnish, J. D., Bates, J. E., & Pettit, G. S. (1997). Reactive and proactive aggression in school children and psychiatrically impaired chronically assaultive youth. *Journal of Abnormal Psychology, 106*, 37–51. https://doi.org/10.1037/0021-843X.106.1.37.

Edwards, A. L. (1953). The relationship between the judged desirability of a trait and the probability that the trait will be endorsed. *Journal of Applied Psychology, 37*, 90–93. https://doi.org/10.1037/h0058073.

Espelage, D., Green, H., & Polanin, J. (2012). Willingness to intervene in bullying episodes among middle school students: Individual and peer-group influences. *Journal of Early Adolescence, 32*, 776–801. https://doi.org/10.1177/0272431611423017.

Ettekal, I., Kochenderfer-Ladd, B., & Ladd, G. W. (2015). A synthesis of person- and relational-level factors that influence bullying and bystanding behaviors: Toward an integrative framework. *Aggression and Violent Behavior, 23*, 75–86. https://doi.org/10.1016/j.avb.2015.05.011.

Evans, C. B. R., & Smokowski, P. R. (2015). Prosocial bystander behavior in bullying dynamics: Assessing the impact of social capital. *Journal of Youth and Adolescence, 44*, 2289–2307. https://doi.org/10.1007/s10964-015-0338-5.

Evans, C. B., & Smokowski, P. R. (2017). Negative bystander behavior in bullying dynamics: Assessing the impact of social capital deprivation and anti-social capital. *Child Psychiatry and Human Development, 48*, 120–135. https://doi.org/10.1007/s10826-018-1078-4.

Gini, G. (2006). Social cognition and moral cognition in bullying: What's wrong? *Aggressive Behaviour, 32*, 528–539. https://doi.org/10.1002/ab.20153.

Gini, G., Albiero, P., Benelli, B., & Altoè, G. (2008). Determinants of adolescents' active defending and passive bystanding behavior in bullying. *Journal of Adolescence, 31*, 93–105. https://doi.org/10.1016/j.adolescence.2007.05.002.

Gini, G., Thornberg, R., & Pozzoli, T. (2018). Individual moral disengagement and bystander behavior in bullying: The role of moral distress and collective moral disengagement. *Psychology of Violence*. Advance online publication. https://doi.org/10.1037/vio0000223.

Goossens, F. A., Olthof, T., & Dekker, P. H. (2006). New participant role scales: Comparison between various criteria for assigning roles and indications for their validity. *Aggressive Behavior, 32*, 343–357. https://doi.org/10.1002/ab.20133.

Grassetti, S., Hubbard, J., Smith, M., Bookhout, M., Swift, L., & Gawrysiak, M. (2018). Caregivers' advice and children's bystander behaviors during bullying incidents. *Journal of Clinical Child & Adolescent Psychology, 47,* 329–340. https://doi.org/10.1080/15374416.2017.1295381.

Gumpel, T. P., Zioni-Koren, V., & Bekerman, Z. (2014). An ethnographic study of participant roles in school bullying. *Aggressive Behavior, 40,* 214–228. https://doi.org/10.1002/ab.21515.

Haddock, A. D., & Jimerson, S. R. (2017). An examination of differences in moral disengagement and empathy among bullying participant groups. *Journal of Relationships Research, 8,* 1–15. https://doi.org/10.1017/jrr.2017.15.

Hara, H. (2002). Justifications for bullying among Japanese schoolchildren. *Asian Journal of Social Psychology, 5,* 197–204. https://doi.org/10.1111/1467-839X.00104.

Holfeld, B. (2014). Perceptions and attributions of bystanders to cyber bullying. *Computers in Human Behavior, 38,* 1–7. https://doi.org/10.1016/j.chb.2014.05.012.

Jeffrey, L. R., Miller, D., & Linn, M. (2001). Middle school bullying as a context for the development of passive observers to the victimization of others. *Journal of Emotional Abuse, 2,* 143–156. https://doi.org/10.1300/J135v02n02_09.

Jenkins, L. N., Demaray, M. K., Frederick, S. S., & Summers, K. H. (2016). Associations among middle school students' bullying roles and social skills. *Journal of School Violence, 15,* 259–278. https://doi.org/10.1080/15388220.2014.986675.

Jenkins, L. N., & Nickerson, A. B. (2017). Bullying participant roles and gender as predictors of bystander intervention. *Aggressive Behavior, 43,* 281–290. https://doi.org/10.1002/ab.21688.

Juvonen, J., & Gross, E. F. (2008). Extending the school grounds?—Bullying experiences in cyberspace. *Journal of School Health, 78,* 496–505. https://doi.org/10.1111/j.1746-1561.2008.00335.x.

Kärnä, A., Voeten, M., Little, T., Poskiparta, E., Kaljonen, A., & Salmivalli, C. (2011). A large-scale evaluation of the KiVa antibullying program. *Child Development, 82,* 311–330. https://doi.org/10.1111/j.1467-8624.2010.01557.x.

Knack, J. M., Vasilinka, T., Vaillancourt, T., Hymel, S., & McDougal, P. (2012). What protects rejected adolescents from also being bullied by their peers? The moderating role of peer-valued characteristics. *Journal of*

Research on Adolescence, 22, 467–479. https://doi.org/10.1111/j.1532-7795. 2012.00792.x.

Kowalski, R. M., Giumetti, G. W., Schroeder, A. N., & Lattanner, M. R. (2014). Bullying in the digital age: A critical review and meta-analysis of cyberbullying research among youth. *Psychological Bulletin, 140,* 1073–1137. https://doi.org/10.1037/a0035618.

Lambe, L. J., Cioppa, V. D., Hong, I. K., & Craig, W. M. (2018). Standing up to bullying: A social ecological review of peer defending in offline and online contexts. *Aggression and Violent Behavior, 45,* 51–74. https://doi.org/10.1016/j.avb.2018.05.007.

Lambe, L. J., Hudson, C. C., Craig, W. M., & Pepler, D. J. (2017). Does defending come with a cost? Examining the psychosocial correlates of defending behaviour among bystanders of bullying in a Canadian sample. *Child Abuse and Neglect, 65,* 112–123. https://doi.org/10.1016/j.chiabu.2017.01.012.

Latané, B., & Darley, J. M. (1968). Bystander intervention in emergencies: Diffusion of responsibility. *Journal of Personality and Social Psychology, 8,* 377–383.

Latané, B., & Darley, J. M. (1970). *The unresponsive bystander: Why doesn't he help?* Englewood Cliffs: Prentice Hall.

Lenhart, A., Madden, M., Smith, A., Purcell, K., Zickuhr, K., & Rainie, L. (2011). *Teens, kindness and cruelty on social network sites.* https://www.pewinternet.org/.

Levasseur, C., Desbiens, N., & Bowen, F. (2017). Moral reasoning about school bullying in involved adolescents. *Journal of Moral Education, 46,* 158–176. https://doi.org/10.1080/03057240.2016.1268113.

Levine, M., Cassidy, C., Brazier, G., & Reicher, S. (2002). Self-categorization and bystander non-intervention: Two experimental studies. *Journal of Applied Social Psychology, 32,* 1452–1463. https://doi.org/10.1111/j.1559-1816.2002.tb01446.x.

Li, Q., Smith, P. K., & Cross, D. (2012). Research into cyberbullying: Context. In Q. Li, D. Cross, & P. K. Smith (Eds.), *Cyberbullying in the global playground: Research from international perspectives* (pp. 3–12). Oxford: Wiley-Blackwell.

Li, Y., Chen, P. Y., Chen, F. L., & Wu, W. C. (2015). Roles of fatalism and parental support in the relationship between bullying victimization and bystander behaviors. *School Psychology International, 36,* 253–267. https://doi.org/10.1177/0143034315569566.

Lucas-Molina, B., Pérez-Albéniz, A., Fonseca-Pedrero, E., & Giménez-Dasí, M. (2018). Bullying, defending, and outsider behaviors: The moderating role of social status and gender in their relationship with empathy. *Scandinavian Journal of Psychology, 59,* 473–482. https://doi.org/10.1111/sjop.12453.

Lucas-Molina, B., Williamson, A. A., Pulido, R., & Calderón, S. (2014). Adaptation of the participant role scale (PRS) in a Spanish youth sample: Measurement invariance across gender and relationship with sociometric status. *Journal of Interpersonal Violence, 29,* 2904–2930. https://doi.org/10.1177/0886260514527822.

Ma, T. L. (2019). Adolescents' willingness to help with peer victimisation in Taiwan: The role of individual and situation-specific characteristics. *International Journal of Psychology, 55,* 1–9. https://doi.org/10.1002/ijop.12565.

Mazzone, A., Camodeca, M., & Salmivalli, C. (2016). Stability and change of outsider behavior in school bullying: The role of shame and guilt in a longitudinal perspective. *The Journal of Early Adolescence, 38,* 164–177. https://doi.org/10.1177/0272431616659560.

Menolascino, N., & Jenkins, L. N. (2018). Predicting bystander intervention among middle school students. *School Psychology Quarterly, 33,* 305–313. https://doi.org/10.1037/spq0000262.

Meter, D. J., & Card, N. A. (2015). Defenders of victims of peer aggression: Interdependence theory and an exploration of individual, interpersonal, and contextual effects on the defender participant role. *Developmental Review, 38,* 222–240. https://doi.org/10.1016/j.dr.2015.08.001.

Moore, S. E., Norman, R. E., Suetani, S., Thomas, H. J., Sly, P. D., & Scott, J. G. (2017). Consequences of bullying victimization in childhood and adolescence: A systematic review and meta-analysis. *World Journal of Psychiatry, 7,* 60–76. https://doi.org/10.5498/wjp.v7.i1.60.

Nansel, T. R., Overpeck, M., & Pilla, R. (2007). Bullying behaviors among U.S. youth: Prevalence and association with psychosocial adjustment. *Journal of the American Medical Association, 285,* 2094–2100. https://doi.org/10.1001/jama.285.16.2094.

Nickerson, A. B., & Mele-Taylor, D. (2014). Empathetic responsiveness, group norms, and prosocial affiliations in bullying roles. *School Psychology Quarterly, 29,* 99–109. https://doi.org/10.1037/spq0000052.

Nickerson, A. B., Mele, D., & Princiotta, D. (2008). Attachment and empathy as predictors of roles as defenders or outsiders in bullying interactions. *Journal of School Psychology, 46,* 687–703. https://doi.org/10.1016/j.jsp.2008.06.002.

Obermann, M. (2011). Moral disengagement among bystanders to school bullying. *Journal of School Violence, 10,* 239–257. https://doi.org/10.1080/15388220.2011.578276.

Oh, I., & Hazler, R. (2009). Contributions of personal and situational factors to bystanders' reactions to school bullying. *School Psychology International, 30,* 291–310. https://doi.org/10.1177/0143034309106499.

Olthof, T., Goossens, F. A., Vermade, M. M., Aleva, E. A., & van der Muelen, M. (2011). Bullying as strategic behavior: Relations with desired and acquired dominance in the peer group. *Journal of School Psychology, 49,* 339–359. https://doi.org/10.1016/j.jsp.2011.03.003.

Polanin, J. R., Espelage, D. L., & Pigott, T. D. (2012). A meta-analysis of school-base bullying prevention program's effects on bystander intervention behavior. *School Psychology Review, 41,* 47–65. https://doi.org/10.1080/02796015.2012.12087375.

Pouwels, J. L., Lansu, T. A. M., & Cillessen, A. H. N. (2016). Participant roles of bullying in adolescence: Status characteristics, social behavior, and assignment criteria. *Aggressive Behavior, 42,* 239–253. https://doi.org/10.1002/ab.21614.

Pouwels, J. L., Lansu, T. A. M., & Cillessen, A. H. N. (2017). Adolescents' explicit and implicit evaluations of hypothetical and actual peers with different bullying participant roles. *Journal of Experimental Child Psychology, 159,* 219–241. https://doi.org/10.1016/j.jecp.2017.02.008.

Pouwels, L., Salmivalli, C., Saarento, S., Van den Berg, Y., Lansu, T. A. M., & Cillessen, A. H. N. (2018). Predicting adolescent's bullying participation from developmental trajectories of social status and behavior. *Child Development, 89,* 1157–1176. https://doi.org/10.1111/cdev.12794.

Pöyhönen, V., Juvonen, J., & Salmivalli, C. (2010). What does it take to stand up for the victim of bullying? The interplay between personal and social factors. *Merrill-Palmer Quarterly, 56,* 143–163. https://doi.org/10.1353/mpq.0.0046.

Pozzoli, T., & Gini, G. (2010). Active defending and passive bystanding behavior in bullying: The role of personal characteristics and perceived peer pressure. *Journal of Abnormal Child Psychology, 38,* 815–827. https://doi.org/10.1007/s10802-010-9399-9.

Pozzoli, T., & Gini, G. (2012). Why do bystanders of bullying help or not? A multidimensional model. *Journal of Early Adolescence, 33,* 315–340. https://doi.org/10.1177/0272431612440172.

Pozzoli, T., Gini, G., & Thornberg, R. (2017). Getting angry matters: Going beyond perspective taking and empathic concern to understand bystanders'

behavior in bullying. *Journal of Adolescence, 61,* 87–95. https://doi.org/10.1016/j.adolescence.2017.09.011.
Pozzoli, T., Gini, G., & Vieno, A. (2012). The role of individual correlates and class norms in defending and passive bystanding behavior in bullying: A multilevel analysis. *Child Development, 83,* 1917–1931. https://doi.org/10.1111/j.1467-8624.2012.01831.x.
Pronk, J., Goossens, F. A., Olthof, T., de Mey, L., & Willemen, A. M. (2013). Children's intervention strategies in situations of victimization by bullying: Social cognitions of outsiders versus defenders. *Journal of School Psychology, 51,* 669–682. https://doi.org/10.1016/j.jsp.2013.09.002.
Pronk, J., Olthof, T., & Goossens, F. A. (2015). Differential personality correlates of early adolescents' bullying-related outsider and defender behavior. *Journal of Early Adolescence, 35,* 1069–1091.
Pronk, J., Olthof, T., & Goossens, F. A. (2016). Factors influencing interventions on behalf of victims of bullying: A counterfactual approach to the social cognitions of outsiders and defenders. *Journal of Early Adolescence, 36,* 267–291. https://doi.org/10.1177/0272431614549628.
Quirk, R., & Campbell, M. (2015). On standby? A comparison of online and offline witnesses to bullying and their bystander behaviour. *Educational Psychology, 35,* 430–448. https://doi.org/10.1080/01443410.2014.893556.
Rieffe, C., & Camodeca, M. (2016). Empathy in adolescence: Relations with emotion awareness and social roles. *British Journal of Developmental Psychology, 34,* 340–353. https://doi.org/10.1111/bjdp.12133.
Rigby, K., & Johnson, B. (2006). Expressed readiness of Australian schoolchildren to act as bystanders in support of children who are being bullied. *Educational Psychology, 26,* 425–440. https://doi.org/10.1080/01443410500342047.
Rivers, I., Poteat, V. P., Noret, N., & Ashurst, N. (2009). Observing bullying at school: The mental health implications of witness status. *School Psychology Quarterly, 24,* 211–223. https://doi.org/10.1037/a0018164.
Ross, S. W., & Horner, R. H. (2009). Bully prevention in positive behavior support. *Journal of Applied Behavior Analysis, 42,* 747–759. https://doi.org/10.1901/jaba.2009.42-747.
Salmivalli, C. (1998). Intelligent, attractive, well-behaving, unhappy: The structure of adolescents' self-concept and its relations to their social behavior. *Journal of Research on Adolescence, 8,* 333–354. https://doi.org/10.1207/s15327795jra0803_3.
Salmivalli, C. (2010). Bullying and the peer group: A review. *Aggression and Violent Behavior, 15,* 112–120. https://doi.org/10.1016/j.avb.2009.08.007.

Salmivalli, C., Huttunen, A., & Lagerspetz, K. M. J. (1997). Peer networks and bullying in schools. *Scandinavian Journal of Psychology, 38,* 305–312. https://doi.org/10.1111/1467-9450.00040.
Salmivalli, C., Kärnä, A., & Poskiparta, E. (2011). Counteracting bullying in Finland: The KiVa program and its effects on different forms of being bullied. *International Journal of Behavioral Development, 35,* 405–411. https://doi.org/10.1177/0165025411407457.
Salmivalli, C., Kaukiainen, A., Kaistaniemi, L., & Lagerspetz, K. M. J. (1999). Self-evaluated self-esteem, peer-evaluated self-esteem, and defensive egotism as predictors of adolescents' participation in bullying situations. *Personality and Social Psychology Bulletin, 25,* 1268–1278. https://doi.org/10.1177/014 6167299258008.
Salmivalli, C., Lagerspetz, K., Björkqvist, K., Österman, K., & Kaukiainen, A. (1996). Bullying as a group process: Participant roles and their relations to social status within the group. *Aggressive Behavior, 22,* 1–15. https://doi.org/ 10.1002/(SICI)1098-2337(1996)22:1%3c1:AID-AB1%3e3.0.CO;2-T.
Salmivalli, C., Lappalainen, M., & Lagerspetz, K. M. J. (1998). Stability and change of behavior in connection with bullying in schools: A two-year follow-up. *Aggressive Behavior, 24,* 205–218. https://doi.org/10.1002/(SIC I)1098-2337(1998)24:3%3c205:AID-AB5%3e3.0.CO;2-J.
Salmivalli, C., & Voeten, M. (2004). Connections between attitudes, group norms, and behaviour in bullying situations. *International Journal of Behavioral Development, 28,* 246–258. https://doi.org/10.1080/016502503440 00488.
Sutton, J., & Smith, P. K. (1999). Bullying as a group process: An adaptation of the participant role approach. *Aggressive Behavior, 25,* 97–111. https://doi.org/10.1002/(SICI)1098-2337(1999)25:2%3c97:AID-AB3%3e3.0.CO;2-7.
Sutton, J., Smith, P. K., & Swettenham, J. (1999a). Bullying and 'theory of mind': A critique of the 'social skills deficit' view of anti-social behavior. *Social Development, 8,* 117–127. https://doi.org/10.1111/1467-9507.00083.
Sutton, J., Smith, P. K., & Swettenham, J. (1999b). Socially undesirable need not be incompetent: A response to Crick and Dodge. *Social Development, 8,* 132–134. https://doi.org/10.1111/1467-9507.00085.
Sutton, J., Smith, P. K., & Swettenham, J. (1999c). Social cognition and bullying: Social inadequacy or skilled manipulation? *British Journal of Developmental Psychology, 17,* 435–450. https://doi.org/10.1348/026151099 165384.

Sutton, J., Smith, P. K., & Swettenham, J. (2001). 'It's easy, it works, and it makes me feel good'—A response to Arsenio and Lemerise. *Social Development, 10*, 74–78. https://doi.org/10.1111/1467-9507.00149.

Tani, F., Greenman, P. S., Schneider, B. H., & Fregoso, M. (2003). Bullying and the big five. *School Psychology International, 24*, 131–146. https://doi.org/10.1177/0143034303024002001.

Thornberg, R., & Jungert, T. (2013). Bystander behavior in bullying situations: Basic moral sensitivity, moral disengagement and defender self-efficacy. *Journal of Adolescence, 36*, 475–483. https://doi.org/10.1016/j.adolescence.2013.02.003.

Thornberg, R., Tenenbaum, L., Varjas, K., Meyers, J., Jungert, T., & Vanegas, G. (2012). Bystander motivation in bullying incidents: To intervene or not to intervene? *Western Journal of Emergency Medicine, 13*, 247–252. https://doi.org/10.5811/westjem.2012.3.11792.

Thornberg, R., Wänström, L., Hong, J. S., & Espelage, D. L. (2017). Classroom relationship qualities and social-cognitive correlates of defending and passive bystanding in school bullying in Sweden: A multilevel analysis. *Journal of School Psychology, 63*, 49–62. https://doi.org/10.1016/j.jsp.2017.03.002.

Valdés-Cuervo, A. A., Alcántar-Nieblas, C., Martínez-Ferrer, B., & Parra-Pérez, L. (2018). Relations between restorative parental discipline, family climate, parental support, empathy, shame, and defenders in bullying. *Children and Youth Services Review, 95*, 152–159. https://doi.org/10.1016/j.childyouth.2018.10.015.

Van Cleemput, K., Vandebosch, H., & Pabian, S. (2014). Personal characteristics and contextual factors that determine "helping", "joining in", and "doing nothing" when witnessing cyberbullying. *Aggressive Behavior, 40*, 383–396. https://doi.org/10.1002/ab.21534.

Wachs, S. (2012). Moral disengagement and emotional and social difficulties in bullying and cyberbullying: Differences by participant role. *Emotional and Behavioural Difficulties, 17*, 347–360. https://doi.org/10.1080/13632752.2012.704318.

Werth, J. M., Nickerson, A. B., Aloe, A. M., & Swearer, S. M. (2015). Bullying victimization and the social and emotional maladjustment of bystanders: A propensity score analysis. *Journal of School Psychology, 53*, 295–308. https://doi.org/10.1016/j.jsp.2015.05.004.

Williford, A., Boulton, A., Noland, B., Little, T. D., Kärnä, A., & Salmivalli, C. (2012). Effects of the KiVa anti-bullying program on adolescents' depression, anxiety, and perception of peers. *Journal of Abnormal Child Psychology, 40*, 289–300. https://doi.org/10.1007/s10802-011-9551-1.

Yang, S. A., & Kim, D. H. (2017). Factors associated with bystander behaviors of Korean youth in school bullying situations. *Medicine, 96*(32), 1–7. https://doi.org/10.1097/MD.0000000000007757.

5

The Defender Vantage Point

Stephanie S. Fredrick, Lyndsay Jenkins, and Cassandra M. Dexter

A small percentage of students engage in bullying behaviors either as the bully or the victim (or both) (Salmivalli, Lagerspetz, Björkqvist, Österman, & Kaukiainen, 1996). The majority of youth are classified as bystanders, in that they have witnessed the bullying behavior in some way (Salmivalli et al., 1996). An individual is considered an active, prosocial bystander, or defender, when they attempt to stop or intervene with bullying behavior and stand up for their peers. Intervention may be direct in which the individual actively stops the bullying behavior through verbal or physical means (i.e., bully-oriented defending; Reijntjes et al., 2016). Intervention may also be indirect, such as comforting the person being bullied after the incident occurred or

S. S. Fredrick (✉)
University at Buffalo, State University of New York, Buffalo, NY, USA
e-mail: ssfredri@buffalo.edu

L. Jenkins
Florida State University, Tallahassee, FL, USA

C. M. Dexter
Central Michigan University, Mt Pleasant, MI, USA

© The Author(s) 2020
L. Rosen et al. (eds.), *Bullies, Victims, and Bystanders*,
https://doi.org/10.1007/978-3-030-52939-0_5

encouraging them to tell an adult (i.e., victim-oriented defending; Reijntjes et al., 2016). Some scholars have suggested that defending a peer or classmate who is being bullied can be risky—since it often involves opposing someone with power—and thus, defending behavior in bullying situations may be considered different from general altruistic or helping behavior (Pozzoli & Gini, 2010).

Research on defending behavior has gained substantial popularity in recent years with good reason, as peer intervention has been found to be an effective means to stop bullying. Hawkins, Pepler, and Craig (2001) found that 60% of ongoing bullying episodes stop within 10 seconds when bystanders actively intervene. Peers who experience bullying also report less negative outcomes when they feel supported or defended (Ma & Chen, 2019). However, this behavior can be difficult to study as it is often contingent on contextual factors, such the setting, the child's peer group, and classroom and school norms (Espelage, Green, & Polanin, 2012). In fact, Peets, Pöyhönen, Juvonen, and Salmivalli (2015) found that 36% of variance within defending behavior was due to differences between classrooms among a large sample ($n = 6708$) of elementary school students, and Salmivalli, Voeten, and Poskiparta (2011) found similar results, with 35% of variance in defending due to classroom differences. The impact of contextual factors on defending behavior will be discussed in more detail later in this chapter.

Prevalence of defending is inconsistent across studies. Lambe, Hudson, Craig, and Pepler (2017) found 64% of children and adolescents reported intervening in the last bullying event they witnessed. Levasseur, Desbiens, and Bowen (2017) found that of those students that peers nominated as being involved in bullying incidents, 37% were classified as defenders in a sample of Canadian adolescents. Other studies have indicated even higher prevalence rates, with Quinn, Fitzpatrick, Bussey, Hides, and Chan (2016) reporting approximately 90% of students in their sample of 1255 Australian adolescents reported engaging in defending behaviors at least once in the past term. However, Quinn and colleagues also indicated that most of these students reported other types of behaviors (victim, outsider, assistant to the bully), in addition to defending.

It is not surprising that prevalence rates regarding defending behavior are inconsistent. As previously indicated, a student choosing to engage in defending behavior may be contingent on: who is being bullied or doing the bullying (Song & Oh, 2017), the number of bystanders (Song & Oh, 2018), the type or severity of bullying (Bastiaensens et al., 2015), and classroom or school level norms (Salmivalli & Voeten, 2004). To date, the majority of research on defending behavior has established this role as separate from other bullying roles (i.e., bully, victim, assistant, reinforcer, outsider). However, this behavior may be more fluid and complex than previously thought. The extant literature on defending has explored characteristics of defenders, which will be summarized in the next sections.

Demographic Characteristics Associated with Defending Behavior

Gender Characteristics

Across studies, girls are more likely to defend than boys (Lambe et al., 2017; Levasseur et al., 2017; Pöyhönen, Juvonen, & Salmivalli, 2010; Salmivalli et al., 1996). Lambe, Cioppa, Hong, and Craig (2019) recently conducted a systematic review of 155 studies that examined peer defending in both offline and online contexts. Lambe and colleagues reported 87.5% of the studies (63 out of 72) that examined gender in offline contexts found that being a girl was positively and significantly associated with defending. There could be a few reasons for this gender difference, one of which is a difference in expectations based on gender (Salmivalli et al., 1996). Girls are often expected to be more nurturing and caring than boys overall, so defending behaviors could be a manifestation of perceived expectations. Additionally, girls tend to report witnessing bullying more than boys (Lambe et al., 2017), and are more likely to notice bullying events and interpret them as emergencies compared to boys (Jenkins & Nickerson, 2017). Taken all together, it could be that girls are more likely to notice bullying, understand that something needs to be done, and may hold preconceived gender expectations regarding helping behavior.

However, there may be some differences regarding defending behavior in offline and online contexts. Lambe et al. (2019) reported in their systematic review that only seven of the 13 studies (54%) that examined gender differences in online contexts found being a girl was positively associated with defending. Thus, further research is needed to examine if gender differences in offline contexts generalize online, as well.

In addition to girls being more likely to defend, differences in types of defending behaviors have also been found in offline contexts. Specifically, an observational study of playground bullying found that girls were more likely to use verbal assertion to defend their peers whereas boys were more likely to use physical aggression (Hawkins et al., 2001). Similarly, when seventh and eighth grade students were given bullying scenarios to read and told to select an effective intervention, girls were more likely than boys to select the verbal assertive strategies, such as telling the bully to stop or explaining that the bully's behavior was wrong (Camodeca & Goossens, 2010). Additionally, peer nomination data from 394 elementary school students in the Netherlands revealed that girls were more likely to engage in victim-oriented defending—such as consoling or being friendly to the victim after they had been bullied—whereas boys were more likely to use bully-oriented strategies, such as running up to the bully and forcing them to leave the victim alone (Reijntjes et al., 2016). Thus, boys may be more likely to use aggressive strategies directed toward the bully whereas girls are more likely to intervene by either verbally asserting themselves or by approaching and helping the victim afterwards.

Age Characteristics

Numerous studies have also found that younger students tend to be more likely to defend than older students (Caravita, Gini, & Pozzoli, 2012; Huang et al., 2016; Pöyhönen et al., 2010; Pozzoli, Gini, & Vieno, 2012b). In their review, Lambe et al. (2019) reported 36 out of 41 studies found a significant age effect in which younger students defended more than older students. Social factors regarding attitudes toward aggressive behavior and peer influences may help to account for this difference. Salmivalli and Voeten (2004) found that anti-bullying attitudes and norms decreased from fourth grade to sixth grade, suggesting that older students were less likely to view bullying as unacceptable in comparison to younger students. Additionally, the younger students were less influenced by class norms overall. Since defending behavior may be viewed as a possible jeopardization of social status, it stands to reason that younger students would be less hesitant to defend. However, a large majority of studies have been conducted among early adolescents and more research is needed with younger and older students, including college and adult samples.

Cultural Characteristics

Most defending research has focused on Western cultures, with little regard for cultural or international differences. However, there may be important differences across cultures, particularly across collectivist or individualist cultures. The few cross-cultural studies conducted on defending behavior have, in fact, found cultural differences (e.g., Ferreira, Simao, Ferreira, Souza, & Francisco, 2016; Monks, Palermiti, Ortega, & Costabile, 2011; Pronk et al., 2017). Pozzoli, Ang, and Gini (2012a) examined defending behavior in Singapore and Italy and found a more robust positive relationship between perceived pressure for intervention and defending among Singaporean students. Pozzoli and colleagues suggest this may be due to an influence of collectivism in Singaporean culture and students may feel a greater need to conform to group norms or expectations. In a more recent study, Pronk et al. (2017) examined bullying role behavior and peer group status (i.e., popularity, peer preference) among Dutch and Indian adolescents and found that defending was positively associated with popularity for Indian adolescents but not for Dutch adolescents. Thus, there may be cultural variations in terms of valued behavior. Pronk and colleagues suggest that the selfless nature of defending may be more associated with a collectivist culture orientation. However, bullying behavior was positively and significantly associated with popularity for both cultures. It is clear more research is needed to provide further insight on these findings.

Attitudes and Motivations Associated with Defending Behavior

Examining individual motivations and attitudes, as well as peer attitudes, is incredibly complex since defending behavior is highly influenced by situational characteristics (e.g., number of bystanders, type of bullying) and environmental norms (e.g., peer expectations). To date, much of the defending research has focused on the impact of empathy and morality on defending behavior (Lambe et al., 2019). Other important characteristics include self-efficacy (Pöyhönen et al., 2010), social status (Yun & Graham, 2018), social skills (Jenkins, Demaray, & Tennant, 2017), quality of relationships with adults and peers (Murphy, Laible, & Augustine, 2017), and personality characteristics (e.g., agreeableness; Tani, Greenman, Schneider, & Fregoso, 2003).

Empathy

Previous research has generally found that higher levels of empathy are related to defending behavior (Caravita, Di Blasio, & Salmivalli, 2009; Correia & Dalbert, 2008; Gini, Albiero, Benelli, & Altoè, 2007; Jolliffe & Farrington, 2011; Nickerson, Mele, & Princiotta, 2008; Nickerson & Mele-Taylor, 2014; Pöyhönen et al., 2010; Pozzoli & Gini, 2013; Zych, Ttofi, & Farrington, 2019). Nickerson, Aloe, and Werth (2015) conducted a meta-analysis that included 20 empirical studies about the relation between empathy and defending. They calculated weighted average correlations of .31 and .33, respectively, for studies that did and did not distinguish gender of the defender. Van Noorden, Haselager, Cillessen, and Bukowski (2015) conducted a systematic review of 40 studies that examined the relation between affective empathy (i.e., feeling emotional concern for another person) and cognitive empathy (i.e., identifying another person's perspective) and involvement in bullying. All but one of the six studies examining cognitive empathy and defending found a positive correlation (*rs* ranging from .14 to .52).

However, other studies have not found a significant relation between defending and empathy (Gini et al., 2007), especially when other factors are controlled (e.g., gender, grade; Pöyhönen et al., 2010). Espelage et al. (2012) reported a positive relation between cognitive empathy and willingness to intervene for boys, but not for girls. Similarly, in the review by Van Noorden et al. (2015), all but one of the 10 studies that examined affective empathy and defending also found positive correlations (*rs* ranging from .12 to .61). Menolascino and Jenkins (2018) recently found that boys with high levels of affective empathy were more likely to intervene with bullying than boys with low levels of affective empathy; however, girls were likely to report intervening at any level of affective empathy. Interestingly, cognitive empathy was not related to any steps of the bystander intervention model (e.g., notice and interpret the event, know how to intervene), including intervening with bullying. Menolascino and Jenkins (2018) suggest that perhaps cognitive empathy by itself is not enough to intervene in bullying situations. This has also been found in longitudinal designs, for example, van der Ploeg, Kretschmer, Salmivalli, and Veenstra (2017) found affective empathy, but not cognitive empathy, was significantly related to defending behavior over time while controlling for gender and stability in defending in a large ($n = 4209$) sample of Finnish youth. Taken together, the connection between empathy and defending is quite strong and affective empathy may be a particularly important predictor of defending behavior.

Morality and Moral Engagement

Moral disengagement is the process of separating one's moral reactions from one's harmful practices, in order to engage in unethical behavior and still maintain a positive self-regard without feeling distressed (Bandura, 1999). Multiple studies have found moral disengagement to be negatively related to defending behaviors (Caravita et al., 2012; Levasseur et al., 2017; Mazzone, Camodeca, & Salmivalli, 2016; Pozzoli, Gini, & Thornberg, 2016); however, this relationship can be contingent on other factors. For example, Mazzone et al. (2016) found that if a child or adolescent reported high levels of guilt, their moral disengagement was no longer significantly related to defending behavior. Additionally, Pozzoli et al. (2016) examined the influence of implicit moral cognition on the relationship between moral disengagement and defending behaviors among 279 middle school students. They found that moral disengagement was negatively associated with defending when the student had high levels of immediate affective reactions, but not at low levels of immediate affective reactions. These results suggest that children with high affective reactions, manifested as a tendency to cue moral intuition during moral events, are more in need of disengagement to refrain from defending a victim (Pozzoli et al., 2016).

In addition to moral disengagement, moral justification, or the process of developing justifications for morally questionable behavior in an attempt to make it appear socially acceptable (Shalvi, Gino, Barkan, & Ayal, 2015), is also related to defending. Levasseur et al. (2017) asked high school students ($n = 626$) to read a bullying scenario, rate the acceptability of both the bullying and the punishment in the scenario, and explain their reasoning behind their rating. Levasseur et al. found that students classified as defenders used more moral justifications than the other bullying roles. Similarly, Kollerová, Janosová, and Rícan (2015) asked 6th grade students ($n = 512$) to imagine themselves as the bully in a provided scenario and asked how they would feel and why. Moral justifications for the provided emotion were correlated, albeit weakly, with defending. Additionally, at high and moderate levels of social preference, moral justifications in this scenario predicted defending.

Self-Efficacy

Several cross-sectional and longitudinal studies have found a positive correlation between perceived self-efficacy in defending and actual defending behavior (Gini et al., 2008; Pöyhönen et al., 2010; Rigby & Johnson, 2006; van der Ploeg et al., 2017). A recent study also suggests that an individual may need high self-efficacy in order to directly, but not indirectly, intervene (van der Ploeg et al., 2017). Direct forms of defending (i.e., confronting the bully) may require high self-efficacy in addition to affective empathy, whereas indirect forms (i.e., comforting the victim) may require affective empathy alone. Interestingly, Barchia and Bussey (2011) found collective efficacy (i.e., students' perception that the school can or will intervene), but not defender efficacy (i.e., self-efficacy to defend victims), predicted defending behavior. This finding highlights the importance of school-wide bullying prevention and intervention efforts and student perceptions of these efforts. Students may be more likely to intervene if they feel that intervention is part of school norms and that they will be supported by staff at their school.

Social Status and Popularity

Although defending a peer being bullied may be perceived as a social risk (Pöyhönen et al., 2010), a few studies have found a positive association between defending and perceived popularity (Caravita et al., 2009; Pöyhönen et al., 2010; Sainio, Veenstra, Huitsing, & Salmivalli, 2010). In fact, defenders tend to be well-liked by their peers (Caravita et al., 2009). When using sociometric techniques in which children nominate their peers that they like the most and least, 43% of identified defenders fell into the popular category (Salmivalli et al., 1996). Similarly, Sainio et al. (2010) found that, although being liked by the class was not significantly associated with defending when popularity was included in the analysis, defenders were very unlikely to be rejected by classmates. As most of these studies are cross-sectional, questions remain regarding the direction of this relationship. In their longitudinal study, van der Ploeg et al. (2017) found perceived popularity to predict defending behavior over time. However, other studies have not found a link between defending and perceived popularity (Caravita et al., 2009, 2012) or have only found they are connected when empathy is high (Pöyhönen et al., 2010).

Unfortunately, although popularity has been associated with defending, it has also been associated with being less likely to notice bullying. Menolascino and Jenkins (2018) surveyed 346 middle school students and found more popular students were less likely to notice bullying than their less popular counterparts. This suggests that though popularity and defending are correlated, popularity could be an inhibiting factor to initially seeing bullying as well. This may be explained by the tendency for popular students to surround themselves with other popular students. In general, popular students are bullied less than students who are less popular, meaning they may not witness bullying as frequently (Pöyhönen et al., 2010; Salmivalli et al., 1996), and may have decreased awareness of potential bullying situations (Jenkins & Nickerson, 2017).

Ecological or Contextual Variables

In addition to individual characteristics, the influence of ecological characteristics, such as classroom or peer group norms, are important to consider. A child or adolescent is more likely to intervene if the perceived classroom norm is to defend the victim (Pozzoli et al., 2012b), if the victim is part of the individual's peer group (Levine, Cassidy, Brazier, & Reicher, 2002), or if other members of their social group engage in defending behavior (Salmivalli, Huttunen, & Lagerspetz, 1997). Several recent studies underscore the importance of the classroom and school context. For example, Lucas-Molina, Giménez-Dasí, Fonseca-Pedrero, and Pérez-Albéniz (2018) examined the interactions between individual variables and classroom norms among 8- to 13-year-old children (n = 2050). They found that classes with more victimization and higher injunctive bullying norms—meaning the classes held more pro-bullying attitudes—had fewer defending behaviors. Further, numerous studies have found that individual characteristics and ecological contexts interact to influence behavior. Peets et al. (2015) looked at the effects of classroom norms, empathy, and self-efficacy on defending in 6708 third to fifth grade students. Findings revealed that classroom norms influenced the degree to which a student's affective empathy predicted defending, such that classes with higher levels of bullying had a stronger link between empathy and defending. Popular students were less likely to defend in classes where bullies were also popular, perhaps due to fear of losing their social standing. In classes where bullies were not popular,

popular students were more likely to defend. Similarly, Yun and Graham (2018) found perceived popularity to interact with classroom prosocial norms—popular students were more likely to defend when classroom-level prosocial norms were high than when prosocial norms were low. These findings suggest that defending behavior is strongly associated with perceived class norms, particularly for students with high social status. Popular students may be less likely to defend in situations that jeopardize their popularity by going against group norms.

Association of Defending Behavior with Physical and Mental Health

Although much of the focus on defending has revolved around the positive effect on the victim or the bullying incident, research has also examined the effect of defending on the physical, mental, and social health for the defender. One area of focus has been on a link between defending and internalizing problems. Wu, Luu, and Luh (2016) found that defending behaviors were positively associated with self-reported social anxiety and depressive symptoms in Taiwanese adolescents. Bistrong, Bottiani, and Bradshaw (2019) also found that overall internalizing problems are linked to defending. They analyzed survey data from 57,314 adolescents in Maryland that included information on bystander behavior and internalizing problems, and they found that for every additional point a student had on their internalizing score, their odds of defending were 38.2% higher. A Canadian study on 5071 children and adolescents in fourth grade through twelfth grade also found that internalizing problems—assessed by asking youth if they have been sad or scared recently—were associated with recent defending behavior (Lambe et al., 2017). However, this relationship was only found for boys, not girls. Another study with 246 middle school students found that defending was associated with emotional difficulties such as internalizing or personal adjustment problems for girls, but not for boys (Jenkins et al., 2017). Lambe et al. (2017) also found that the youth that reported defending during their last observed bullying episode were more likely to experience anger problems than their peers that had not defended.

When pulling together the information from these studies, it is apparent that defending behaviors are at least related to mental health concerns; however, due to the cross-sectional nature of these studies, it is impossible to determine the directionality of this relationship. Although it could be possible that defending leads to increased anger or internalizing problems, it is just as possible that those with anger or internalizing problems are more likely to act against bullies.

It is unsurprising that defending behaviors are associated with negative outcomes. As Lambe et al. (2017) explained, bullying could potentially be a traumatic event, and one would expect negative outcomes to be associated with viewing or being involved in bullying. Additionally, although the majority of peer defending in bullying tends to stop the bully (Hawkins et al., 2001), there is still the possibility that the would-be defender could fail to stop the bullying and then become the target of future bullying themselves. The relationship could also be more complex than defending directly causing mental health problems or vice versa. For example, Jenkins and Fredrick (2017) found that internalizing problems acted as a mediator in the relationship between social capital (i.e., resources and benefits gained from interpersonal relationships, shared experiences, and social interactions) and defending behavior, such that internalizing problems inhibited defending behavior. More research is needed to help determine the relationship between defending and mental health and the directions of those relationships.

In addition to the above concerns, some attention has also been given to possible links between defending and substance use, particularly alcohol and cigarette use. Quinn et al. (2016) administered a survey to 1255 ninth and eleventh grade students and found that defending was significantly but weakly correlated with smoking after controlling for grade, gender, and other participant role behaviors. Additionally, among the 672 students that reported lifetime alcohol use, higher defending scores were associated with higher alcohol-related harm. Further research is needed to understand this relationship, as this is the only known study to look at the association between defending and substance abuse.

A possible benefit to defending is increased self-esteem. Salmivalli, Kaukiainen, Kaistaniemi, and Lagerspetz (1999) looked at three measures of self-esteem—peer-evaluated, self-evaluated, and defensive egotism (i.e., having an inflated self-image and being overly reactive or defensive in response to criticism)—to determine what relationship these had with bullying roles. They found that peer-evaluated self-esteem was significantly and positively correlated with defending behavior. Additionally, they found that students that were high in both self-evaluated and peer-evaluated self-esteem and low in defensive egotism were more likely to be defenders than any other combination of self-esteem ratings. This could suggest that students who defend benefit from elevating self-esteem, or that students with higher self-esteem are just more likely to defend. However, self-esteem has also been found to be unrelated to defending behavior, as nominated by peers (Sainio et al., 2010). Regardless, more research is needed on the relationship between self-esteem and defending, specifically looking at the direction of any such relationship.

Implications for Prevention and Intervention

As demonstrated above, there are risks and benefits to defending victims of bullying. Despite the potential risks, there is evidence that increasing active bystander intervention in bullying can reduce bullying perpetration and victimization above and beyond the effects of programs that do not focus on defending (Merrell, Gueldner, Ross, & Isava, 2008). Meta-analyses and systematic reviews suggest that many anti-bullying programs yield small to modest effects (Merrell et al., 2008; Smith, Schneider, Smith, & Ananiadou, 2004), and even harmful effects in high school (Yeager, Fong, Lee, & Espelage, 2015). However, bystander intervention programs (i.e., those explicitly teaching students the importance of intervening) have shown greater promise (Polanin, Espelage, & Pigott, 2012). There is research to suggest that defending can stop bullying. For example, Hawkins et al. (2001) found that when youth intervene, bullying stops within 10 seconds 60% of the time. Taken together, there is evidence that bystander intervention by defenders is an effective way to stop peer victimization.

Despite the promising findings about the role of defenders, there are few evidence-based training programs aimed specifically at increasing defending behavior in bullying, particularly for K-12 schools. Training for the purpose of increasing bystander intervention in interpersonal violence is not a novel concept and has been used to reduce hazing and sexual violence on college campuses (Banyard, 2008, 2015; Burn, 2009; Moynihan, Eckstein, Banyard, & Plante, 2010). Polanin et al. (2012) conducted a meta-analysis of 12 school-based programs that sought to increase bystander intervention in bullying situations. Overall, they found that these programs were effective at increasing intention to intervene or actual intervention. Of the 12 studies included in the meta-analysis, only eight of them were published in peer-reviewed journals and many of the programs were not readily available to schools and practitioners. They also found that the programs worked better with the high school samples compared to the elementary and middle school samples, indicating that bystander intervention behavior may be a developmental process. Thus, the effectiveness of defender training with elementary and middle school is still uncertain.

Though not included in the Polanin et al. (2012) meta-analysis, there are two promising programs, Green Dot and STAC, that incorporate bystander intervention elements to address interpersonal violence or bullying in youth and adolescents. Green Dot is a widely used bystander intervention training program on many college campuses, which focuses on engaging college students to prevent sexual violence (Coker et al., 2011). There are published studies demonstrating the effectiveness of Green Dot on increasing active bystander behavior to prevent interpersonal violence among college-age students. Green Dot trains students how to reduce high-risk situations or "Red Dots," by using two types of intervening behaviors: "Proactive Green Dot" behaviors (i.e., attending violence prevention events) and "Reactive Green Dot" behaviors (i.e., utilizing emergency services, intervening in bullying). Even though Green Dot has been adapted for use in K-12 schools, there are only two published studies showing the effectiveness of the program, which was focused on high school. Coker, Bush, Brancato, Clear, and Recktenwald (2018; Coker et al., 2017) conducted a randomized controlled trial of Green Dot with a high school in Kentucky. They found that Green Dot reduced overall interpersonal violence in the treatment schools, but the researchers did not measure bullying specifically. There are no published studies about the effectiveness of the Green Dot program for students in elementary or middle school (Grades K-8).

STAC (Midgett, Doumas, & Johnston, 2018; Midgett, Doumas, & Trull, 2016; Midgett, Doumas, Trull, & Johnson, 2017) is the only intervention program focused on training defenders that has published evidence of its effectiveness in increasing bystander interventions. The researchers who developed the STAC program have published very promising findings. Results from their studies have shown that both elementary (Midgett & Doumas, 2016) and middle school (Midgett, Doumas, Sears, Lundquist, & Hausheer, 2015) students can increase their knowledge of intervention options and defending strategies and have greater confidence about intervening in bullying. The STAC program is described in greater detail below.

Though there is not extensive empirical support for prevention and intervention programs assessing the effectiveness and impact of defender training programs, there is evidence that defending usually has a positive impact (Banyard, 2008, 2015; Hawkins et al., 2001). In addition, suggestions for prevention and intervention can be gleaned when looking at the Green Dot and STAC programs, as well as from the broader literature on the role of defenders in interpersonal violence (e.g., Banyard, 2008, 2015). First, potential defenders should be taught multiple strategies for intervening. The STAC program teaches four strategies: "stealing the show," "turning it over," "accompanying others," and "coaching compassion." In the interpersonal violence literature, Banyard, Plante, and Moynihan (2004) and Berkowitz (2004) use the Four Ds: direct, distract, delegate, and delay. Teaching multiple strategies is important because there are different types of bullying (e.g., physical, relational/social, verbal), the perpetrator and/or victim may or may not be a friend to the potential defender, and youth have very different skill sets (e.g., social skills, emotional skills) and may not feel comfortable or be able to intervene the same way in all situations. Though all forms of defending may be beneficial under certain circumstances, few individuals can successfully engage in all types because most students are not socially or emotionally equipped to use all defending strategies. We need to teach students multiple ways to intervene or defend. Teaching one strategy is not sufficient if we expect all students to support victims of bullying.

Second, we should not rely solely on defenders to reduce bullying. That is, we cannot only teach students some defending strategies and expect to see drastic reductions in bullying at a school. Increasing defending behavior by peers should help to reduce bullying, but it should be one piece of a much larger comprehensive social-emotional learning program (Durlak, Weissberg, Dymnicki, Taylor, & Schellinger, 2011). Increasing social and emotional skills from an early age could prevent negative peer interactions from occurring, which would reduce the need for defending. By using a tiered, comprehensive approach teaching social and emotional learning, schools may be able to prevent problems before they occur. Then intervention efforts involving bullying reduction and increasing defending can be used more strategically on a fewer number of youth.

Finally, there are risks to defending that should be anticipated and addressed in future defender intervention training programs. Though defending is typically thought of as a prosocial act by empathetic individuals with good social standing and social support, there is plenty of evidence that this is not the case for all defenders (Bistrong et al., 2019; Jenkins et al., 2017; Lambe et al., 2017; Wu et al., 2016). Many youth who engage in defending are also the victim (Demaray, Summers, Jenkins, & Becker, 2014). Training programs aimed at increasing defending behavior should also teach potential defenders coping strategies and how to decide if they should intervene themselves or alert others. Recognizing the potential risk to defenders should be a salient discussion in defender training programs so we are not putting undue pressure on youth to intervene or inadvertently hurting defenders for the sake of intervening on behalf of victims.

Future Issues

There has been a surge in recent years on research focusing on defender behavior, as peers are an effective means to prevent and intervene with bullying behavior (Lambe et al., 2019; Lucas-Molina et al., 2018). However, the majority of this research has focused on individual traits in order to identify specific characteristics of youth who may be more likely to defend their peers. Some of these traits include gender (i.e., being a girl), age (i.e., being younger), having higher levels of empathy, morality, and self-efficacy, and being well-liked by peers (Huang et al., 2016; Lambe et al., 2017; Murphy et al., 2017; Nickerson & Mele-Taylor, 2014; Pöyhönen et al., 2010; Yun & Graham, 2018). There is some evidence to suggest that youth that engage in defending behavior report higher levels of internalizing problems (Bistrong et al., 2019; Wu et al., 2016), although longitudinal studies are needed to further explore these relationships. Though these traits are certainly important in creating a picture of youth who defend, predicting defender behavior is incredibly complex and goes well beyond individual correlates. As individual traits and contextual factors likely interact to further complicate this picture, further research is needed that takes into account both individual traits and ecological characteristics within longitudinal designs.

Given that we now know that peer group processes are dynamic, a social network perspective is a promising approach that can help researchers account for these dynamic processes. This approach is beginning to gain traction among researchers as a means to understand the variability and interdependency of friendship networks (for a more in-depth overview, see Snijders, van de Bunt, & Steglich, 2010). This is particularly important for researchers and practitioners attempting to predict and ultimately encourage defender behavior. Within bullying dynamics, the social network perspective allows researchers to obtain a detailed picture of the connections between classmates based on bullying role behavior. This is typically obtained through a combination of self-report and peer nominations, in which youth indicate their own experiences with bullying and then identify specific classmates who have bullied or defended them. Through this networking perspective, it has been found that classmates who are victimized from the same bully tend to defend one another, and classmates who perpetrate bullying tend to defend one another, suggesting there may be supportive defender subgroups within bullying roles (Huitsing, Snijders, Van Duijn, & Veenstra, 2014; Huitsing & Veenstra, 2012). The main advantage of using a social network approach to study defender behavior is that youth do not need to be designated into fixed roles and potentially be inaccurately identified (Huitsing et al., 2014).

Regardless, rigorous research is needed to examine the interplay of factors that may influence defending behavior, including the impact of online contexts. Cross-cultural studies are needed to determine if this behavior is universal across cultures, and this is especially important for creating culturally sensitive prevention and intervention programs. Despite promising results, more rigorous research on the effectiveness of programs training defenders of bullying in K-12 settings is essential (Banyard, 2008, 2015; Hawkins et al., 2001). Even studies of the STAC program, which has been studied to the greatest degree, have used fairly small samples and the outcome has typically been knowledge of strategies and intention to intervene, not actual defending (Midgett & Doumas, 2016; Midgett et al., 2015). Thus, although there is a wealth of knowledge regarding defending behavior, there is still much work to be done.

References

Bandura, A. (1999). Moral disengagement in the perpetration of inhumanities. *Personality and Social Psychology Review: An Official Journal of the Society for Personality and Social Psychology, Inc, 3*(3), 193–209. https://doi.org/10.1207/s15327957pspr0303_3.

Banyard, V. L. (2008). Measurement and correlates of pro-social bystander behavior: The case of interpersonal violence. *Violence and Victims, 23*, 85–99. https://doi.org/10.1891/0886-6708.23.1.83.

Banyard, V. L. (2015). *Toward the next generation of bystander prevention of sexual and relationship violence: Action coils to engage communities*. New York: Springer.

Banyard, V. L., Plante, E. G., & Moynihan, M. M. (2004). Bystander education: Bringing a broader community perspective to sexual violence prevention. *Journal of Community Psychology, 32*, 61–79. https://doi.org/10.1002/jcop.10078.

Barchia, K., & Bussey, K. (2011). Predictors of student defenders of peer aggression victims: Empathy and social cognitive factors. *International Journal of Behavioral Development, 35*, 289–297. https://doi.org/10.1177/0165025410396746.

Bastiaensens, S., Vendebosch, H., Poels, K., Van Cleemput, K., DeSmet, A., & De Bourdeaudhuij, I. (2015). 'Can I afford to help?' How affordances of communication modalities guide bystanders' helping intentions towards harassment on social network sites. *Behaviour and Information Technology, 34,* 425–435. https://doi.org/10.1080/0144929X.2014.983979.

Berkowitz, A. D. (2004). *The social norms approach: Theory, research and annotated bibliography.* Newton, MA: Higher Education Center. Retrieved from www.alanberkowitz.com/articles/social_norms.pdf.

Bistrong, E., Bottiani, J. H., & Bradshaw, C. P. (2019). Youth reactions to bullying: Exploring the factors associated with students' willingness to intervene. *Journal of School Violence, 18,* 522–535. https://doi.org/10.1080/15388220.2019.1576048.

Burn, S. M. (2009). A situational model of sexual assault prevention through bystander intervention. *Sex Roles: a Journal of Research, 60,* 779–792. https://doi.org/10.1007/211199-008-9581-5.

Camodeca, M., & Goossens, F. A. (2010). Children's opinions on effective strategies to cope with bullying: The importance of bullying role and perspective. *Educational Research, 47,* 93–105. https://doi.org/10.1080/0013188042000337587.

Caravita, S. C. S., Di Blasio, P., & Salmivalli, C. (2009). Unique and interactive effects of empathy and social status on involvement in bullying. *Social Development, 18,* 140–163. https://doi.org/10.1111/j.1467-9507.2008.00465.x.

Caravita, S. C. S., Gini, G., & Pozzoli, T. (2012). Main and moderated effects of moral cognition and status on bullying and defending. *Aggressive Behavior, 38,* 456–468. https://doi.org/10.1002/ab.21447.

Coker, A. L., Bush, H. M., Brancato, C. J., Clear, E. R., & Recktenwald, E. A. (2018). Bystander program effectiveness to reduce violence acceptance: RCT in high schools. *Journal of Family Violence, 34,* 153–164. https://doi.org/10.1007/s10896-018-9961-8.

Coker, A. L., Bush, H. M., Cook-Craig, P. G., DeGue, S. A., Clear, E. R., Brancato, ... Recktenwald, E. A. (2017). RCT testing bystander effectiveness to reduce violence. *American Journal of Preventative Medicine, 52,* 566–578. https://doi.org/10.1016/j.amepre.2017.01.020.

Coker, A. L., Cook-Craig, P. G., Williams, C. M., Fisher, B. S., Clear, E. R., Garcia, L. S., & Hegge, L. M. (2011). Evaluation of Green Dot: An active bystander intervention to reduce sexual violence on college campuses. *Violence against Women, 17,* 776–796. https://doi.org/10.1177/1077801211410264.

Correia, I., & Dalbert, C. (2008). School bullying: Belief in a personal just world of bullies, victims, and defenders. *European Psychologist, 13,* 248–254. https://doi.org/10.1027/1016-9040.13.4.248.

Demaray, M. K., Summers, K. H., Jenkins, L. N., & Becker, L. (2014). The Bully Participant Behavior Questionnaire (BPBQ): Establishing a reliable and valid measure. *Journal of School Violence, 15,* 158–188. https://doi.org/10.1080/15388220.2014.964801.

Durlak, J. A., Weissberg, R. P., Dymnicki, A. B., Taylor, R. D., & Schellinger, K. B. (2011). The impact of enhancing students' social and emotional learning: A meta-analysis of school-based universal interventions. *Child Development, 82,* 405–432. https://doi.org/10.1111/j.1467-8624.2010.01564.x.

Espelage, D., Green, H., & Polanin, J. (2012). Willingness to intervene in bullying episodes among middle school students: Individual and peer-group influences. *The Journal of Early Adolescence, 32,* 776–801. https://doi.org/10.1177/0272431611423017.

Ferreira, P. C., Simao, A. M. V., Ferreira, A., Souza, S., & Francisco, S. (2016). Student bystander behavior and cultural issues in cyberbullying: When actions speak louder than words. *Computers in Human Behavior, 60,* 301–311. https://doi.org/10.1016/j.chb.2016.02.059.

Gini, C., Albiero, P., Benelli, B., & Altoè, G. (2007). Does empathy predict adolescents' bullying and defending behavior? *Aggressive Behavior, 33,* 467–476. https://doi.org/10.1002/ab.20204.

Gini, G., Albiero, P., Benelli, B., & Altoè, G. (2008). Determinants of adolescents' active defending and passive bystanding behavior in bullying. *Journal of Adolescence, 31,* 93–105. https://doi.org/10.1016/j.adolescence.2007.05.002.

Hawkins, D. L., Pepler, D. J., & Craig, W. M. (2001). Naturalistic observations of peer interventions in bullying. *Social Development, 10,* 512–527. https://doi.org/10.1111/1467-9507.00178.

Huang, Z., Liu, Z., Liu, X., Lv, L., Zhang, Y., Ou, L., & Li, L. (2016). Risk factors associated with peer victimization and bystander behaviors among adolescent students. *International Journal of Environmental Research and Public Health, 13,* 759. https://doi.org/10.3390/ijerph13080759.

Huitsing, G., Snijders, T. A. B., Van Duijn, M. A. J., & Veenstra, R. (2014). Victims, bullies, and their defenders: A longitudinal study of the coevolution of positive and negative networks. *Development and Psychopathology, 26,* 645–659. https://doi.org/10.1017/S0954579414000297.

Huitsing, G., & Veenstra, R. (2012). Bullying in the classrooms: Participant roles from a social network perspective. *Aggressive Behavior, 38,* 494–509. https://doi.org/10.1002/ab.21438.
Jenkins, L. N., Demaray, M. K., & Tennant, J. (2017). Social, emotional, and cognitive factors associated with bullying. *School Psychology Review, 46,* 42–64. https://doi.org/10.17105/SPR46-1.42-64.
Jenkins, L. N., & Fredrick, S. S. (2017). Social capital and bystander behavior in bullying: Internalizing problems as a barrier to prosocial intervention. *Journal of Youth and Adolescence, 46,* 757–771. https://doi.org/10.1007/s10 964-017-0637-0.
Jenkins, L. N., & Nickerson, A. B. (2017). Bullying participant roles and gender as predictors of bystander intervention. *Aggressive Behavior, 43,* 281–290. https://doi.org/10.1002/ab.21688.
Jolliffe, D., & Farrington, D. P. (2011). Is low empathy related to bullying after controlling for individual and social background variables? *Journal of Adolescence, 34,* 59–71. https://doi.org/10.1016/j.adolescence.2010.02.001.
Kollerová, L., Janosová, P., & Rícan, P. (2015). Moral motivation in defending classmates victimized by bullying. *European Journal of Developmental Psychology, 12,* 297–309. https://doi.org/10.1080/17405629.2015.1006125.
Lambe, L. J., Cioppa, V. D., Hong, I. K., & Craig, W. M. (2019). Standing up to bullying: A social ecological review of peer defending in offline and online contexts. *Aggression and Violent Behavior, 45,* 51–74. https://doi.org/ 10.1016/j.avb.2018.05.007.
Lambe, L. J., Hudson, C. C., Craig, W. M., & Pepler, D. J. (2017). Does defending come with a cost? Examining the psychosocial correlates of defending behaviour among bystanders of bullying in a Canadian sample. *Child Abuse and Neglect, 65,* 112–123. https://doi.org/10.1016/j.chiabu. 2017.01.012.
Levasseur, C., Desbiens, N., & Bowen, F. (2017). Moral reasoning about school bullying in involved adolescents. *Journal of Moral Education, 46,* 158–176. https://doi.org/10.1080/03057240.2016.1268113.
Levine, M., Cassidy, C., Brazier, G., & Reicher, S. (2002). Self-categorization and bystander non-intervention: Two experimental studies. *Journal of Applied School Psychology, 32,* 1452–1463. https://doi.org/10.1111/j.1559-1816.2002.tb01446.x.
Lucas-Molina, B., Giménez-Dasí, M., Fonseca-Pedrero, E., & Pérez-Albéniz, A. (2018). What makes a defender? A multilevel study of individual correlates and classroom norms in explaining defending behaviors. *School Psychology Review, 47,* 34–44. https://doi.org/10.17105/SPR-2017-0011.V47-1.

Ma, T., & Chen, W. (2019). The benefits of being defended: Perceived bystander participant roles and victims' emotional and psychosocial adjustment. *Journal of School Violence, 18,* 77–91. https://doi.org/10.1080/15388220.2017.1387132.

Mazzone, A., Camodeca, M., & Salmivalli, C. (2016). Interactive effects of guilt and moral disengagement on bullying, defending and outsider behavior. *Journal of Moral Education, 45,* 419–432. https://doi.org/10.1080/03057240.2016.1216399.

Menolascino, N., & Jenkins, L. N. (2018). Predicting bystander intervention among middle school students. *School Psychology Quarterly, 33,* 305–313. https://doi.org/10.1037/spq0000262.

Merrell, K. W., Gueldner, B. A., Ross, S. W., & Isava, D. M. (2008). How effective are school bullying intervention programs? A meta-analysis of intervention research. *School Psychology Quarterly, 23,* 26–42. https://doi.org/10.1037/1045-3830.23.1.26.

Midgett, A., & Doumas, D. M. (2016). Training elementary school students to intervene as peer-advocates to stop bullying at school: A pilot study. *Journal of Creativity in Mental Health, 11,* 353–365. https://doi.org/10.1080/15401383.2016.1164645.

Midgett, A., Doumas, D. M., & Johnston, A. D. (2018). Establishing school counselors as leaders in bullying curriculum delivery: Evaluation of a brief, school-wide bystander intervention. *Professional School Counseling, 2,* 1–9. https://doi.org/10.1177/2156759X18778781.

Midgett, A., Doumas, D., Sears, D., Lundquist, A., & Hausheer, R. (2015). A bystander bullying psychoeducation program with middle school students: A preliminary report. *Professional Counselor, 5,* 486–500. https://doi.org/10.15241/am.5.4.486.

Midgett, A., Doumas, D., & Trull, R. (2016). Evaluations of a brief, school-based bystander intervention for elementary school students. *Professional School Counseling, 20,* 172–183. https://doi.org/10.5330/1096-2409-20.1.172.

Midgett, A., Doumas, D. M., Trull, R., & Johnson, J. (2017). Training students who occasionally bully to be peer advocates: Is a bystander intervention effective in reducing bullying behavior? *Journal of Child and Adolescent Counseling, 3,* 1–13. https://doi.org/10.1080/23727810.2016.1277116.

Monks, C. P., Palermiti, A., Ortega, R., & Costabile, A. (2011). A cross-national comparison of aggressors, victims and defenders in preschools in England, Spain and Italy. *The Spanish Journal of Psychology, 14,* 133–144. https://doi.org/10.5209/rev_SJOP.2011.v14.n1.11.

Moynihan, M. M., Eckstein, R. P., Banyard, V. L., & Plante, E. G. (2010). *Facilitator's guide for Bringing in the Bystander™: A prevention workshop for establishing a community of responsibility* (Rev. version). Durham, NH: Prevention Innovations, University of New Hampshire.

Murphy, T. P., Laible, D., & Augustine, M. (2017). The influences of parent and peer attachment on bullying. *Journal of Child and Family Studies, 26,* 1388–1397. https://doi.org/10.1007/s10826-017-0663-2.

Nickerson, A. B., Aloe, A. M., & Werth, J. M. (2015). The relation of empathy and defending in bullying: A meta-analytic investigation. *School Psychology Review, 44,* 372–390. https://doi.org/10.17105/spr-15-0035.1.

Nickerson, A. B., & Mele-Taylor, D. (2014). Empathic responsiveness, group norms, and prosocial affiliations in bullying roles. *School Psychology Quarterly, 29,* 99–109. https://doi.org/10.1037/sqp0000052.

Nickerson, A. B., Mele, D., & Princiotta, D. (2008). Attachment and empathy as predictors of roles as defenders or outsiders in bullying interactions. *Journal of School Psychology, 46,* 687–703. https://doi.org/10.1016/j.jsp.2008.06.002.

Peets, K., Pöyhönen, V., Juvonen, J., & Salmivalli, C. (2015). Classroom norms of bullying alter the degree to which children defend in response to their affective empathy and power. *Developmental Psychology, 51,* 913–920. https://doi.org/10.1037/a0039287.

Polanin, J. R., Espelage, D. L., & Pigott, T. D. (2012). A meta-analysis of school-based bullying prevention programs' effects on bystander intervention behavior. *School Psychology Review, 41,* 47–65.

Pöyhönen, V., Juvonen, J., & Salmivalli, C. (2010). What does it take to stand up for the victim of bullying? The interplay between personal and social factors. *Merrill-Palmer Quarterly, 56,* 143–163. https://doi.org/10.1353/mpq.0.0046.

Pozzoli, T., Ang, R. P., & Gini, G. (2012a). Bystanders' reactions to bullying: A cross-cultural analysis of personal correlates among Italian and Singaporean students. *Social Development, 21,* 686–703. https://doi.org/10.1111/j.1467-9507.2011.00651.x.

Pozzoli, T., & Gini, G. (2010). Active defending and passive bystanding behavior in bullying: The role of personal characteristics and perceived peer pressure. *Journal of Abnormal Child Psychology, 38,* 815–827. https://doi.org/10.1007/s10802-010-939909.

Pozzoli, T., & Gini, G. (2013). Friend similarity in attitudes toward bullying and sense of responsibility to intervene. *Social Influence, 8,* 161–176. https://doi.org/10.1080/15534510.2012.716372.

Pozzoli, T., Gini, G., & Thornberg, R. (2016). Bullying and defending behavior: The role of explicit and implicit moral cognition. *Journal of School Psychology, 59,* 67–81. https://doi.org/10.1016/j.jsp.2016.09.005.

Pozzoli, T., Gini, G., & Vieno, A. (2012b). The role of individual correlates and class norms in defending and passive bystanding behavior in bullying: A multilevel analysis. *Child Development, 83,* 1917–1931. https://doi.org/10.1111/j.1467-8624.2012.01831.x.

Pronk, J., Lee, N., Sandhu, D., Kaur, K., Olthof, S., & Goossens, T. (2017). Associations between Dutch and Indian adolescents' bullying role behavior and peer-group status: Cross-culturally testing an evolutionary hypothesis. *International Journal of Behavioral Development, 41,* 735–742. https://doi.org/10.1177/0165025416679743.

Quinn, C. A., Fitzpatrick, S., Bussey, K., Hides, L., & Chan, G. C. K. (2016). Associations between the group processes of bullying and adolescent substance use. *Addictive Behaviors, 62,* 6–13. https://doi.org/10.1016/j.addbeh.2016.06.007.

Reijntjes, A., Vermande, M., Olthof, T., Goossens, F. A., Aleva, L., & van der Meulen, M. (2016). Defending victimized peers: Opposing the bully, supporting the victim, or both? *Aggressive Behavior, 42,* 585–597. https://doi.org/10.1002/ab21653.

Rigby, K., & Johnson, B. (2006). Expressed readiness of Australian schoolchildren to act as bystanders in support of children who are being bullied. *Educational Psychology, 26,* 425–440. https://doi.org/10.1080/01443410500342047.

Sainio, M., Veenstra, R., Huitsing, G., & Salmivalli, C. (2010). Victims and their defenders: A dyadic approach. *International Journal of Behavioral Development, 35,* 144–151. https://doi.org/10.1177/0165025410378068.

Salmivalli, C., Huttunen, A., & Lagerspetz, K. (1997). Peer networks and bullying in schools. *Scandinavian Journal of Psychology, 38,* 305–312. https://doi.org/10.1111/1467-9450.00040.

Salmivalli, C., Kaukiainen, A., Kaistaniemi, L., & Lagerspetz, K. (1999). Self-evaluated self-esteem, peer-evaluated self-esteem, and defensive egotism as predictors of adolescents' participation in bullying situations. *Personality and Social Psychology Bulletin, 25,* 1268–1278. https://doi.org/10.1177/0146167299258008.

Salmivalli, C., Lagerspetz, K., Björkqvist, K., Österman, K., & Kaukiainen, A. (1996). Bullying as a group process: Participant roles and their relations to social status within the group. *Aggressive Behavior, 22,* 1–15. https://doi.org/10.1002/(SICI)1098-2337(1996)22:1.

Salmivalli, C., & Voeten, M. (2004). Connections between attitudes, group norms, and behaviour in bullying situations. *International Journal of Behavioral Development, 28,* 246–258. https://doi.org/10.1080/10650250344000488.

Salmivalli, C., Voeten, M., & Poskiparta, E. (2011). Bystanders matter: Associations between reinforcing, defending, and the frequency of bullying behavior in classrooms. *Journal of Clinical Child and Adolescent Psychology, 40,* 668–676. https://doi.org/10.1080/15374416.2011.597090.

Shalvi, S., Gino, F., Barkan, R., & Ayal, S. (2015). Self-serving justifications: Doing wrong and feeling moral. *Current Directions in Psychological Science, 24*(2), 125–130. https://doi.org/10.1177/0963721414553264.

Smith, J. D., Schneider, B. H., Smith, P. K., & Ananiadou, K. (2004). The effectiveness of whole-school antibullying programs: A synthesis of evaluation research. *School Psychology Review, 33,* 547–560. Retrieved from naspon line.org.

Snijders, T. A. B., van de Bunt, G. G., & Steglich, C. E. G. (2010). Introduction to stochastic actor-based models for network dynamics. *Social Networks, 32,* 44–60. https://doi.org/10.1016/j.socnet.2009.02.004.

Song, J., & Oh, I. (2017). Investigation of the bystander effect in school bullying: Comparison of experiential, psychological and situational factors. *School Psychology International, 38,* 319–336. https://doi.org/10.1177/0143034317699997.

Song, J., & Oh, I. (2018). Factors influencing bystanders' behavioral reactions in cyberbullying situations. *Computers in Human Behavior, 78,* 273–282. https://doi.org/10.1016/j.chb.2017.10.008.

Tani, F., Greenman, P. S., Schneider, B. H., & Fregoso, M. (2003). Bullying and the Big Five: A study of childhood personality and participant roles in bullying incidents. *School Psychology International, 24,* 131–146. https://doi.org/10.1177/0143034303023002001.

van der Ploeg, R., Kretschmer, T., Salmivalli, C., & Veenstra, R. (2017). Defending victims: What does it take to intervene in bullying and how is it rewarded by peers? *Journal of School Psychology, 65,* 1–10. https://doi.org/10.1016/j.jsp.2017.06.002.

Van Noorden, T., Haselager, G., Cillessen, A., & Bukowski, W. (2015). Empathy and involvement in bullying in children and adolescents: A systematic review. *Journal of Youth and Adolescence, 44,* 637–657. https://doi.org/10.1007/s10964-014-0135-6.

Wu, W., Luu, S., & Luh, D. (2016). Defending behaviors, bullying roles, and their associations with mental health in junior high school students:

A population-based study. *BMC Public Health, 16,* 1–10. https://doi.org/10.1186/s12889-016-3721-6.

Yeager, D. S., Fong, C. J., Lee, H. Y., & Espelage, D. L. (2015). Declines in efficacy of anti-bullying programs among older adolescents: Theory and a three-level meta-analysis. *Journal of Applied Developmental Psychology, 37,* 36–51. https://doi.org/10.1016/j.appdev.2014.11.005.

Yun, H., & Graham, S. (2018). Defending victims of bullying in early adolescence: A multilevel analysis. *Journal of Youth and Adolescence, 47,* 1926–1937. https://doi.org/10.1007/s10964-018-0869-7.

Zych, I., Ttofi, M. M., & Farrington, D. P. (2019). Empathy and callous-unemotional traits in different bullying roles: A systematic review and meta-analysis. *Trauma, Violence, & Abuse, 20,* 3–21. https://doi.org/10.1177/1524838016683456.

6

The Vantage Point of a Victim

David Schwartz, Luiza Mali, and Annemarie Kelleghan

In this chapter, we will be focusing specifically on children and adolescents who emerge as disproportionate targets of peer aggression. That is, we will be considering those youths who are frequently conceptualized as "victims" in the extant literature. Over the course of development, most children will experience some form of verbal or physical mistreatment by peers (Card & Hodges, 2008; Hong & Espelage, 2012). As we will discuss, however, a relatively small subgroup of youths are victimized by peers on a frequent (and perhaps chronic) basis (Bowes et al., 2013; Telzer, Miernicki, & Rudolph, 2018). The plight of these children certainly warrants attention, but victims of bullying are not a homogenous group (e.g., Barboza, 2015; Wang, Iannotti, Luk, & Nansel, 2010). The bully/victim phenomenon is complicated, multifaceted, and involves distinct subgroups of youths.

Although we will endeavor to avoid conclusions that are universal in nature, throughout the chapter we will emphasize the involuntary

D. Schwartz (✉) · L. Mali · A. Kelleghan
University of Southern California, Los Angeles, CA, USA
e-mail: davschw@usc.edu

nature of the victim role. Peer victimization is a highly aversive experience that nearly all children will attempt to avoid insofar as possible. We contend that the victim's role differs from any of the other involved actors in bullying incidents. Many children who have mixed feelings about bullying in their school will still be actively (as bullies or reinforcers) or passively (as onlookers) involved (O'Connell, Pepler, & Craig, 1999; Salmivalli, 1999). The victimized youth, in contrast, is an unwilling participant who will be motivated to avoid further abuse (for a worthwhile contradicting argument, see Pepler, Craig, & O'Connell, 1999).

Guided by this conceptualization, we begin by delineating the behaviors that typically constitute peer victimization and we identify common attributes, correlates, and features of victimized youths. We will then move on to identify other factors (e.g., gender and age group) that might shape the prevalence of victimization. We will conclude by describing some potential longer-term implications and briefly suggesting areas for further inquiry.

Definitional Criteria and the Topography of Peer Victimization

What does it mean to define a child as a victim of bullying? Olweus' (1993) influential definitional criteria (see Kim and colleagues, this volume) portrays bullying as a specific subtype of aggression that is malicious, repeated, and rooted in an imbalance of power. The imbalance might incorporate any disparities that allow one peer to dominate another. For example, the bully might have more social power (e.g., a preeminent position in the peer group hierarchy) or physical strength than the victim.

The existing definitional criteria were developed primarily by researchers but may not map closely onto children's own perspective. In a small number of existing studies, researchers used semi-structured interviews, cartoon stimuli, or open-ended questions to assess children's understanding of the components of bullying (see Monks & Smith, 2006 for examples). Children do not necessarily conceptualize the victim role in terms of the features identified by Olweus (Cuadrado-Gordillo, 2012; Guerin & Hennessy, 2002; Monks & Smith, 2006).

Bullying also involves diverse forms of aggression. Initially, researchers focused primarily on youths who were victimized via overt forms of aggression (Olweus, 1978; Perry, Kusel, & Perry, 1988; Schwartz, Dodge, & Coie, 1993). By the 1990s, investigators began to emphasize relational forms of victimization—gossiping, exclusion, and social manipulation (Crick & Grotpeter, 1995). More recently, the information revolution has fostered a focus on youths who experience victimization in digital contexts (i.e., "cyberbullying;" see Kowalski, Giumetti, Schroeder, & Lattanner, 2014).

Regardless of the dimensions of aggressive behavior, bullying can involve large groups of children or one specific peer. The initial work in this domain was influenced by the "mobbing" concept (small animals grouping together as a unit to defend against potential attackers; Heinemann, 1972) from the animal behavior literature. Accordingly, the emphasis was on youths who are victimized by a sizeable percentage of their peers (e.g., Boulton, Smith, & Cowie, 2010). More recently, there has been an increasing dyadic focus in the literature, the idea that bullying can be restricted to particular relationships (Card & Hodges, 2010; Rodkin, Hanish, Wang, & Logis, 2014; Veenstra et al., 2007). Whether the features of dyadic victimization differ from the larger peer group process remains an open question. For example, bullying that occurs within a bully-victim dyad could involve unique motivations.

As noted above, most children encounter some form of bullying at one time or another during their school years. The seminal work of Olweus (1978) and other pioneering investigators (e.g., Perry et al., 1988) helped draw attention to the plight of youths who are victimized by peers on a persistent or extreme basis. These victims of bullying have traditionally been identified on ad hoc criteria selected by investigators. For example, peer nomination researchers have often relied on standardized cutoff scores (e.g., Schwartz, 2000). More recently, analysts have begun to identify victimized children using multivariate techniques such as Latent Class Analysis (LCA; Lovegrove, Henry, & Slater, 2012). LCA is a technique that allows for membership in victim subgroups to be identified based on observed scores across multiple indicators.

For some youths, bullying and related social difficulties may be relatively short-lived phenomena. Unfortunately, however, victimized youths can also continue to be targeted by their peers over long periods. In correlational analyses, year-to-year stabilities are moderate to high (generally in the .50 range; Pouwels, Souren, Lansu, & Cillessen, 2016). As latent profile analysis and related methodologies have been more widely implemented, analysts have been able to identity youths who experience high levels of victimization over multiple waves (Williford, Brisson, Bender, Jenson, & Forrest-Bank, 2011). Bullying by peers may be a daily reality for some children and could be a near constant stressor throughout their school years.

To this point, we have implicitly portrayed victims as a qualitatively distinct subgroup of children. Nonetheless, we argue that categorical perspectives of this nature are not necessarily supported by available data. Assessments of victimization typically yield estimates with continuous distributions (Schwartz, Lansford, Dodge, Pettit, & Bates, 2018). Depending on the measurement approach, peer victimization could be operationalized as a dimensional construct that tends to be distributed with positive skew (many children being rarely victimized and a small number of children being frequently victimized; e.g., Malcolm, Jensen-Campbell, Rex-Lear, & Waldrip, 2006). The concept of "victim" as a discrete category could be more theoretical than empirical.

An additional caveat relates to the assumption that victims, as a group, lack social power. Youths who have achieved a degree of dominance in the peer group can also experience some forms of bullying (Andrews, Hanish, Updegraff, Martin, & Santos, 2016). There has been growing interest in the construct of popularity (often referred to as "perceived popularity" in the extant literature; Cillessen & Marks, 2011), which denotes high status, prestige, and visibility. Popular youths wield considerable social power and can often use aggression successfully when confronted (Mayeux, Houser, & Dyches, 2011). Although the preeminent social position enjoyed by these youths would seem to preclude emergence as a persistent victim of bullying, ethnographic researchers have described the jockeying for power that occurs within popular cliques (Merten, 2011). Some socially elite youths might experience relational forms of aggression because of this ongoing struggle for control (Cillessen & Mayeux, 2004).

To illustrate this point, consider Hillary and Nancy, two adolescent girls who are popular cheerleaders at the top of the peer group social hierarchy. Hillary views Nancy as a potential rival and worries that Nancy's social status might eventually eclipse her own. Accordingly, she constantly gossips about Nancy and works hard to spread derisive rumors behind Nancy's back. We contend that Nancy has effectively emerged as a popular victim in this situation as she is subject to persistent mistreatment by a peer.

Popular victims are likely to be targeted for very specific subtypes of aggression and, on that level, could differ from other victimized subgroups (Dawes & Malamut, 2018; Malamut, Dawes, & Xie, 2018). Their dominance in the peer group will preclude frequent challenges in the form of overt bullying or physical aggression. Some relational forms of victimization (e.g., exclusion) are also unlikely given the centrality of these youths in the peer group. Instead, popular adolescents will be vulnerable to behaviors (e.g., gossip) that are intended to covertly degrade their overall standing in the peer group. Although a youth with high status may, indeed, experience peer victimization, we would expect a very narrow subset of aggressive behaviors to be involved.

This brief discussion illustrates some of the complexities underlying the victim concept. The subgroup definition can incorporate youths who experience distinct forms of mistreatment (relational, overt, or electronic). These social problems can be bound to specific dyadic relationships or could be manifestations of a wider group process. We also contend that social power and position in the peer group hierarchy can be a variable dimension with victims representing a full spectrum of social status outcomes.

Who Is the Victim?

Peer victimization is not distributed randomly in the peer group. Instead, the propensity to be victimized by peers is pronounced for children and adolescents who are characterized by specific patterns of attributes.

Understanding the behavioral, psychological, and physical factors that may be linked to vulnerability to bullying is critical for the efficient design of prevention and intervention programs. Identifying these correlates will also be a central issue for those investigators who seek to understand the underlying mechanisms of risk.

Before we attempt to delineate a representative portrait of a victimized youth, we will pause to remind the reader that the victim concept should not be viewed as indicative of a "type" of child. Victim status is not akin to a stable personality constellation. Bullying is a peer group process, and we use the term "victim" to refer to youths who experience this form of mistreatment by peers on a persistent or extreme basis. We will argue that there are specific behavioral tendencies that can be linked to victimization. However, social outcomes with peers can be viewed as an interaction between child attributes and features of the peer group (Hodges, Malone, & Perry, 1997; Kochenderfer-Ladd, Ladd, & Kochel, 2009). Youths who are seen as "misfits" in a specific context may experience more positive outcomes under different conditions (Wright, Giammarino, & Parad, 1986).

The association between academic competence and bully/victim problems presents one clear example of cross-context variability. Achievement is highly valued in some cultural contexts (Duong, Badaly, Liu, Schwartz, & McCarty, 2016). Reflecting the broader societal pressures, these dominant norms will begin to shape the values of the proximal peer group. Deficient academic performance might thus be associated with rejection and victimization by peers (Nakamoto & Schwartz, 2010). Conversely, attitudes toward academic engagement tend to be much more negative in some North American communities (particularly impoverished urban neighborhoods; e.g., Ceballo, McLoyd, & Toyokawa, 2004). Adolescents with studious dispositions can be unpopular and victimized in these settings (Schwartz, Kelly et al., 2013).

One implication of environment/person interactions is that victim status may be bound to very specific social contexts. Children can quickly replicate some aspects of their experience with peers when placed in a new context (Coie & Kupersmidt, 1983; Dodge, 1983; Dodge, Coie, Pettit, & Price, 1990). Still, a child or adolescent who emerges as a victim in the school peer group may encounter a much different social situation in other contexts. For example, a child who is a frequent target of bullies at school may be in a more advantageous social position in summer camp or in after school activities.

Contextual variability notwithstanding, there is compelling evidence linking specific patterns of social behavior to risk for victimization. In particular, submissive, passive, or anxious behavior seems to signal vulnerability to potential bullies (Schwartz, Chang et al., 2001). Youths who reward aggressors with crying or other overt signs of pain are also likely to emerge as persistent victims (Hodges & Perry, 1999). In terms of a developmental sequence, submissive behavior in nonaggressive exchanges appears to signal defenselessness and acquiescence to aggression, which maintains the cycle of mistreatment (Schwartz et al., 1993).

Although a submissive disposition characterizes many victims of frequent bullying, a subgroup of these youths will exhibit a more aggressive or reactive presentation. Based on open-ended descriptions obtained from secondary school teachers, Olweus (1978) reported that a very small percentage of "whipping boys" were provocative and characterized by restless or irritable behavior. Subsequent investigators also identified aggressive victims (Salmivalli & Nieminen, 2002; Schwartz, Proctor et al., 2001), but theoretical conceptualizations of the features of this subgroup differ across research teams.

Youths who are concurrently aggressive and victimized are often categorized as "bully/victims" (e.g., Veenstra et al., 2005). The underlying assumption seems to be that some youths fluctuate between the roles of perpetrator and target (Hanish & Guerra, 2004). We are resistant to this portrayal because we argue that bullying requires specific skills and psychological capacities that do not typify persistently victimized youths. Rather than engaging in goal-oriented bullying (e.g., using aggression as an efficacious strategy for dominating peers), aggressive victims are more likely to exhibit explosive, irritable, or impulsive behavior (Schwartz, 2000). Our conceptualization echoes Perry et al.'s (1992) early portrayal of aggressive victims as "dysregulated aggressors" and resonates with related models (Schwartz, Proctor et al., 2001). Perry et al. (1992) noted that aggressive victims react quickly to perceived provocations and then lose conflicts with exaggerated displays of distress.

A theme that is consistent across both aggressive and nonaggressive subgroups of victims is deficient emotion regulation (Shields & Cicchetti, 2001). Children and adolescents who do not effectively modulate powerful emotional states (including anger, sadness, or anxiety; e.g., Hanish et al., 2004) are relatively more likely to experience mistreatment by peers. The process linking impaired modulation of affect to victimization could be reciprocal. Displays of distress or anger can simultaneously signal vulnerability, reward potential aggressors, and be a response to persistent negative treatment by peers.

Given their deficits in self-regulation, it is perhaps not surprising that these youths also experience a wide array of related social difficulties in the peer group. Victims are often quite unpopular with their peers and tend to be socially rejected (Card & Hodges, 2008; Gorman, Schwartz, Nakamoto, & Mayeux, 2011). Dyadic relationships can also be compromised (Boulton, Trueman, Chau, Whitehand, & Amatya, 1999), although some victimized youths do succeed in establishing a small number of close friendships (Schacter & Juvonen, 2018). Rejection and friendlessness are likely to be particular issues for aggressive victims, who tend to be highly disliked by their peers (Kochel, Ladd, Bagwell, & Yabko, 2015).

Earlier in this chapter, we suggested that some victimized youths might occupy high positions in the peer group hierarchy. Our contention is that some victims could be quite popular but are bullied in the context of struggles for social power (Dawes & Malamut, 2018). Because high status victims have only rarely been examined by past investigators (Andrews et al., 2016), we know relatively little about these youths. Some popular youths may be especially likely to emerge as persistent targets of gossip and other forms of relational victimization. Given the influence of popular students (Sandstrom, 2011), understanding the processes through which these socially elite youths encounter victimization would likely be a worthwhile objective for future research.

Beyond the issue of social behavior, other factors may have a role in helping to determine a child's propensity to be victimized by peers. Media images of victimized youths often emphasize physical deviances of one kind or another. Consistent with these stereotyped perceptions, a number of investigators have considered links between obesity and peer victimization (Juvonen, Lessard, Schacter, & Suchilt, 2017; Puhl, Luedicke, & Heuer, 2011). Investigators have also expressed concerns that some victims of bullying may go on to develop problems with body image (Lunde, Frisén, & Hwang, 2007; Lunde & Frisén, 2011). Moreover, both children and adolescents describe physical deviances as one determinant of peer victimization (Erling & Hwang, 2004; Frisén, Jonsson, & Persson, 2007).

In the larger literature on peer relationships, attractiveness is well investigated as an important predictor of positive social outcomes (e.g., acceptance and popularity; Boyatzis, Baloff, & Durieux, 1998; LaFontana & Cillessen, 2002; Vannatta, Gartstein, Zeller, & Noll, 2009). Some preliminary evidence suggests children who are perceived as being unattractive by peers may be especially likely to be targeted for victimization. In a particularly well-designed project, Rosen, Underwood, and Beron (2011) demonstrated that facial attractiveness predicts internalized distress through the mediation of victimization by peers. We suspect that the importance of attractiveness has generally been understated in the extant bully/victim literature, given existing evidence with regard to closely related social outcomes (e.g., popularity and status; e.g., Borch, Hyde, & Cillessen, 2011).

Olweus (1978) initially focused his research efforts on the role of physical strength and size in predicting bully/victim outcomes. Not surprisingly, Olweus found that large or physically imposing youths tend not to be favored targets of aggressive peers. This result is consistent with dominance perspectives that view bullying as an efficacious social strategy used to exert control over subservient peers (Reijntjes et al., 2016).

Anxiety and distress have also been viewed as potential determinants of peer victimization. Not surprisingly, there is ample evidence that bullied youths are vulnerable to depression, low self-esteem, and anxiety (e.g., Schwartz, Lansford, Dodge, Pettit, & Bates, 2015). There are certainly compelling reasons to view these dimensions of internalized distress as potential products of stressful experiences in the peer group. However, there is also evidence for reciprocal relations between internalizing symptoms and bullying by peers (Reijntjes et al., 2010). Models that emphasize the social origins of depression often incorporate an awareness of the pernicious implications of the associated symptoms for social functioning (Kochel, Ladd, & Rudolph, 2012). Low self-esteem might also potentiate submissive behaviors that increase likelihood of victimization (Egan & Perry, 1998).

There has been less emphasis in the bully/victim literature on schemas, beliefs, and expectations that might eventually shape the social behavior of victimized youths. For several decades, research on aggression and peer rejection was guided by models that stressed social-cognitive mechanisms (Crick & Dodge, 1994). Commonly examined mechanisms include attributional biases, outcome beliefs, values and goals, response generation, and response enactment (Dodge et al., 2003; Graham & Juvonen, 2001; Lemerise & Arsenio, 2000). Given the influence of social-information-processing models in the broader peer relations literature, it seems somewhat surprising that these models have not had a greater impact in research on victims of bullying. There is evidence that victimized youths are characterized by some specific cognitive biases (including hostile attributions; Perren, Ettekal, & Ladd, 2013), but this area of inquiry is generally under elaborated.

To summarize, the concept of a "victim" should not be viewed as a reference to a "type" of child. Instead, this label denotes a persistent pattern of negative social experiences. Frequently victimized youths tend to be characterized by a specific constellation of behavioral, social, psychological, and physical attributes. However, each of these factors may have social implications that are more benign in a different peer group context. We suggest that peer victimization is best conceptualized as an interaction between vulnerabilities and peer group features.

Group Differences

Bullying is not a random process, and there are behavioral and psychosocial mechanisms that are systematically linked to frequent victimization by peers. Demographic and contextual factors may also shape the prevalence of peer victimization across particular subgroups. Group difference variables could be critical to consider as we seek to understand the processes that are predictive of vulnerability. In this next section of our chapter, we will consider gender, ethnicity, and cultural context.

Gender

Research on peer victimization initially emphasized the potential for boys to emerge as either victims or bullies. Girls were generally viewed as less likely to be directly involved in peer victimization. In fact, early studies in this area sometimes excluded girls altogether (Olweus, 1983; Schwartz et al., 1993, 1997). The literature has subsequently evolved in a more inclusive direction. As relational subtypes of aggression became the focus of increased empirical attention, investigators have been in a stronger position to examine bully/victim problems among girls (e.g., Crick, Casas, & Nelson, 2002; Henington, Hughes, Cavell, & Thompson, 1998). When relationally aggressive behaviors (e.g., exclusion, gossip, and social manipulation) are considered, gender disparities in prevalence rates of victimization are not always pronounced (Prinstein, Boergers, & Vernberg, 2001; Sullivan, Farrell, & Kliewer, 2006).

The role of girls in bully/victim interactions could continue to expand as a reflection of the ubiquitous nature of electronic communication technologies. Modern adolescents are reliant on digital communication technologies for their day-to-day interactions with peers, with social networking platforms (e.g., Snapchat, Instagram, and Twitter) playing an increasingly influential role. Girls are particularly avid users of these communication modalities (Anderson & Jiang, 2018). As the digital world becomes a new frontline in the phenomenon of peer victimization, girls may begin to play an increasingly central role in victim/bully interactions

One caveat with regard to electronic forms of bullying is that gender disparities may be dependent on the specific modality of communication. For example, video games may have been once viewed as a solitary pursuit but modern gaming consoles often include chat clients and are oriented toward multiplayer. Boys are more likely than girls to communicate through these platforms (Anderson & Jiang, 2018). The incidence of digital harassment could be influenced by the gender distribution within each technological modality.

Regardless of broad trends and shifts, gender differences are not likely to be constant across victim subtypes. Even when relational forms of aggression are taken into account, boys are more likely than girls to have concurrent problems with aggression and victimization (Toblin, Schwartz, Gorman, & Abou-ezzeddine, 2005). The over-reactive and emotionally dysregulated presentation of aggressive victims could be more common for boys than girls. Aggressive victims are at higher risk for some forms of dysfunction than either passive victims or bullies (Haynie et al., 2001). Accordingly, gender disparities in the composition of this subgroup are critical to recognize.

Age Trends

What developmental period represents the peak occurrence of victimization in the peer group? The pattern in the extant survey data suggests that bullying is a particular common social behavior during early to mid-adolescence (Boulton & Underwood, 1992; Scheithauer, Hayer, Petermann, & Jugert, 2006). One potential complication with these data is that findings with regard to age group differences rely exclusively on self-report data (Smith, Madsen, & Moody, 1999). We know that a relatively high percentage of children perceive themselves to be victimized during the middle school years, but self-reports do not always accurately tap real world experiences (Graham, Bellmore, Nishina, & Juvonen, 2009).

Other assessment approaches are often relativized so that developmental changes are not preserved. As an example, peer nomination inventories are widely used to identify victimized youths (Schwartz, Lansford, Dodge, Pettit, & Bates, 2018). These reputational assessments are well validated but do not provide insight into absolute levels, and instead index individual differences in a specific peer group. A child who is viewed as being highly victimized by peers in one classroom might have a much different social reputation in other classrooms.

Another measurement complexity is that the form and function of bullying is likely to evolve across development. Physical aggression occurs with relative frequency early in development (Cummings, Iannotti, & Zahn-Waxler, 1989). Adult sanctions and socializing processes counter the underlying behavioral tendencies during the transition to middle childhood. Conversely, relationally aggressive forms of victimization may be more prevalent during adolescence due to growing cognitive and social sophistication (Banny, Heilbron, Ames, & Prinstein, 2011). Some forms of bullying may also persist into young adulthood, as digital communications become efficient tools for aggression. In light of these complexities, we believe that caution should be exercised before making strong inferences regarding developmental trends. Normative trajectories for distinct forms of victimization (relational, overt, and electronic) will not necessarily overlap. In addition, behaviors that are more closely associated with vulnerability may not be constant across the lifespan.

Ethnic/Racial Backgrounds

Victimization can be viewed as a process that is partially driven by social power or dominance (Vaillancourt, McDougall, Hymel, & Sunderani, 2010). Youths who occupy low positions in the peer group hierarchy are particularly vulnerable (Card & Schwartz, 2009). As an extension of these mechanisms to the larger social environment, children and adolescents who are from minority ethnic/racial backgrounds have sometimes been presumed to be especially likely to be targeted by their peers (Xu, Macrynikola, Waseem, & Miranda, in press). The underlying hypothesis is that social injustice will result in youths from underrepresented groups being marginalized by their peers.

In considering this issue, we will need to recognize the primacy of the proximal microsystem. In the United States, European American cultural values can have a dominating influence given efficient transmission through mass media. Still, in a diverse society, European American youths will be a numerical minority in many schools. A group that is underrepresented in society as a whole may have a large presence in specific school districts. Vulnerability to victimization is likely an interaction between the youths own ethnic/racial background and the composition of the immediate peer group (Vervoort, Scholte, & Overbeek, 2010). Minority youths will not necessarily be at elevated risk for bullying in diverse settings.

Youths may also derive information about their social experience based on the ethnicity of their peers. Graham, Bellmore, Nishina, and Juvonen

(2009) concluded that victimized adolescents whose background is well represented in their classroom would tend to attribute their mistreatment to their own personal qualities. Conversely, victims who are in the numerical minority are more likely to attribute their social difficulties to external factors (e.g., social prejudice) and will not encapsulate the experience as a threat to the self.

In any case, we suspect that the detection of ethnic/racial group differences in peer victimization will be complicated by racial stereotypes and related cognitive biases (for a similar argument, see Peguero, & Williams, 2013). Researchers often rely on assessments that are derived from peer nominations, self-reports, or other questionnaires. The extent to which these measurement approaches are biased by existing schemas regarding ethnicity is not yet clear. For example, societally based stereotypes may assign particular behavioral attributes (e.g., aggression or withdrawal) to specific cultural subgroups. This typecasting might then help determine whether peers identify a child as a victim.

An additional assessment concern is that variability within group is likely to be as significant as variability between groups (Costigan, Bardina, Cauce, Kim, & Latendresse, 2006). Ethnic/racial groups are not homogenous with regard to critical constructs like ethnic identity and acculturation (Schwartz, Des Rosiers et al., 2013). Discussion of broad-based differences between groups is not necessarily meaningful unless group membership is truly indicative of shared experience. We suggest that a more meaningful approach might be to consider the influence of cultural values embedded in the macrosystem.

Cultural Context

Bullying has emerged as a major social problem in many countries and research has been conducted across international boundaries. Indeed, victimized youths have been the subject of ongoing empirical research in numerous cultures (e.g., Craig et al., 2009). Efforts toward comparing prevalence rates and correlates will be challenged by the underlying conceptualizations that typify bullying in each culture. Smith et al.

(2002) reported evidence that the cultural context can frame understanding of the specific features of peer victimization. For example, the behaviors that are generally viewed as being aspects of bullying are not equivalent across countries.

Definitional challenges notwithstanding, we suggest that a "social misfit" model (Wright et al., 1986) could help to identify children who are at risk for victimization in many different cultures. Cultural perspectives on peer relationships emphasize the idea that the values embedded in the broader society are likely to influence the attitudes of the peer group toward specific attributes (Chen & Liu, 2016). Behaviors that are discouraged by the cultural beliefs implicit in the macrosystem will lead to social sanctions (including peer group victimization) in the microsystem. The findings that we previously reviewed regarding achievement and peer victimization support this suggestion. As we described, academically inclined students tend to emerge as frequent targets of their peers in community settings characterized by negative attitudes toward school. Conversely, high achieving youths are unlikely to be bullied in cultures that are strongly oriented toward academic achievement (Nakamoto & Schwartz, 2010).

Developmental Impact

Developmental psychopathology perspectives on the bully/victim phenomenon have emphasized potential links between mistreatment by peers and later maladjustment (e.g., McDougall & Vaillancourt, 2015). The core underlying assumption is that victimization in the peer group is a stressful experience that can exert a pernicious influence on development. Concerns regarding developmental impact appear to be well founded. As we will discuss, there is growing evidence that persistent bullying during childhood and adolescence can have effects that extend into the adult years.

The initial studies in this domain emphasized cross-sectional and short-term relations between peer victimization and psychosocial maladjustment. The evidence emerging from this work highlights potential links to both internalizing and externalizing disorders. Over two to four-year periods, victims of bullying are likely to experience symptoms of depression and anxiety as well as related difficulties that might include low self-esteem and loneliness (Reijntjes et al., 2010). In addition, some victimized youths develop disruptive externalizing problems that include aggression, hyperactivity/impulsiveness, and delinquency (Reijntjes et al., 2011). By the early adolescent years, victimization can also predict affiliation with deviant peer groups (Rudolph et al., 2014).

Because school is a primary context for both education and socialization, a degree of "spillover" across academic and peer domains could be expected. Not surprisingly, victimization by peers is associated with poor academic functioning and negative attitudes toward school (Schwartz et al., 2005; Wang et al., 2014). These relations are most consistent during the elementary school years. The findings in middle school and beyond (i.e., early to middle adolescence) appear to be more variable and may be shaped by the academic values embedded in the proximal context (Schwartz, Kelly et al., 2013).

Regardless of the adjustment domain examined, main-effect relations between peer victimization and functioning difficulties have consistently been modest in magnitude (Casper, Card, Bauman, & Toomey, 2017). A stronger pattern of effects has probably not emerged because the implications of bullying are not equivalent across all victimized youths. For this reason, interactive models of risk which incorporate critical moderator constructs (i.e., factors that exacerbate or mitigate risk) have become increasingly influential (e.g., Schwartz et al., 2008). Some factors examined in this work include relationships with teachers (Elledge, Elledge, Newgent, & Cavell, 2016), coping strategies (Erath, Kaeppler, & Tu, 2019) and involvement in extracurricular activities (McConnell & Erath, 2018).

Investigators who have sought to identify relevant moderators have often focused on the potential role of friends and friendship. An underlying presumption in this work is that the social support associated with friendship functions to buffer youths against the distress associated with peer victimization (Schmidt & Bagwell, 2007). The extant findings do provide some support for this hypothesis but the eventual implications of friendship for bullied youths will likely depend on the behavioral characteristics of the child's friends. Schwartz et al. (2008) reported that friendships mitigate associations between peer victimization and academic difficulties, but only when the victim's friends are not characterized by aggression or other antisocial attributes. Friendships with aggressive peers may actually intensify risk for some negative outcomes by providing victimized youths with maladaptive socializing influences (Zhu et al., 2016).

Of course, friendships are not the only close relationships in a child's life. Adult caregivers, like teachers and parents, are also important sources of social support. There is evidence that warm relationships with teachers alleviate some of the stress associated with victimization by peers (Elledge et al., 2016; Galand & Hospel, 2013). On the other hand, investigators have yet to demonstrate conclusively that parents are important mechanisms of resilience for bullied youths (Stadler, Feifel, Rohrmann, Vermeiren, & Poustka, 2010). Arguably, there is stronger evidence relating to the pernicious influence of harsh or punitive parents. For example, Schwartz, Landsford et al. (2013) found that restrictive discipline and victimization by peers interact in the prediction of declines in achievement.

Relationship processes can be subsumed efficiently under the broader rubric of stress and coping models. Victims of bullying may rely on a variety of strategies to mitigate the effects of negative experiences in the peer group (Erath et al., 2019). Researchers have sought to identify the most efficient coping styles, with some evidence suggesting that girls and boys tend to rely on different coping strategies. For example, support seeking appears to have greater efficacy for girls than boys (Kochenderfer-Ladd & Skinner, 2002).

Regardless of coping strategies and available social resources, aggressive victims are far more likely to encounter adjustment problems than any other victim/bully subgroup (Haynie et al., 2001). Aggressive victims often experience pervasive forms of maladjustment that include a mixed pattern of internalizing and externalizing disorders. Unfortunately, these youths will also have difficulty marshaling social support in the peer group, as they tend to be highly disliked and have difficulty developing friendships (Schwartz, 2000).

To some extent, recent public concern with bully/victim problems may have been motivated by fears concerning extreme behaviors. The popular media has sometimes portrayed victimization in the peer group as a root cause of mass shootings in schools (e.g., Columbine; see Langman, 2009). In fact, the perpetrators in these tragic events often do have histories of ostracism, social rejection, bullying by peers, and isolation (Leary, Kowalski, Smith, & Phillips, 2003). Still, tragic events of this nature are complex and the evidence regarding the role of bullying or other peer relationship difficulties at this time remains anecdotal. We would also note that extreme violence is (fortunately) a very rare outcome whereas bullying is a very common event.

The link between peer victimization and mass shootings has not been clearly demonstrated but related findings suggest that some victims of bullying may resort to carrying weapons to school. Recent meta-analyses indicate peer victimization does have a modest relation with weapon carrying (van Geel, Vedder, & Tanilon, 2014). Victimized youths may feel vulnerable or helpless and view weapons as a means of self-defense.

Public attention has also focused on relations between victimization and self-harm, suicidal ideation, and suicidal behavior. Modest relations between self-harm and bullying have been demonstrated by a number of researchers (see van Geel et al., 2015; Victor, Hipwell, Stepp, & Scott, 2019). In addition, victimization has been linked to suicidal thoughts and suicide attempts. Nonetheless, we caution against strong interpretation of these findings, because self-harm and suicidal behavior are unlikely to occur in the absence of other mental health problems (Baldwin et al., 2019).

From a public health perspective, the short-term findings certainly warrant attention. However, questions remain regarding longer-term impact. To what extent do adjustment problems experienced by victimized youths extend beyond childhood and adolescence? Prospective studies suggest that the risk for anxiety, depression and other distress-related disorders can persist into the adult years. For example, Sourander et al. (2007) described a longitudinal study with bully/victim assessment conducted at age 8 and follow-up psychiatric interviews in early adulthood (10–15 years later). Participants who were classified as victims or bully-victims during childhood had elevated levels of anxiety in adulthood. Consistent with these findings, Schwartz et al. (2015) conducted analyses with peer victimization scores in middle childhood predicting outcomes on a structured clinical interview in early adulthood. High levels of victimization were linked to diagnoses of major depression. Copeland, Wolke, Angold, and Costello (2013) reported that victim and victim-bully status in childhood predicted anxiety disorders, depression, and suicidality in adulthood.

Investigators have also examined long-term risk for antisocial personality, criminal justice outcomes, and various forms of violent behavior. As might be expected, victimized youths who are not concurrently aggressive are unlikely to experience antisocial outcomes during adulthood. The findings for aggressive victims are less clear with some paradoxical results emerging. Schwartz et al. (2018) found that childhood aggression was linked to adult arrest only when rates of victimization by peers were low. Schwartz et al. speculated that the problems with self-regulation experienced by aggressive victims might preclude exposure to contexts in which violent crime is likely to occur later in development. Some forms of criminal activity require efficacious use of goal-oriented forms of aggression rather than the emotionally explosive behavior that tends to characterize aggressive victims (Schwartz, Proctor et al., 2001). An implication of these findings is that bullies may be at higher risk for long-term antisocial outcomes than aggressive victims may.

Taken together, the long-term pattern presents a troubling picture that portends serious functioning difficulties that persist through adulthood. Nonetheless, much remains to be learned about processes underlying the outcomes experienced by victimized youths. It seems reasonable to speculate that frequent mistreatment by peers might serve as an insult to normative development processes. Alternatively, a parsimonious hypothesis might hold that victimization by peers is a "marker" construct that is a lead indicator of later maladjustment. For example, victimization may be indicative of specific child attributes that increase vulnerability to disorder (e.g., deficits in self-regulation).

A related issue is that we know very little about the eventual social experiences of victims as they transition into adulthood. For some youths, victimization by peers will be an ongoing stressor through childhood and adolescence (Pouwels et al., 2016). Indicators of maladjustment may be stable across development because of the chronicity of negative experiences in the peer group. Clearly, however, the context and organization of an adult's social interactions differ from adolescent peer relationships. We do not yet know if bullied youths eventually encounter social problems in adulthood, which then contribute to the prediction of dysfunction.

Peer victimization could also serve as one-step in a cascade of developmental processes (Masten & Cicchetti, 2010) that influence distal outcomes through the mediation of more proximal mechanisms. As an example of how this progression might unfold, consider early links between bullying by peers and academic problems in the classroom. Academic difficulties could then portent other difficulties (e.g., affiliations with academically disengaged antisocial peers). The resulting negative socializing influences could then have implications for other competencies.

Future Directions

Before we move to our concluding comments, we will pause to identify the areas that we see as critical for future investigation. Since the publication of Olweus' (1978) seminal work, the plight of victimized youths has attracted considerable empirical attention. There is now an extensive body of relevant findings and we have learned much about the underlying dynamics. During the period of active inquiry, powerful social changes have continued to impact the structure of young people's interactions with peers. Research on victimization in the peer group will need to evolve to reflect new developments.

Over the last few decades, new communication technologies have assumed a ubiquitous presence in young people's social lives. Social networking platforms, texting, instant messaging, and media sharing applications are now central components of day-to-day interaction in the peer group (Schwartz et al., 2019). This increasing connectivity brings new opportunities for interaction and friendships but has also become a powerful new conduit for bullying (Livingstone & Smith,

2014). To some extent, the digital world may be a mirror of existing peer group processes with bullying simply moving to a new forum (Perren, Dooley, Shaw, & Cross, 2010). Electronic interactions do incorporate novel features though that could potentially intensify the distress that a victimized youth experiences. Aggressors can no longer be left behind at school, insofar as bullying occurs through mobile technologies that follow the child home.

Researchers have not been slow to respond to these technological developments. In fact, young people's electronic interactions have attracted considerable empirical attention (e.g., Nesi, Choukas-Bradley, & Prinstein, 2018a, 2018b). Nevertheless, we do not yet understand the full implication of electronic communications for bully/victim dynamic. Technology is also a dynamic force with electronic modalities constantly shifting in and out of prominence. The challenges ahead for researchers who seek to examine bullying in digital contexts will be substantial.

A related point is that new findings suggest moderately strong associations between activity on social networking platforms and popularity in adolescent peer groups (Schwartz et al., 2019). Digital communications could provide a powerful forum for relational aggression and bullying within high status cliques, as battles for power, visibility, and reputation unfolds. As we noted earlier in this chapter, popular victims are an understudied subgroup. We suggest that online interactions could provide a powerful window into the social lives of these youths.

We also contend that peer victimization specific to particular relationships (both in online and offline contexts) is an understudied problem. The majority of the research cited in this chapter adopts the implicit perspective that bullying is a group process (e.g., an individual child who has been mistreated by many peers and has a widely accepted reputation as an *easy mark*). Only a handful of studies have focused on bullying as a dyadic interaction. We know relatively little about the dynamics underlying these bully-victim relationships and there is a dearth of relevant prospective data.

Likewise, we believe that there is a need for further prospective research that addresses long-term impacts of victimization. Relevant projects are now becoming available, but most of the existing work has focused on main-effect relations. Investigations are needed that reveal mediating processes and identify moderators that promote resilience or intensify risk. What factors lie beneath the long-term risk associated with peer victimization in childhood and adolescence? We suspect that there will be very specific developmental pathways for distinct subgroups of victims (e.g., passive victims, aggressive victims, and popular victims) and contend that exploration of these trajectories will be critical for intervention and prevention efforts.

Conclusion

We began this chapter by recognizing the unique plight of the victimized child. Some children will find themselves trapped in a chronic cycle of mistreatment by peers. These stressful experiences appear to predict long-term risk and can have developmental implications that persist into adulthood. Although the literature on persistently bullied youths is quite extensive, unanswered questions remain. Moreover, profound cultural shifts (e.g., the digital world becoming an organizing aspect of young people's social lives) are transforming the nature of bullying. The challenges ahead are substantial and further inquiry is certainly warranted.

References

Anderson, M. & Jiang, J. (2018). *Teens, social media, & technology 2018*. Pew Research Center. Retrieved from http://www.pewinternet.org/2018/05/31/teens-social-media-technology-2018/.

Andrews, N. C. Z., Hanish, L. D., Updegraff, K. A., Martin, C. L., & Santos, C. E. (2016). Targeted victimization: Exploring linear and curvilinear associations between social network prestige and victimization. *Journal of Youth and Adolescence, 45*, 1772–1785. https://doi.org/10.1007/s10964-016-0450-1.

Baldwin, J. R., Arseneault, L., Caspi, A., Moffitt, T. E., Fisher, H. L., Odgers, C. L., ... Richmond-Rakerd, L. S. (2019). Adolescent victimization and self-injurious thoughts and behaviors: A genetically sensitive cohort study.

Journal of the American Academy of Child & Adolescent Psychiatry, 58, 506–513. https://doi.org/10.1016/j.jaac.2018.07.903.
Banny, A. M., Heilbron, N., Ames, A., & Prinstein, M. J. (2011). Relational benefits of relational aggression: Adaptive and maladaptive associations with adolescent friendship quality. *Developmental Psychology, 47,* 1153–1166. https://doi.org/10.1037/a0022546.
Barboza, G. E. (2015). The association between school exclusion, delinquency and subtypes of cyber- and F2F-victimizations: Identifying and predicting risk profiles and subtypes using latent class analysis. *Child Abuse & Neglect, 39,* 109–122. https://doi.org/10.1016/j.chiabu.2014.08.007.
Borch, C., Hyde, A., & Cillessen, A. H. N. (2011). The role of attractiveness and aggression in high school popularity. *Social Psychology of Education: an International Journal, 14,* 23–39. https://doi.org/10.1007/s11218-010-9131-1.
Boulton, M. J., Smith, P. K., & Cowie, H. (2010). Short-term longitudinal relationships between children's peer victimization/bullying experiences and self-perceptions: Evidence for reciprocity. *School Psychology International, 31,* 296–311. https://doi.org/10.1177/0143034310362329.
Boulton, M. J., Trueman, M., Chau, C. A. M., Whitehand, C., & Amatya, K. (1999). Concurrent and longitudinal links between friendship and peer victimization: Implications for befriending interventions. *Journal of Adolescence, 22,* 461–466. https://doi.org/10.1006/jado.1999.0240.
Boulton, M. J., & Underwood, K. (1992). Bully/victim problems among middle school children. *British Journal of Educational Psychology, 62,* 73–87. https://doi.org/10.1111/j.2044-8279.1992.tb01000.x.
Bowes, L., Maughan, B., Ball, H., Shakoor, S., Ouellet-Morin, I., Caspi, A., … Arseneault, L. (2013). Chronic bullying victimization across school transitions: The role of genetic and environmental influences. *Development and Psychopathology, 25,* 333–346. https://doi.org/10.1017/S095457941200 1095.
Boyatzis, C. J., Baloff, P., & Durieux, C. (1998). Effects of perceived attractiveness and academic success on early adolescent peer popularity. *The Journal of Genetic Psychology, 159,* 337–344. https://doi.org/10.1080/002213298095 96155.
Card, N. A., & Hodges, E. V. (2008). Peer victimization among schoolchildren: Correlations, causes, consequences, and considerations in assessment and intervention. *School Psychology Quarterly, 23,* 451–461. https://doi.org/10.1037/a0012769.

Card, N. A., & Hodges, E. V. (2010). It takes two to fight in school, too: A social relations model of the psychometric properties and relative variance of dyadic aggression and victimization in middle school. *Social Development, 19*, 447–469. https://doi.org/10.1111/j.1467-9507.2009.00562.x.

Card, N. A., & Schwartz, D. (2009). Social networks and peer victimization: The contexts of children's victimization by peers. In M. J. Harris (Ed.), *Bullying, rejection, and peer victimization: A social cognitive neuroscience perspective* (pp. 319–344). New York: Spring.

Casper, D. M., Card, N. A., Bauman, S., & Toomey, R. B. (2017). Overt and relational aggression participant role behavior: Measurement and relations with sociometric status and depression. *Journal of Research on Adolescence, 27*, 661–673. https://doi.org/10.1111/jora.12306.

Ceballo, R., McLoyd, V. C., & Toyokawa, T. (2004). The influence of neighborhood quality on adolescents' educational values and school effort. *Journal of Adolescent Research, 19*, 716–739. https://doi.org/10.1177/0743558403260021.

Chen, X., & Liu, C. H. (2016). Culture, peer relationships, and developmental psychopathology. In D. Cicchetti (Ed.), *Developmental psychopathology: Risk, resilience, and intervention* (Vol. 4, 3rd ed., pp. 723–769, Chapter xiii, 1137 Pages). Hoboken: Wiley.

Cillessen, A. H., & Mayeux, L. (2004). From censure to reinforcement: Developmental changes in the association between aggression and social status. *Child development, 75*, 147–163.

Cillessen, A. H. N., & Marks, P. E. L. (2011). Conceptualizing and measuring popularity. In A. H. N. Cillessen, D. Schwartz, & L. Mayeux (Eds.), *Popularity in the peer system; popularity in the peer system* (pp. 25–56, Chapter xiv, 306 Pages). New York: Guilford Press.

Coie, J. D., & Kupersmidt, J. B. (1983). A behavioral analysis of emerging social status in boys' groups. *Child Development, 54*, 1400–1416. https://doi.org/10.2307/1129803.

Copeland, W. E., Wolke, D., Angold, A., & Costello, E. J. (2013). Adult psychiatric outcomes of bullying and being bullied by peers in childhood and adolescence. *JAMA Psychiatry, 70*, 419–426. https://doi.org/10.1001/jamapsychiatry.2013.504.

Costigan, C. L., Bardina, P., Cauce, A. M., Kim, G. K., & Latendresse, S. J. (2006). Inter- and intra-group variability in perceptions of behavior among Asian Americans and European Americans. *Cultural Diversity and Ethnic Minority Psychology, 12*(4), 710–724. https://doi.org/10.1037/1099-9809.12.4.710.

Craig, W., Harel-Fisch, Y., Fogel-Grinvald, H., Dostaler, S., Hetland, J., Simons-Morton, B., ... Pickett, W. (2009). A cross-national profile of bullying and victimization among adolescents in 40 countries. *International Journal of Public Health, 54,* 216–224. https://doi.org/10.1007/s00038-009-5413-9.

Crick, N. R., Casas, J. F., & Nelson, D. A. (2002). Toward a more comprehensive understanding of peer maltreatment: Studies of relational victimization. *Current Directions in Psychological Science, 11,* 98–101. https://doi.org/10.1111/1467-8721.00177.

Crick, N. R., & Dodge, K. A. (1994). A review and reformulation of social information-processing mechanisms in children's social adjustment. *Psychological Bulletin, 115,* 74–101. https://doi.org/10.1037/0033-2909.115.1.74.

Crick, N. R., & Grotpeter, J. K. (1995). Relational aggression, gender, and social-psychological adjustment. *Child Development, 66,* 710–722. https://doi.org/10.2307/1131945.

Cuadrado-Gordillo, I. (2012). Repetition, power imbalance, and intentionality: Do these criteria conform to teenagers' perception of bullying? A role-based analysis. *Journal of Interpersonal Violence, 27,* 1889–1910. https://doi.org/10.1177/0886260511431436.

Cummings, E. M., Iannotti, R. J., & Zahn-Waxler, C. (1989). Aggression between peers in early childhood: Individual continuity and developmental change. *Child Development, 60,* 887–895. https://doi.org/10.2307/1131030.

Dawes, M., & Malamut, S. (2018). No one is safe: Understanding risk for victimization for low-status and high-status adolescents. *Adolescent Research Review.* https://doi.org/10.1007/s40894-018-0103-6.

Dodge, K. A. (1983). Behavioral antecedents of peer social status. *Child Development, 54,* 1386–1399. https://doi.org/10.2307/1129802.

Dodge, K. A., Coie, J. D., Pettit, G. S., & Price, J. M. (1990). Peer status and aggression in boys' groups: Developmental and contextual analyses. *Child Development, 61,* 1289–1309. https://doi.org/10.2307/1130743.

Dodge, K. A., Lansford, J. E., Burks, V. S., Bates, J. E., Pettit, G. S., Fontaine, R., & Price, J. M. (2003). Peer rejection and social information-processing factors in the development of aggressive behavior problems in children. *Child development, 74,* 374–393.

Duong, M. T., Badaly, D., Liu, F. F., Schwartz, D., & McCarty, C. A. (2016). Generational differences in academic achievement among immigrant youths: A meta-analytic review. *Review of Educational Research, 86,* 3–41. https://doi.org/10.3102/0034654315577680.

Egan, S. K., & Perry, D. G. (1998). Does low self-regard invite victimization? *Developmental Psychology, 34,* 299–309. https://doi.org/10.1037/0012-1649.34.2.299.

Elledge, L. C., Elledge, A. R., Newgent, R. A., & Cavell, T. A. (2016). Social risk and peer victimization in elementary school children: The protective role of teacher-student relationships. *Journal of Abnormal Child Psychology, 44,* 691–703. https://doi.org/10.1007/s10802-015-0074-z.

Erath, S. A., Kaeppler, A. K., & Tu, K. M. (2019). Coping with peer victimization predicts peer outcomes across the transition to middle school. *Social Development, 28,* 22–40. https://doi.org/10.1111/sode.12330.

Erling, A., & Hwang, C. P. (2004). Swedish 10-year-old children's perceptions and experiences of bullying. *Journal of School Violence, 3,* 33–43. https://doi.org/10.1300/J202v03n01_04.

Frisén, A., Jonsson, A. K., & Persson, C. (2007). Adolescents' perception of bullying: who is the victim? Who is the bully? What can be done to stop bullying? *Adolescence, 42,* 749–761.

Galand, B., & Hospel, V. (2013). Peer victimization and school disaffection: Exploring the moderation effect of social support and the mediation effect of depression. *British Journal of Educational Psychology, 83,* 569–590. https://doi.org/10.1111/j.2044-8279.2012.02077.x.

Gorman, A. H., Schwartz, D., Nakamoto, J., & Mayeux, L. (2011). Unpopularity and disliking among peers: Partially distinct dimensions of adolescents' social experiences. *Journal of Applied Developmental Psychology, 32,* 208–217. https://doi.org/10.1016/j.appdev.2011.05.001.

Graham, S., Bellmore, A., Nishina, A., & Juvonen, J. (2009). "It must be me": Ethnic diversity and attributions for peer victimization in middle school. *Journal of Youth and Adolescence, 38*(4), 487–499. https://doi.org/10.1007/s10964-008-9386-4.

Graham, S., & Juvonen, J. (2001). An attributional approach to peer victimization. In J. Juvonen & S. Graham (Eds.), *Peer harassment in school: The plight of the vulnerable and victimized; peer harassment in school* (pp. 49–72, Chapter xix, 440 Pages). New York: Guilford Press.

Guerin, S., & Hennessy, E. (2002). Pupils' definitions of bullying. *European Journal of Psychology of Education, 17,* 249–261. https://doi.org/10.1007/BF03173535.

Hanish, L. D., Eisenberg, N., Fabes, R. A., Spinrad, T. L., Ryan, P., & Schmidt, S. (2004). The expression and regulation of negative emotions: Risk factors for young children's peer victimization. *Development and Psychopathology, 16,* 335–353. https://doi.org/10.1017/S0954579404044542.

Hanish, L. D., & Guerra, N. G. (2004). Aggressive victims, passive victims, and bullies: Developmental continuity or developmental change? *Merrill-Palmer Quarterly, 50,* 17–38. https://doi.org/10.1353/mpq.2004.0003.

Haynie, D. L., Nansel, T., Eitel, P., Crump, A. D., Saylor, K., Yu, K., & Simons-Morton, B. (2001). Bullies, victims, and bully/victims: Distinct groups of at-risk youth. *The Journal of Early Adolescence, 21,* 29–49. https://doi.org/10.1177/0272431601021001002.

Heinemann, P.P. (1972). *Mobbning-Gruppvåld bland barn och vuxna.* Stockholm: Natur & Kultur.

Henington, C., Hughes, J. N., Cavell, T. A., & Thompson, B. (1998). The role of relational aggression in identifying aggressive boys and girls. *Journal of School Psychology, 36,* 457–477. https://doi.org/10.1016/S0022-4405(98)00015-6.

Hodges, E. V., Malone, M. J., & Perry, D. G. (1997). Individual risk and social risk as interacting determinants of victimization in the peer group. *Developmental Psychology, 33,* 1032–1039. https://doi.org/10.1037/0012-1649.33.6.1032.

Hodges, E. V., & Perry, D. G. (1999). Personal and interpersonal antecedents and consequences of victimization by peers. *Journal of Personality and Social Psychology, 76,* 677–685. https://doi.org/10.1037/0022-3514.76.4.677.

Hong, J. S., & Espelage, D. L. (2012). A review of research on bullying and peer victimization in school: An ecological system analysis. *Aggression and Violent Behavior, 17,* 311–322. https://doi.org/10.1016/j.avb.2012.03.003.

Juvonen, J., Lessard, L. M., Schacter, H. L., & Suchilt, L. (2017). Emotional implications of weight stigma across middle school: The role of weight-based peer discrimination. *Journal of Clinical Child and Adolescent Psychology, 46,* 150–158. https://doi.org/10.1080/15374416.2016.1188703.

Kochel, K. P., Ladd, G. W., Bagwell, C. L., & Yabko, B. A. (2015). Bully/victim profiles' differential risk for worsening peer acceptance: The role of friendship. *Journal of Applied Developmental Psychology, 41,* 38–45. https://doi.org/10.1016/j.appdev.2015.05.002.

Kochel, K. P., Ladd, G. W., & Rudolph, K. D. (2012). Longitudinal associations among youth depressive symptoms, peer victimization, and low peer acceptance: An interpersonal process perspective. *Child Development, 83,* 637–650. https://doi.org/10.1111/j.1467-8624.2011.01722.x.

Kochenderfer-Ladd, B., Ladd, G. W., & Kochel, K. P. (2009). A child and environment framework for studying risk for peer victimization. In M. J. Harris (Ed.), *Bullying, rejection and peer victimization: A social cognitive neuroscience perspective* (pp. 27–52). New York:

Springer. Retrieved from http://libproxy.usc.edu/login?url=https://search-proquest-com.libproxy2.usc.edu/docview/621992144?accountid=14749.

Kochenderfer-Ladd, B., & Skinner, K. (2002). Children's coping strategies: Moderators of the effects of peer victimization? *Developmental Psychology, 38,* 267–278. https://doi.org/10.1037/0012-1649.38.2.267.

Kowalski, R. M., Giumetti, G. W., Schroeder, A. N., & Lattanner, M. R. (2014). Bullying in the digital age: A critical review and meta-analysis of cyberbullying research among youth. *Psychological Bulletin, 140,* 1073–1137. https://doi.org/10.1037/a0035618.

LaFontana, K. M., & Cillessen, A. H. (2002). Children's perceptions of popular and unpopular peers: A multimethod assessment. *Developmental Psychology, 38,* 635–647. https://doi.org/10.1037/0012-1649.38.5.635.

Langman, P. (2009). *Why kids kill: Inside the minds of school shooters.* New York: Macmillan.

Leary, M. R., Kowalski, R. M., Smith, L., & Phillips, S. (2003). Teasing, rejection, and violence: Case studies of the school shootings. *Aggressive Behavior, 29,* 202–214. https://doi.org/10.1002/ab.10061.

Lemerise, E. A., & Arsenio, W. F. (2000). An integrated model of emotion processes and cognition in social information processing. *Child Development, 71,* 107–118. https://doi.org/10.1111/1467-8624.00124.

Livingstone, S., & Smith, P. K. (2014). Annual research review: Harms experienced by child users of online and mobile technologies: The nature, prevalence and management of sexual and aggressive risks in the digital age. *Journal of Child Psychology and Psychiatry, 55,* 635–654. http://dx.doi.org.libproxy2.usc.edu/10.1111/jcpp.12197.

Lovegrove, P. J., Henry, K. L., & Slater, M. D. (2012). Examination of the predictors of latent class typologies of bullying involvement among middle school students. *Journal of School Violence, 11,* 75–93. https://doi.org/10.1080/15388220.2011.631447.

Lunde, C., & Frisén, A. (2011). On being victimized by peers in the advent of adolescence: Prospective relationships to objectified body consciousness. *Body Image, 8,* 309–314. https://doi.org/10.1016/j.bodyim.2011.04.010.

Lunde, C., Frisén, A., & Hwang, C. P. (2007). Ten-year-old girls' and boys' body composition and peer victimization experiences: Prospective associations with body satisfaction. *Body Image, 4,* 11–28. https://doi.org/10.1016/j.bodyim.2006.10.002.

Malamut, S., Dawes, M., & Xie, H. (2018). Characteristics of rumors and rumor victims in early adolescence: Rumor content and social impact. *Social Development, 27,* 601–618. https://doi.org/10.1111/sode.12289.

Malcolm, K. T., Jensen-Campbell, L., Rex-Lear, M., & Waldrip, A. M. (2006). Divided we fall: Children's friendships and peer victimization. *Journal of Social and Personal Relationships, 23,* 721–740. https://doi.org/10.1177/026 5407506068260.

Masten, A. S., & Cicchetti, D. (2010). Developmental cascades. *Development and Psychopathology, 22,* 491–495. https://doi.org/10.1017/S09545794100 00222.

Mayeux, L., Houser, J. J., & Dyches, K. D. (2011). Social acceptance and popularity: Two distinct forms of peer status. In A. H. N. Cillessen, D. Schwartz, & L. Mayeux (Eds.), *Popularity in the peer system* (pp. 79–102, Chapter xiv, 306 Pages) New York: Guilford Press.

McConnell, L. M., & Erath, S. A. (2018). Affiliation value and extracurricular commitment moderate associations between peer victimization and depression. *Journal of Applied Developmental Psychology, 58,* 49–56. https://doi.org/ 10.1016/j.appdev.2018.08.006.

McDougall, P., & Vaillancourt, T. (2015). Long-term adult outcomes of peer victimization in childhood and adolescence: pathways to adjustment and maladjustment. *American Psychologist, 70,* 300–310. https://doi.org/10. 1037/a0039174.

Merten, D. E. (2011). Being there awhile: An ethnographic perspective on popularity. In A. H. N. Cillessen, D. Schwartz, & L. Mayeux (Eds.), *Popularity in the peer system* (pp. 57–76, Chapter xiv, 306 Pages). New York: Guilford Press.

Monks, C. P., & Smith, P. K. (2006). Definitions of bullying: Age differences in understanding of the term, and the role of experience. *British Journal of Developmental Psychology, 24,* 801–821. https://doi.org/10.1348/026151 005X82352.

Nakamoto, J., & Schwartz, D. (2010). Is peer victimization associated with academic achievement? A meta-analytic review. *Social Development, 19,* 221–242. https://doi.org/10.1111/j.1467-9507.2009.00539.x.

Nesi, J., Choukas-Bradley, S., & Prinstein, M. J. (2018a). Transformation of adolescent peer relations in the social media context: Part 1—A theoretical framework and application to dyadic peer relationships. *Clinical Child and Family Psychology Review, 21,* 267–294. https://doi.org/10.1007/s10 567-018-0261-x.

Nesi, J., Choukas-Bradley, S., & Prinstein, M. J. (2018b). Transformation of adolescent peer relations in the social media context: Part 2—Application to peer group processes and future directions for research. *Clinical*

Child and Family Psychology Review, 21, 295–319. https://doi.org/10.1007/s10567-018-0262-9.

O'Connell, P., Pepler, D., & Craig, W. (1999). Peer involvement in bullying: Insights and challenges for intervention. *Journal of Adolescence, 22,* 437–452. https://doi.org/10.1006/jado.1999.0238.

Olweus, D. (1978). *Aggression in the schools: Bullies and whipping boys.* Washington: Hemisphere (Wiley).

Olweus, D. (1983). Testosterone in the development of aggressive antisocial behavior in adolescents. In *Prospective studies of crime and delinquency* (pp. 237–247). Dordrecht: Springer.

Olweus, D. (1993). *Bullying at school: What we know and what we can do.* Malden: Blackwell.

Peguero, A. A., & Williams, L. M. (2013). Racial and ethnic stereotypes and bullying victimization. *Youth & Society, 45,* 545–564. https://doi.org/10.1177/0044118X11424757.

Pepler, D., Craig, W. M., & O'Connell, P. (1999). Understanding bullying from a dynamic systems perspective. In A. Slater & D. Muir (Eds.), *The Blackwell reader in development psychology* (pp. 440–451, Chapter xxi, 558 Pages). Malden: Blackwell.

Perren, S., Dooley, J., Shaw, T., & Cross, D. (2010). Bullying in school and cyberspace: Associations with depressive symptoms in Swiss and Australian adolescents. *Child and Adolescent Psychiatry and Mental Health, 4.* https://doi.org/10.1186/1753-2000-4-28.

Perren, S., Ettekal, I., & Ladd, G. (2013). The impact of peer victimization on later maladjustment: Mediating and moderating effects of hostile and self-blaming attributions. *Journal of Child Psychology and Psychiatry, 54,* 46–55. https://doi.org/10.1111/j.1469-7610.2012.02618.x.

Perry, D. G., Kusel, S. J., & Perry, L. C. (1988). Victims of peer aggression. *Developmental Psychology, 24,* 807–814. https://doi.org/10.1037/0012-1649.24.6.807.

Perry, D. G., Perry, L. C., & Kennedy, E. (1992). Conflict and the development of anti-social behavior. In C. U. Shantz & W. W. Hartup (Eds.), *Conflict in child and adolescent development* (pp. 301–329). Cambridge: Cambridge University Press.

Pouwels, J. L., Souren, P. M., Lansu, T. A. M., & Cillessen, A. H. N. (2016). Stability of peer victimization: A meta-analysis of longitudinal research. *Developmental Review, 40,* 1–24. https://doi.org/10.1016/j.dr.2016.01.001.

Prinstein, M. J., Boergers, J., & Vernberg, E. M. (2001). Overt and relational aggression in adolescents: Social-psychological adjustment of aggressors and victims. *Journal of Clinical Child Psychology, 30,* 479–491. https://doi.org/10.1207/S15374424JCCP3004_05.

Puhl, R. M., Luedicke, J., & Heuer, C. (2011). Weight-based victimization toward overweight adolescents: Observations and reactions of peers. *Journal of School Health, 81,* 696–703. https://doi.org/10.1111/j.1746-1561.2011.00646.x.

Reijntjes, A., Kamphuis, J. H., Prinzie, P., Boelen, P. A., Van der Schoot, M., & Telch, M. J. (2011). Prospective linkages between peer victimization and externalizing problems in children: A meta-analysis. *Aggressive Behavior, 37,* 215–222. https://doi.org/10.1002/ab.20374.

Reijntjes, A., Kamphuis, J. H., Prinzie, P., & Telch, M. J. (2010). Peer victimization and internalizing problems in children: A meta-analysis of longitudinal studies. *Child Abuse and Neglect, 34,* 244–252. https://doi.org/10.1016/j.chiabu.2009.07.009.

Reijntjes, A., Vermande, M., Thomaes, S., Goossens, F., Olthof, T., Aleva, L., & Meulen, M. (2016). Narcissism, bullying, and social dominance in youth: A longitudinal analysis. *Journal of Abnormal Child Psychology, 44,* 63–74. https://doi.org/10.1007/s10802-015-9974-1.

Rodkin, P. C., Hanish, L. D., Wang, S., & Logis, H. A. (2014). Why the bully/victim relationship is so pernicious: A gendered perspective on power and animosity among bullies and their victims. *Development and Psychopathology, 26,* 689–704. https://doi.org/10.1017/s0954579414000327.

Rosen, L. H., Underwood, M. K., & Beron, K. J. (2011). Peer victimization as a mediator of the relation between facial attractiveness and internalizing problems. *Merrill-Palmer Quarterly, 57,* 319–347. https://doi.org/10.1353/mpq.2011.0016.

Rudolph, K. D., Lansford, J. E., Agoston, A. M., Sugimura, N., Schwartz, D., Dodge, K. A., ... Bates, J. E. (2014). Peer victimization and social alienation: Predicting deviant peer affiliation in middle school. *Child Development, 85,* 124–139. https://doi.org/10.1111/cdev.12112.

Salmivalli, C. (1999). Participant role approach to school bullying: Implications for interventions. *Journal of Adolescence, 22,* 453–459. https://doi.org/10.1006/jado.1999.0239.

Salmivalli, C., & Nieminen, E. (2002). Proactive and reactive aggression among school bullies, victims, and bully-victims. *Aggressive Behavior, 28,* 30–44. https://doi.org/10.1002/ab.90004.abs.

Sandstrom, M. J. (2011). The power of popularity: Influence processes in childhood and adolescence. In A. H. N. Cillessen, D. Schwartz, & L.

Mayeux (Eds.), *Popularity in the peer system; popularity in the peer system* (pp. 219–244, Chapter xiv, 306 Pages). New York: Guilford Press.

Schacter, H. L., & Juvonen, J. (2018). Dynamic changes in peer victimization and adjustment across middle school: Does friends' victimization alleviate distress? *Child Development*. https://doi.org/10.1111/cdev.13038.

Scheithauer, H., Hayer, T., Petermann, F., & Jugert, G. (2006). Physical, verbal, and relational forms of bullying among German students: Age trends, gender differences, and correlates. *Aggressive Behavior, 32,* 261–275. https://doi.org/10.1002/ab.20128.

Schmidt, M. E., & Bagwell, C. L. (2007). The protective role of friendships in overtly and relationally victimized boys and girls. *Merrill-Palmer Quarterly,* 439–460. https://doi.org/10.1353/mpq.2007.0021.

Schwartz, D. (2000). Subtypes of victims and aggressors in children's peer groups. *Journal of Abnormal Child Psychology, 28,* 181–192. https://doi.org/10.1023/A:1005174831561.

Schwartz, D., Chang, L., & Farver, J. M. (2001). Correlates of victimization in Chinese children's peer groups. *Developmental Psychology, 37,* 520. https://doi.org/10.1037//0012-1649.37.4.520.

Schwartz, D., Dodge, K. A., & Coie, J. D. (1993). The emergence of chronic peer victimization in boys' play groups. *Child Development, 64,* 1755–1772. https://doi.org/10.2307/1131467.

Schwartz, D., Dodge, K. A., Pettit, G. S., & Bates, J. E. (1997). The early socialization of aggressive victims of bullying. *Child Development, 68,* 665–675.

Schwartz, D., Gorman, A. H., Dodge, K. A., Pettit, G. S., & Bates, J. E. (2008). Friendships with peers who are low or high in aggression as moderators of the link between peer victimization and declines in academic functioning. *Journal of Abnormal Child Psychology, 36,* 719–730. https://doi.org/10.1007/s110802-007-9200-x.

Schwartz, D., Gorman, A. H., Nakamoto, J., & Toblin, R. L. (2005). Victimization in the peer group and children's academic functioning. *Journal of Educational Psychology, 97,* 425–435. https://doi.org/10.1037/0022-0663.97.3.425.

Schwartz, D., Kelleghan, A., Malamut, S., Mali, L., Ryjova, Y., Hopmeyer, A., & Luo, T. (2019). Distinct modalities of electronic communication and school adjustment. *Journal of Youth and Adolescence, 48,* 1452–1468. https://doi.org/10.1007/s10964-019-01061-8.

Schwartz, D., Kelly, B. M., & Duong, M. T. (2013). Do academically-engaged adolescents experience social sanctions from the peer group? *Journal of Youth and Adolescence, 42,* 1319–1330. https://doi.org/10.1007/s10964-012-9882-4.

Schwartz, D., Lansford, J. E., Dodge, K. A., Pettit, G. S., & Bates, J. E. (2013). The link between harsh home environments and negative academic trajectories is exacerbated by victimization in the elementary school peer group. *Developmental Psychology, 49,* 305–316. https://doi.org/10/1037/a0028249.

Schwartz, D., Lansford, J. E., Dodge, K. A., Pettit, G. S., & Bates, J. E. (2015). Peer victimization during middle childhood as a lead indicator of internalizing problems and diagnostic outcomes in late adolescence. *Journal of Clinical Child & Adolescent Psychology, 44,* 393–404. https://doi.org/10.1080/15374416.2014.881293.

Schwartz, D., Lansford, J. E., Dodge, K. A., Pettit, G. S., & Bates, J. E. (2018). Peer victimization during middle childhood as a marker of attenuated risk for adult arrest. *Journal of Abnormal Child Psychology, 46,* 57–65. https://doi.org/10.1007/s10802-017-0354-x.

Schwartz, D., Proctor, L. J., & Chien, D. H. (2001). The aggressive victim of bullying: Emotional and behavioral dysregulation as a pathway to victimization by peers. In J. Juvonen & S. Graham (Eds.), *Peer harassment in school: The plight of the vulnerable and victimized* (pp. 147–174). New York: Guilford Press. https://doi.org/10.1037/e322202004-007.

Schwartz, S. J., Des Rosiers, S., Huang, S., Zamboanga, B. L., Unger, J. B., Knight, G. P., ... Szapocznik, J. (2013). Developmental trajectories of acculturation in Hispanic adolescents: Associations with family functioning and adolescent risk behavior. *Child Development, 84*(4), 1355–1372. https://doi.org/10.1111/cdev.12047.

Shields, A., & Cicchetti, D. (2001). Parental maltreatment and emotion dysregulation as risk factors for bullying and victimization in middle childhood. *Journal of Clinical Child Psychology, 30,* 349–363. https://doi.org/10.1207/s15374424jccp3003_7.

Smith, P. K., Cowie, H., Olafsson, R. F., Liefooghe, A. P. D., Almeida, A., Araki, H., ... Wenxin, Z. (2002). Definitions of bullying: A comparison of terms used, and age and gender differences, in a fourteen-country international comparison. *Child Development, 73,* 1119–1133. https://doi.org/10.1111/1467-8624.00461.

Smith, P. K., Madsen, K., & Moody, J. (1999). What causes the age decline in reports of being bullied at school? Towards a developmental analysis of risks of being bullied. *Educational Research, 41,* 267–285. https://doi.org/10.1080/0013188990410303.

Snyder, J., Brooker, M., Patrick, M. R., Snyder, A., Schrepferman, L., & Stoolmiller, M. (2003). Observed peer victimization during early elementary school: Continuity, growth, and relation to risk for child antisocial and depressive behavior. *Child Development, 74,* 1881–1898. https://doi.org/10.1046/j.1467-8624.2003.00644.x.

Solberg, M. E., & Olweus, D. (2003). Prevalence estimation of school bullying with the Olweus Bully/Victim Questionnaire. *Aggressive Behavior, 29,* 239–268. https://doi.org/10.1002/ab.10047.

Sourander, A., Jensen, P., Rönning, J. A., Niemelä, S., Helenius, H., Sillanmäki, L., ... Almqvist, F. (2007). What is the early adulthood outcome of boys who bully or are bullied in childhood? The finnish "From a Boy to a Man" study. *Pediatrics, 120,* 397–404. https://doi.org/10.1542/peds.2006.2704.

Stadler, C., Feifel, J., Rohrmann, S., Vermeiren, R., & Poustka, F. (2010). Peer-victimization and mental health problems in adolescents: Are parental and school support protective? *Child Psychiatry and Human Development, 41,* 371–386. https://doi.org/10.1007/s10578-010-0174-5.

Sullivan, T. N., Farrell, A. D., & Kliewer, W. (2006). Peer victimization in early adolescence: Association between physical and relational victimization and drug use, aggression, and delinquent behaviors among urban middle school students. *Development and Psychopathology, 18,* 119–137. https://doi.org/10.1017/s095457940606007x.

Telzer, E. H., Miernicki, M. E., & Rudolph, K. D. (2018). Chronic peer victimization heightens neural sensitivity to risk taking. *Development and Psychopathology, 30,* 13–26. https://doi.org/10.1017/s0954579417000438.

Toblin, R. L., Schwartz, D., Gorman, A. H., & Abou-ezzeddine, T. (2005). Social-cognitive and behavioral attributes of aggressive victims of bullying. *Journal of Applied Developmental Psychology, 26,* 329–346. https://doi.org/10.1016/j.appdev.2005.02.004.

Vaillancourt, T., McDougall, P., Hymel, S., & Sunderani, S. (2010). Respect or fear? The relationship between power and bullying behavior. In S. R. Jimerson, S. M. Swearer, & D. L. Espelage (Eds.), *Handbook of bullying in schools: An international perspective* (pp. 211–222, Chapter x, 614 Pages). New York: Routledge and Taylor & Francis Group.

van Geel, M., Goemans, A., & Vedder, P. (2015). A meta-analysis on the relation between peer victimization and adolescent non-suicidal self-injury. *Psychiatry Research, 230,* 364–368. https://doi.org/10.1016/j.psychres.2015.09.017.

van Geel, M., Vedder, P., & Tanilon, J. (2014). Bullying and weapon carrying: A meta-analysis. *JAMA Pediatrics, 168,* 714–720. https://doi.org/10.1001/jamapediatrics.2014.213.

Vannatta, K., Gartstein, M. A., Zeller, M., & Noll, R. B. (2009). Peer acceptance and social behavior during childhood and adolescence: How important are appearance, athleticism, and academic competence? *International Journal of Behavioral Development, 33,* 303–311. https://doi.org/10.1177/0165025408101275.

Veenstra, R., Lindenberg, S., Oldehinkel, A. J., De Winter, A. F., Verhulst, F. C., & Ormel, J. (2005). Bullying and victimization in elementary schools: a comparison of bullies, victims, bully/victims, and uninvolved preadolescents. *Developmental Psychology, 41,* 672–682. https://doi.org/10.1037/0012-1649.41.4.672.

Veenstra, R., Lindenberg, S., Zijlstra, B. J., De Winter, A. F., Verhulst, F. C., & Ormel, J. (2007). The dyadic nature of bullying and victimization: Testing a dual-perspective theory. *Child Development, 78,* 1843–1854. https://doi.org/10.1111/j.1467-8624.2007.01101.x.

Vervoort, M. H., Scholte, R. H., & Overbeek, G. (2010). Bullying and victimization among adolescents: The role of ethnicity and ethnic composition of school class. *Journal of Youth and Adolescence, 39,* 1–11. https://doi.org/10.1007/s10964-008-9355-y.

Victor, S. E., Hipwell, A. E., Stepp, S. D., & Scott, L. N. (2019). Parent and peer relationships as longitudinal predictors of adolescent non-suicidal self-injury onset. *Child and Adolescent Psychiatry and Mental Health, 13,* 1–13. https://doi.org/10.1186/s1304-018-0261-0.

Wang, J., Iannotti, R. J., Luk, J. W., & Nansel, T. R. (2010). Co-occurrence of victimization from five subtypes of bullying: Physical, verbal, social exclusion, spreading rumors, and cyber. *Journal of Pediatric Psychology, 35,* 1103–1112. https://doi.org/10.1093/jpepsy/jsq048.

Wang, W., Vaillancourt, T., Brittain, H. L., McDougall, P., Krygsman, A., Smith, D., ... Hymel, S. (2014). School climate, peer victimization, and academic achievement: Results from a multi-informant study. *School Psychology Quarterly, 29,* 360–377. https://doi.org/10.1037/e57424 2014-057.

Williford, A. P., Brisson, D., Bender, K. A., Jenson, J. M., & Forrest-Bank, S. (2011). Patterns of aggressive behavior and peer victimization from childhood to early adolescence: A latent class analysis. *Journal of Youth and Adolescence, 40,* 644–655. https://doi.org/10.1007/s10964-010-9583-9.

Wright, J., Giammarino, M., & Parad, H. (1986). Social status in small groups: Individual-group similarity and the social "misfit". *Journal of Personality and Social Psychology, 50,* 523–536. https://doi.org/10.1037/0022-3514.50.3.523.

Xu, M., Macrynikola, N., Waseem, M., & Miranda, R. (in press). Racial and ethnic differences in bullying: Review and implications for intervention. *Aggression and Violent Behavior.*

Zhu, J., Yu, C., Zhang, W., Bao, Z., Jiang, Y., Chen, Y., & Zhen, S. (2016). Peer victimization, deviant peer affiliation and impulsivity: Predicting adolescent problem behaviors. *Child Abuse & Neglect, 58,* 39–50. https://doi.org/j.chiabu.2016.06.008.

7

Role of Adults in Prevention and Intervention of Peer Victimization

Jina Yoon, Sheri Bauman, and Colleen Corcoran

As others have highlighted in this book, the phenomenon of bullying and peer victimization is influenced by many factors and involves many individuals in various contexts (school, family, and community). Within the socio-ecological framework, Swearer and Espelage (2004) proposed concentric layers of influence that affect bullying behaviors, with family, school, and peers in overlapping layers surrounding the participants in bullying. Among these influences, research has identified contextual factors, including the peer ecology (Doll, Song, & Siemers, 2004; Swearer & Espelage, 2004; Rodkin & Hodges, 2003) and school climate (Gendron, Williams, & Guerra, 2011; Klein, Cornell, & Konold, 2012) that are important elements. This body of literature underscores the importance of ecological influences on the development and maintenance of bullying.

J. Yoon (✉)
College of Education, University of Arizona, Tucson, AZ, USA
e-mail: jinayoon@email.arizona.edu

S. Bauman · C. Corcoran
University of Arizona, Tucson, AZ, USA

Although bullying intervention efforts have identified teachers and parents as key players in reducing bullying incidents (Swearer & Espelage, 2004) and have acknowledged their support as critical for a victim's adjustment, the roles of parents and teachers in the dynamics of bullying are not well documented (Troop-Gordon & Ladd, 2015; Yoon, Sulkowski, & Bauman, 2016). The chapter presents theoretical frameworks and reviews existing literature that highlights parental and teacher influences on the peer ecology and victimization, with a particular emphasis on the roles of parents and teachers in prevention and intervention efforts against bullying. We posit that both parents' and teachers' roles are similar to the peers' roles as bystanders, but their roles are unique in that they have clear responsibilities and authority and thus they can have an impact on broader contexts of peer victimization (e.g., peer ecology, classroom dynamics, school climate, family processes, and home-school collaboration).

Adults as Bystanders and Beyond

Pioneering works by Salmivalli and her colleagues (e.g., Saarento & Salmivalli, 2015; Salmivalli, Lagerspetz, Björkqvist, Österman, & Kaukiainen, 1996) found that peers participate in bullying by taking various roles when bullying occurs: assistants, reinforcers, defenders, and outsiders. Although adult roles differ from peer roles in that they may not be physically present when a bullying incident occurs, responses by teachers and parents serve comparable functions as do those of peers. For example, many studies have documented that some teachers do not respond to the report of victimization and others intentionally ignore it (e.g., Ellis & Shute, 2007; Kochenderfer-Ladd & Pelletier, 2008; Rigby & Bauman, 2010). Clearly, they become outsiders or passive bystanders. Some teachers comfort victims and address perpetrators, which describes the actions of defenders.

Another unique aspect of teacher and parent roles in peer victimization is that adults have a responsibility to ensure students' safety. Physical and psychological safety is a core foundation for one's learning and functioning, and children rely on adults to maintain a safe environment on their behalf. Adults' failure to protect them from bullying and to support them in a bullying incident is likely to add a sense of danger and fear in addition to the direct impact of victimization experience.

In some cases, adults participate as perpetrators in their relationships with children as in cases of child maltreatment. A few studies have noted teachers' verbal abuse of students in their interactions (Brendgen, Wanner, & Vitaro, 2006; Brendgen, Wanner, Vitaro, Bukowski, & Tremblay, 2007). Casarjian (2000) found that about 34% of students reported psychological abuse by the teacher in a school year, which was defined as verbal attacks and acts of neglect. Framed as a hidden trauma by Twemlow, Fonagy, Sacco, and Brethour (2006), victimization by teachers has been associated with academic, emotional, and social maladjustment (Brendgen et al., 2006; Twemlow et al., 2006) and with somatic symptoms (Baier, Hong, Kliem, & Bergmann, 2018). More alarming is that a systematic approach to address victimization by teachers (e.g., school policies or reporting procedures) is non-existent (McEvoy, 2005). Khoury-Kassabri (2011) found in a sample of Israeli children that those who are verbally victimized by peers were more likely to experience emotional victimization by teachers (e.g., verbal humiliation and calling names). This finding is particularly harmful for the victimized students, not only because of the possible additive impacts of peer and teacher victimization, but also considering that teachers' victimization is likely to provide a tacit encouragement of peer victimization.

Theoretical Framework

While the role of adults in a bullying dynamic can be broadly understood in a socio-ecological framework, we draw from several theoretical frameworks to conceptualize how parents and teachers may shape the experiences of peer victimization. Significant adults such as parents and teachers have been long recognized as important key figures in building social competence and facilitating social adjustment among children. One theoretical approach that attempts to delineate the process of that influence describes significant adults as socializing agents, prominent adults who communicate rules and values through their interpersonal interactions and relationships (Grusec & Hastings, 2015). For example, parenting styles research (based on the work of Baumrind, 1971) has contributed to the knowledge base regarding parents' role in children's peer relationships. A typology of four styles, based on the intersection of parental responsiveness and parental demandingness (Darling, 1999), is widely known: authoritarian (high expectations and low warmth), authoritative (high expectations and high warmth), indulgent (permissive, high warmth, and low expectations), and indifferent-uninvolved (neglectful, low warmth, low expectations) (Duncan, 2004). Children of authoritative parents tend to have good social skills and good relationships with peers, while the other three styles more often lead to aggressive behavior in the children.

Another perspective on how parents influence the peer relations of their children was proposed by Ladd, LeSieur, and Profilet (1993). In their review of direct parental influences on peer relations of younger children, they categorized direct parental strategies into the roles of *designer, mediator, supervisor,* and *consultant.* Designer activities include such important tasks as choosing a neighborhood in which to raise the child, choosing a preschool, and seeking out community opportunities for peer contact and interaction. Mediator functions involve finding suitable peers with whom the child may play and arrange playdates. In the role of supervisor, parents may react to inappropriate behaviors the child displays or to praise and encourage prosocial actions. Parents may use what Ladd et al. (1993) call *interactive interventions,* which are supervisory functions enacted by participating in the play with the children. Supervision may also take the form of monitoring the child's activities and associates, but this is more common in older children who have more autonomy. The object of parental consulting is to directly instruct the child in the skills of peer relations, either to prepare the child in advance of peer activities, or to reflect with the child on peer problems that the child has experienced. Parent-as-consultant may seek expert advice in particularly challenging situations.

With respect to teachers' socialization, Wentzel (2003) argued that students' interpersonal interactions and relationships with teachers and peers influence their social behaviors by two mechanisms: direct influence (e.g., modeling, advice, information) and indirect influence of the "socialization process as one of adults communicating goals and expectations for specific behaviors and then providing a context where these goals are learned and subsequently internalized" (p. 322). Through this process, it is obvious that teachers play a similar role to those by parents outlined by Ladd et al. (1993).

When it is applied to the ecology of peer victimization, parents and teachers in their family and classroom/school contexts are thought to model caring relationships, communicate behavioral expectations, and offer experiences to practice and demonstrate their concern for others. The goal framing theory (Lindenberg, as cited in Veenstra, Lindenberg, Huitsing, Sainio, & Salmivalli, 2014) suggests that significant others such as parents and teachers serve as an "active agent" (Veenstra et al., 2014, p. 3) who consistently activates the norms and goals when relevant situations arise (e.g., an incident of peer victimization). That is, this level of ongoing and consistent socialization around the anti-bullying norms and goals is required beyond just having rules and policies.

The notion of parents and teachers as socializing agents raises several important points. According to this theoretical approach, parents' and teachers' responses to victimization are extremely important not only for bullies and victims, but also for others in the peer ecology (Duncan, 2004; Grusec & Hastings, 2015). Adults' responses are a part of socialization that serves as a salient experience, strengthening or weakening the expectation about how to interact with others (e.g., victimizing or defending). The theoretical approach presented above further underscores adults' role in promoting a positive social climate where negative peer interactions are discouraged and defending and other prosocial behaviors are facilitated, a preventive approach to addressing bullying.

Roles of Parents

The impact of parents on all aspects of a child's development has been a topic of interest to researchers and the public for many years. Parenting is a complex endeavor, arguably more so in the complicated context of the twenty-first century. In this section, we examine what is known about parental influences on peer relations in general, and then focus more specifically on parents' influence on bullying and victimization by peers. We then examine how parents react to knowledge of their child's involvement in bullying and conclude with a discussion of parental options for both prevention of and intervention in bullying situations.

Parental Influences on Peer Relations

A body of scholarly work has consistently found that parenting practices are relevant for understanding bullying (Haynie et al., 2001). Olweus (1980), a pioneer in bullying research, conducted parent (mother alone, or mother and father) interviews with two samples of Swedish male students: 76 boys in Grade 6 (12–14 years old) and 51 boys in Grade 9 (15–17 years old). The most robust predictors of aggression in boys were mothers' permissive attitude toward aggression, mothers' negativism, the boys' temperament, and parental use of punitive, authoritarian methods of discipline. Olweus cites earlier work (Sears, Maccoby, & Levin, 1957) that found similar predictors of aggression in young children: lack of maternal warmth, use of physical punishment, and a permissive parental attitude toward aggression.

In her review of studies about family influences on school bullies and victims, Duncan (2004) extends Ladd et al.'s review by expanding the list of theories that can be applied. Attachment theory (Bowlby, 1969) proposes that a child develops a mental template of relationships with others based on the early relationship with parents. In a review and study reported by Elicker, Englund, and Sroufe (1992), the importance of the infant-parent relationship as a model for future relationships is emphasized. When the relationship is positive, the child expects that future relationships will be positive and will have internalized the basic patterns of reciprocity with others. When the child is prized and has efforts at autonomy supported, the child also develops self-worth and self-efficacy. These characteristics are needed for satisfactory peer relationships, and the way these functions are enacted varies with the developmental stage of the child. Negative parenting is associated with victims and bully/victims, while positive parenting characterized by warmth and cohesion, open communication within the family, and parental supervision were protective factors (Lereya, Samara, & Wolke, 2013).

Numerous studies have found that securely attached infants had better peer competence ratings in early childhood. Elicker et al. (1992) studied 47 ten-and eleven-year-old children whose attachment style had been determined via the Strange Situation at 12 and 18 months (classified as secure, anxious-resistant, or anxious-avoidant). They were assessed at a one-month long summer camp by the camp counselors and observers and via interviews with the child. As expected, they found that those children with secure attachments as babies were more socially competent, were more involved in peer activities, and were more engaged with peers. When the parent (usually the mother) is nurturing and sensitive to the child's needs, the child develops a *secure* attachment, and approaches novel situations with confidence (Dunst & Kassow, 2008; Etzion-Carasso & Oppenheim, 2000). When the parental care is inconsistent or unresponsive to the child, the child may develop an *insecure* attachment, and approach to new situations is likely to be characterized by upset and anxiety. The child may also become aggressive to garner attention from the insensitive parent (Belsky, 2002).

Another approach to understand parental influences on social competence emphasizes interactions between parents and children. Social learning theory (Bandura & Walters, 1977) claims that children learn interpersonal behaviors by modeling behaviors they observe, and through operant conditioning (e.g., reinforcement or punishment, direct or vicarious). Duncan (2004) observes that there is good evidence that children who experience abuse or receive physical or verbal aggression from parents adopt aggressive behaviors in their peer relations. From this perspective, the family provides a model of relationships that children then employ in their peer contexts, sometimes in the role of bully or bully-victim.

Family systems theory emphasizes the interconnection among members of the family, meaning that the family is a unit whose parts are interdependent. Research reported by Duncan (2004) found that when warmth, harmony, and affinity were absent or low, and conflict was high, children were more likely to have poor relationships with peers. Regarding bullying roles, families of victims tended to be unified but enmeshed (relationships in which personal boundaries are unclear and easily permeated), especially so for mothers and male children, whereas families of bullies were low on both cohesion and warmth, and less likely to have a father in the home.

The work of Finnegan, Hodges, and Perry (1998) illuminated the sex-linked associations between maternal parenting practices and children's peer relationships in a study with students in grades four through seven. They observed that social competencies needed with peers are different for boys and girls: boys are expected to be independent and assertive with peers, while girls are socialized to form close and intense relationships with same sex peers. Parenting practices that inhibit boys' development of "autonomy and assertion" (p. 1077) and interfere with acquisition of conflict management skills predispose them to peer victimization, while for girls, parenting (particularly lack of interest and threatened rejection) that impedes the development of close relationships with others serves to increase their risk of peer victimization. Mothers' behaviors were measured by child-report, self-report was used to assess child coping strategies for conflict, and peer-report identified victimization. Consistent with previous research, Finnegan et al. (1998) found that maternal overprotection predicted victimization of boys, and that the relation of overprotection and victimization varied by the degree to which boys reported being fearful during conflict with mother. Findings for girls also confirmed prior research, in that when girls feared rejection by their mothers, they were more likely to be victimized. The researchers theorized that for girls, their fears led to difficulties in communicating about feelings, in self-regulation, and in empathy, all of which are needed for successful peer relationships.

Another perspective on parental influence on peer relationships is offered by McDowell and Parke (2009), who suggest that parental influence occurs via three elements: the nature of parent-child interactions, offering advice regarding peer relationships, and providing opportunities for peer social interactions. They see these factors as being particularly critical during upper elementary school, as peer relationships increase in importance. The optimal nature of parent-child interactions is proposed to be one of warmth and positivity, and while explicit advice from parents is associated with good outcomes in preschoolers, advice in middle childhood may function to remediate observed difficulties. In their study of 159 4th and 5th grade children and their families, all three parental elements predicted children's social competence one year later. The quality of parent-child interactions and the opportunities for peer interaction were predictive of higher levels of social competence in the child, but advice-giving predicted lower levels of peer competence; these findings were not affected by parent gender.

Parental Influences on Bullying Involvement

Smith (2014) summarized the findings of extant research on parental factors in bullying involvement: positive parenting (warmth, secure attachment relationships, and non-intrusive supervision) seems to protect youth from becoming involved in bullying. Overprotection, especially maternal overprotection of boys, tends to be associated with being victimized, and harsh discipline in the home—or abuse—is a predictor of bully-victim status of the child. However, Smith notes that many of the studies finding such relations between parent behavior and children's involvement in bullying have rather small effect sizes. Earlier work by Besag (1989) emphasizes the impact of dysfunctional families on bullies and victims. She considers the following characteristics to place children at risk for involvement in bullying as bully, victim, or bully-victim: negative relationship between child and parent, reliance on physical and or harsh discipline or inconsistent discipline in the family, an acceptance of aggression, conflict or hostility between parents, and the child's temperament. Although Besag's work pre-dates Smith's by decades, the same factors are identified. Furthermore, Hong and Espelage (2012) also summarized parental influences on bullying, observing that lack of parental involvement and support have been identified as risk factors for perpetrating bullying.

A recent systematic review of the literature (Nocentini, Fiorentini, DePaola, & Menesini, 2019) examined the parental variables of interest here. Summarizing their findings, the researchers observed that a violent family context has been shown to predict bullying and victimization, and that variations in parenting style, the quality of attachment, parental attitudes and beliefs about bullying, and parent knowledge of bullying have been found to be influential on children's roles in peer bullying. There is some discordance among study findings, but parental mental health problems were associated with both bullying and victimization in the majority of studies. Conflict and violence in the family were more strongly associated with bullying than victimization, but both were impacted. This was also true for family communication, which was negatively associated with bullying more strongly than victimization. Findings on the effects of authoritative parenting were mixed, but the authors suggest this parenting style could be a protective factor against involvement in bullying/victimization. Punitive parenting, however, was consistently associated with bullying. Overall, it seemed that parental support, solid family relationships, and parental engagement with school predicted lower levels of bullying and victimization. Furthermore, parental supervision and monitoring of the child's activities and relationships were related to lower rates of bullying and victimization.

Duncan (2004) notes other research that found the neglectful parenting style to be associated with bully-victims, while parents of bullies were most like the authoritarian and neglectful models. Parents of bullies were found in some studies to be aggressive with their children while also being over-indulgent, but other studies found that the parents of bullies exhibited fewer negative behaviors than did parents of victims or bully-victims. Parents of bullies may also fail to curtail aggression in the children. Mothers who are overly involved and controlling of their children (the authoritarian style) often raise children who are either aggressive with peers or submissive to peers. Several studies have examined the two variations of insecure attachment, anxious-avoidant or anxious-resistant, and found that they both tend to exhibit characteristics (anxiety, crying, hesitant to explore) that bullies target. The importance of warmth and cohesion, along with parental monitoring was associated with lower rates of cyberbullying involvement as bullies and victims (Elsaesser, Russell, Ohannessian, & Patton, 2017).

Duncan (2004) speculates that restricting a child's autonomy may leave the child to question their own feelings and to develop internalizing problems, which are common among victims. She reports on several studies that find overinvolvement of the parents to be associated with children who become victims of bullying; boys of overprotective and overly controlling mothers were often victims. Fathers of victimized boys, on the other hand, tended to be remote and critical, or absent from the family. Victimized girls reported more negative feelings toward mothers and described family interactions as unhealthy.

Witnessing parental violence has been associated with involvement in bullying, but findings have been contradictory (Hong & Espelage, 2012). While one study found that youth who witness such violence were more likely to assume the role of bully than their peers who had not witnessed parental violence, another study concluded that witnesses were at greater risk of being victimized by peers.

To summarize, bullies are more likely to exhibit avoidant attachment styles and to experience less support from parents, who are more likely to use physical punishment and to have less empathy. Victims' insecure attachment may be either avoidant or ambivalent. Boy victims are found to have enmeshed relations with parents, especially their mothers. Bully-victims also tend toward avoidant attachment with low level of parental support and inconsistent disciplinary practices (Nickerson, Mele, & Osborne-Oliver, 2010). Authoritative parenting, with high warmth and collaborative discipline, is associated with non-involved children.

Parental Reactions to Victimization

There is a small body of research that addresses parental reactions to their child's victimization. In one of the few quantitative studies with a large sample of parents who indicated their child had been bullied at school in the previous month, the most common responses were talking to their child and contacting a teacher or administrator (Waasdorp, Bradshaw, & Duong, 2011). They also found that parents who had a less favorable perception of school climate were more likely to contact school personnel when their child was victimized. It might be that those parents who had a positive impression of the school ethos believed the school would help their child without prompting from parents, whereas those whose view of the climate were less positive felt a need to bring attention to the situation. Furthermore, parents more often contacted the school about direct bullying than indirect bullying, in which case the parent was more likely to talk to the child.

A similar study was conducted in Spain with 1044 students in grades 7–10 and their parents (Larrañaga, Yubero, & Navarro, 2018). The most common parental response was to contact school personnel, then monitoring/limiting internet access, and talking to the parents of the bully. There were differences related to the age of the child: when children were younger, parents were more likely to contact schools and control digital access, while for older children, parents tended to advise the child to defend themselves or talk to the bully. Bradshaw (2014) also notes that parent advice and assistance when bullying does occur not only affects the child's response to the current situation but can also influence the child's future decisions about disclosing victimization to the parent.

Unfortunately, some parents encourage children to retaliate if they are targeted (Lereya et al., 2013), although many parents instruct youth not to initiate a fight or bullying episode. This puts parents at odds with the messages disseminated at school: don't fight back, tell an adult. Examples of such a message were illustrated by parents' responses to hypothetical bullying and victimization. To the scenario in which the child was the bully, one parent said, "I'd spank her and I'd tell her that, um, not to hit no one because she won't want no one to hit her." When the child was victimized, another parent offered, "I'd have to beat my kid for getting beaten up cause that's the only way I can teach him to stick up for himself" (Curtner-Smith, Smith, & Porter, 2010, pp. 75–76).

In qualitative studies, parents reported negative emotional reactions to their child's victimization, including feeling "angry, helpless, frustrated, guilty, worried, and stressed" (Harcourt, Jasperse, & Green, 2014, p. 382), and when they took action, some parents questioned themselves and wondered if their action was the best thing to do. Parents also reported feeling disappointed that the child's school did not respond effectively and expressed dismay that the school did not contact them when bullying or victimization occurred. A qualitative study based on focus groups and interviews with 21 mothers whose children each attended a different school (Hale, Fox, & Murray, 2017) identified two main themes: institutional factors and concerns about being a good parent. The parents expressed the expectation that the school would discipline the bullies, keep the students safe, and communicate with parents when bullying occurred. The last expectation was often unmet, leading to feelings of frustration in the parents. Parents did not think the school's bullying policies were implemented and so had no confidence in the policy, and by association, with the school's commitment to addressing bullying. Participants also expressed they felt discounted by the school. Either the school did not believe their report of victimization or considered it to be less serious than did the parent. Some parents resorted to gathering evidence to support their case. In a few cases, the parents began to blame themselves for being unable to keep their child safe from bullies at school and questioned their efforts to handle the situation. Some of the parents' frustration turned to anger and resentment toward the bully. On the other hand, several participants in the Hale et al. (2017) study reported being quite pleased with the actions taken by the school; this was more evident among mothers whose children were in elementary schools than those in secondary schools. Harcourt et al. (2014) noted that some parents blamed the victim, but others focused their efforts on providing support and comfort to the child, and still others enrolled children in martial arts classes in an effort to build the child's self-confidence. Some of the studies reviewed by Harcourt et al. (2014) reported that in extreme cases, parents changed their child's school to protect them from further victimization.

Roles of Teachers

Much of current efforts to address and prevent bullying involve school-based interventions, with a specific emphasis on cultivating a positive school climate. A recent meta-analysis identified a positive school climate as a protective factor against bullying and cyberbullying (Zych, Farrington, & Ttofi, 2019), which highlights the importance of the school context in bullying dynamics. It has been generally accepted that teachers play a critical role in positive climate; yet, specific aspects of direct and indirect influences of teachers on school climate and peer victimization (various roles) are less explored. Based on the theoretical notion of teachers as socializing agents, this section reviews current literature on teachers' influences on peer relations in general and bullying involvement.

Teachers' Influences on Peer Relations

Many studies have documented that the teachers' interactions characterized as emotionally responsive and instructionally supportive are associated with positive social/emotional outcomes (Merritt, Wanless, Rimm-Kaufman, Cameron, & Peugh, 2012; NICHD ECCRN, 2002). Gest and Rodkin (2011) found higher rates of reciprocated friendships in classrooms with teachers who are supportive and sensitive to students' needs; Luckner and Pianta (2011) also found greater prosocial behaviors among students in similar classrooms. Chang (2003) found that teachers with strong disapproval of aggression had students who rejected their aggressive peers, whereas students were more tolerant of aggressive peers when teachers showed high levels of warmth and support to students in general. Positive interactions between a teacher and a student are likely to communicate a level of teacher liking of the student, which influences peer liking of the student (Hendrickx, Mainhard, Boor-Klip, & Brekelmans, 2017).

In contrast, White, Sherman, and Jones (1996) found that teachers' derogatory feedback to students was related to the students' peer likeability and reputation. Taylor (1989) also found that lower teacher preference was related to peer rejection after taking the previous level of peer rejection into consideration. In a longitudinal analysis of school adjustment, Mercer and DeRosier (2008) found that baseline and declining teacher preference predicted increased social loneliness. These findings demonstrate that class level social experiences with teachers via teacher-student relationships and interactions have both positive and negative impacts on the quality of peer relations.

In addition to teachers' direct impact on peer relations, researchers have examined teachers' active role in peer group affiliation and acceptance. Teacher attunement, defined as "the extent to which teachers agree with students' perspectives on relationships within the peer ecology"

(Hoffman, Hamm, & Farmer, 2015, p. 14), is believed to be necessary for teachers to guide the peer ecology (Rodkin & Gest, 2010). Audley-Piotrowski, Singer, and Patterson (2015) argue that based on teachers' understanding of social network and peer affiliations, teachers should shape students' peer relationships by utilizing intentional strategies (e.g., classroom management). Although current research highlights the importance of teacher attunement (Farmer, Hall, Petrin, Hamm, & Dadisman, 2010; Hamm, Farmer, Dadisman, Gravelle, & Murray 2011), the question of how teachers should use their knowledge to promote positive peer relations appears to be in need of careful consideration. For example, Gest and Rodkin (2011) found that teachers' efforts to form new friendships by strategic use of grouping assignment was not effective.

Teachers' Influences on Bullying Involvement

A few studies suggest that classroom level social dynamics are unique in each class (Khoury-Kassabri, 2011; Oldenburg et al., 2015; Sentse, Veenstra, Kiuru, & Salmivalli, 2015), and as a primary socializing agent in the class, what teachers do specifically may help explain these differences. For example, Gage, Prykanowski, and Larson (2014) found that teachers' respect for diversity and student differences (e.g., racial diversity) predicted within-class decreases in victimization whereas Reis, Trockel, and Mulhall (2007) found less aggression in middle school classrooms when students participated in rule making and teachers cultivated cultural sensitivity. In a sample of Filipino high school students, Banzon-Librojo, Garabiles, and Alampay (2017) found that teachers' harsh discipline was associated with more victimization.

Classroom management, in particular, appears to be an important component of teachers' potential influence on victimization. Casas, Ortega-Ruiz, and Del Rey (2015) found that positive class management was related to less victimization, and teachers' apathy or disinterest to more aggression. Roland and Galloway (2002) tested a path model that describes the direct and indirect (via social structure of class) effects of teachers' classroom management on bullying. In a large sample of children in Grades 4–6, they found that classroom management (characterized as caring for students, effective instructional activities, monitoring, and responding to unacceptable behaviors) was directly linked to less bullying, but also indirectly via social structure of class as measured by cohesion among students, behavioral engagement, and class level norms about peers and teacher. Through certain approaches to classroom management, teachers are likely to develop and foster classroom level norms and social dynamics. In a large sample of Finnish students, Garandeau, Lee, and Salmivalli, (2014) found that classrooms with greater social hierarchy in mid-year were likely to have higher bullying at the end of year. Similarly, Serdiouk, Rodkin, Madill, Logis, and Gest (2015) found in a study of 54 classrooms and teachers that peer rejection in Fall was linked to peer victimization in Spring in classrooms where teachers made fewer efforts to address social status/hierarchy (e.g., making "social status less relevant, offering opportunities for low status children to receive recognition and have positive experiences with high status children," p. 14). These findings further illustrate the importance of teachers' awareness of these social hierarchy and social networks and efforts to create a positive peer ecology.

Emerging evidence indicates that the link between the classroom level interactions and victimization and defending behaviors may be mediated by cognitive processes. In a sample of Italian students in Grades 5–9, Jungert, Piroddi, and Thornberg (2016) examined the extent to which three aspects of teacher-student relationships (warm relationship, autonomous relationship, and conflictual relationship) are related to defending, passive bystanding, and pro-bullying behaviors. Although they found no support for autonomous relationships between teachers and students to be related to student behaviors, both warm and conflictual relationships were related to defending and pro-bullying, respectively. The link between warm relationships and defending behavior was mediated by autonomous motivation (i.e., motivated by one's values and beliefs: "Because I am the kind of kid who cares about others,") whereas the relation between conflictual relationships and pro-bullying behaviors was mediated by extrinsic motivation (i.e., "to become popular," "to be rewarded by a teacher," or "because I would get into trouble if I didn't help"). These findings provide empirical support for the types of teacher-student interactions that have impacts on students' motivation and social behaviors with peers, giving further support to the significance of classroom level socialization in peer victimization and defending behaviors.

Teacher Reactions to Victimization

Troop-Gordon and Ladd (2015) argued that how teachers handle bullying incidents contributes to a certain school climate that deters or encourages victimization among peers. Meanwhile, students' reports have raised several concerns regarding teacher responses to peer victimization. Students expect teachers to intervene in victimization incidents (Crothers & Kolbert, 2008), but some students believe that teachers make bullying situations worse when they intervene (Bradshaw, Sawyer, & O'Brennan, 2007). In a large survey of UK adolescents, about 56% of those who reported their own victimization to teachers were satisfied with the outcome and only 31% reported talking to adults when witnessing a bullying incident (Iurino, 2020). Wachs, Bilz, Niproschke, and Schubarth (2018) found that 12–15-year-old students reported that teachers were unaware of bullying in about 30% of bullying incidents in German schools. Students' decisions not to talk to teachers may be due to multiple reasons such as ineffective handling of previous reports, lack of warm relationships, or even possible consequences of reporting. Regardless, this presents significant challenges in intervening and preventing victimization incidents because teachers' limited awareness is likely to lead to low teacher attunement about peer relations/dynamics. Thus, opportunities to address victimization are lost and a cycle of victimization is perpetuated.

Studies have documented that teachers significantly vary in their responses to incidents of peer victimization, ranging from ignoring/dismissing, disciplining perpetrators, developing social skills, involving class/peer, and involving other adults (Yoon et al., 2016). Burger, Strohmeier, Spröber, Bauman, and Rigby (2015) and Seidel and Oertel (2017) categorized teacher responses into three major categories: authoritarian-punitive strategies (e.g., threatening, expelling, disciplining), supportive-individual strategies (e.g., talking to victims or bullies, emotionally supporting victims), and supportive-cooperative strategies (e.g., class level intervention, collaboration with parents and others). To date, only a few studies offer empirical evidence that links teacher responses to peer victimization. Marachi, Astor, and Benbenishty (2007) found that a teacher's inaction or avoidance in response to students' violent behaviors was associated with higher levels of peer victimization. In a sample of high school students in Kenya, Mucherah, Finch, White, and Thomas (2018) found that teachers' efforts to stop perpetration (teacher defending) was related to lower reports of perpetration and victimization. In a sample of middle school students, Troop-Gordon and Ladd (2015) found that teachers' efforts to separate the perpetrator and victim were associated with reduced aggression and victimization in the class, whereas contacting parents and reprimanding the aggressor were not related to lower aggression. Garandeau, Vartio, Poskiparta, and Salmivalli (2016) found that students who victimized other students were more likely to stop when teachers highlighted victims' feelings and expressed strong disapproval for the behavior. In Wachs et al. (2018), students' reports indicated no short- or long-term success from teachers' authoritarian-punitive approaches, but greater long-term success associated with supportive-individual and supportive-cooperative responses.

Less is known about teachers' responses to peer victimization and their impact on bystander behaviors. Hektner and Swenson (2012) found that students who had a group of teachers with a normative belief about bullying (i.e., bullying is a part of growing up) reported fewer interventions from these teachers and less likelihood to intervene themselves. These students were less likely to empathize with victims. These findings indicate that teachers' beliefs and actions may be related to the extent to which students feel empathic toward victims and are willing to intervene to stop bullying. However, this socializing mechanism by teachers and its impact on students' bystander behaviors awaits further investigation.

A Case in Point: Adult Roles in LGBTQ Victimization

LGBTQ students experience higher rates of victimization in comparison to their heterosexual and cisgender peers, with nearly 60% of LGBTQ youth reporting feeling unsafe on their school campuses (Kosciw, Greytak, Zongrone, Clark, & Truong, 2018; Toomey & Russell, 2016). Prevalence rates for physical assault and cyber bullying among sexual minority youth far exceed that of heterosexual youth and LGB students are nearly twice as likely to experience bullying at school (Kann et al., 2016). Despite the heightened incidence of peer victimization, LGBTQ youth experience low adult support and intervention in instances of bullying (Crothers et al., 2017). The findings from Kosciw et al. (2018) describe a difficult reality for LGBTQ youth in which repeated victimization is likely to be experienced. Students reported that school personnel typically do not intervene when victimization is reported or even when they witness use of homo-prejudiced and trans-prejudiced language by other students, and that when they shared victimization experiences with adult family members, school personnel were rarely notified. Adult responses included encouraging LGBTQ students to disregard the victimization and to modify their own behaviors, whereas bullies were rarely identified and disciplined.

Lack of responsive and effective adult responses is a serious concern, but more alarming is evidence that teachers actively contribute to this negative climate and culture. Kosciw et al. (2018) found that over half of LGBTQ students surveyed report that they have heard teachers make homo-prejudicial statements, and 71% have heard school staff comment negatively on students' gender expression. This type of interaction with school personnel is a clear example of socialization that not only affects LGBTQ students' sense of belonging and safety, but also shapes how other students perceive them, thus contributing to their social vulnerability.

Given adults' consistent failure to respond to victimization and protect them from future victimization, it is not surprising that LGBTQ students are less likely to report bullying to their teachers in comparison to their heterosexual and cisgender peers (Crothers et al., 2017). Similarly, disclosure of a victimization experience to parents is also less likely when the bullying was related to sexual orientation, with the majority of LGBTQ individuals who have experienced harassment at school reporting that they have not discussed the incidents with their parents, possibly out of fear that their sexual orientation or gender identity will be disclosed (Bauman, Meter, Nixon, & Davis, 2016).

Support from teachers and other school staff members is particularly critical, considering their vulnerable position in school environments. The number of supportive school staff personnel identified by LGBTQ youth has increased significantly over the last fifteen years, with nearly all LGBTQ students able to identify one or more supportive adults on their school campus (Kosciw et al., 2018). Emotional support from teachers and other school personnel has also been identified as a significant moderator, decreasing the likelihood of emotional and behavioral problems in students who have experienced various forms of bullying (Yeung & Leadbearer, 2010). School staff intervention in response to peer victimization on the basis of sexual orientation and gender identity has been found to predict higher self-esteem (Dessel, Kulick, Wernick, & Sullivan, 2017), higher incidence of victimization reporting (Berger, Poteat, & Dantas, 2019), and increased sense of safety (Toomey, McGuire, & Russell, 2012).

A few studies suggest several factors associated with low involvement from teachers. First, teachers often misjudge the frequency and extent of bullying that LGBTQ students experience. Crothers et al. (2017) found a significant discrepancy between school personnel and youth reports of LGBTQ peer victimization, which suggests low teacher attunement. The most common reason cited for failure to recognize and intervene in instances of victimization is lack of knowledge regarding the specific needs of this population, teacher homo-prejudice, and low self-efficacy (Nappa, Palladino, Menesini, & Baiocco, 2018; Swanson & Gettinger, 2016). However, brief, action-oriented school personnel trainings that target these areas have been proven to have positive impacts on teacher responses to LGBTQ students. Participation in such trainings was associated with increased engagement in supportive behaviors and improved self-efficacy regarding intervening in LGBTQ specific bullying (Greytak,

Kosciw, & Boesen, 2013; Swanson & Gettinger, 2016). Additionally, clear policies specific to intervention in bullying and harassment related to sexual orientation or gender identity were associated with increased supportive teacher behaviors (Swanson & Gettinger, 2016).

Parents also play a critical role in LGBTQ youths' experiences with victimization. Individuals who have high levels of parental support experience lesser degrees of victimization motivated by homo-prejudice and trans-prejudice (Poteat, Mereish, DiGiovanni, & Koenig, 2011). Additionally, parent emotional support has been identified as an important factor that moderates the relationship between victimization and future emotional and behavioral problems. The moderating effect of parent support was found to be particularly impactful when the parental support was received from the father (Yeung & Leadbearer, 2010). While parent support and acceptance has been identified as a factor contributing to positive youth adjustment, limitations to parent support in buffering the impacts of LGBTQ victimization have been identified (Snapp, Watson, Russell, Diaz, & Ryan, 2015). Parent support has not been found to moderate the relationship between homo-prejudice and trans-prejudice victimization and student suicidality or school belonging (Hatchel, Merrin, & Espelage, 2019; Poteat et al., 2011). The limited impact of parent support following instances of LGBTQ peer victimization may be directly related to student concerns regarding the disclosure of their sexual orientation or gender identity. Additionally, youth may fear parental rejection or doubt parents' ability to effectively address the problem (Poteat et al., 2011). Despite the identified limitations, parents serve as important social supports for victimized LGBTQ youth, mitigating negative social outcomes.

Implications for Practice and Future Directions

We have made a case for the important role of parents and teachers in promoting prosocial attitudes and behaviors, and in socializing children toward anti-bullying values and defending behaviors. We have examined theories that purport to explain the mechanisms by which parents and teachers exert their influence and provided research evidence to support these frameworks. What does this mean for reducing bullying in schools?

Both parents' and teachers' direct influences on peer relations indicate their potential to prevent peer victimization and promote positive peer relationships. Parents and teachers model behaviors that promote healthy relationships (McCallum & Bracken, 1993). This happens in the home and at school. Children look to these important adults for examples of how to manage friendships, navigate conflicts, and show empathy for others. When authoritarian discipline is the usual approach of the adults, children learn that aggressive use of power results in getting one's way and are more likely to enact this with peers. As argued above, an authoritative approach by parents and teachers is likely to promote empathy and prosocial behaviors. We argue that a preventive approach to anti-bullying should carefully target promoting positive interactions with these critical socializing agents, through which prosocial and anti-bullying values and beliefs are instilled, and empathic and caring behaviors are modeled.

Both parents and teachers need to be *with it* (Kounin, 1977)—aware of what is going on in the classroom or in their child's peer relationships. In the classroom, when students realize that the teacher is always attentive to what is going on all over the room, they may be less likely to misbehave or bully. At home, the parents need to know what their children are doing (with friends, with siblings, online, in their rooms) without violating norms of privacy—a tall order. Furthermore, parents' and teachers' awareness of peer relationships and social dynamics (e.g., power hierarchy) could be achieved through open communications and ongoing monitoring. Given not all victims come to adults, parents of students who witness bullying incidents may learn about them and communicate with teachers and school personnel.

In response to bullying incidents, adults' responsive and sensitive intervention is of particular significance. Both parents and teachers need training on how to best handle incidents of bullying (Bauman & Del Rio, 2005). Ideally, teacher training would occur as part of their instruction in overall classroom management strategies. Given that the dynamics of bullying involves peers with various roles and reflects contextual variables (e.g., class, school, home, and community), determining what is an appropriate response to bullying incidents requires a thorough understanding various influential forces so that adult responses do not perpetuate a cycle of victimization and that the responses prevent further incidents. For example, adults tend to think that punishing the bully will stop the bullying, but often the bully only becomes more secretive about the behavior and/or blames the victim for getting him or her in trouble. What often is overlooked is the importance of teaching the bully alternative behaviors for getting his or her needs met, developing empathy, and accepting responsibility for behaviors. Adult responses often reflect blaming victims, which are implicitly and explicitly communicated to all students. Adults' victim blaming has serious consequences, as highlighted by Schwartz and colleagues (this volume), perpetuating the victim's social status and legitimizing the bullying behaviors. These examples underscore the importance of effective adult responses and challenge us to consider the complex nature of adult responses and their potential impact on current and future bullying dynamics.

A recent meta-analysis indicates that anti-bullying programs overall have a small to moderate effect on teachers' responsiveness to bullying as reported by students (van Verseveld, Fukkink, Fekkes, & Oostdam, 2019). However, the study noted a significant variability in effect sizes among eight programs, with one large scale study explaining the significant overall effect. It is possible that the programs do not specifically target teachers' ability to respond to bullying incidents or consider the socialization processes that we highlighted in this chapter. Our review demonstrated the importance of appropriate adult responses in creating classroom climate and developing a class level norm where students are encouraged to stand up and support victims. Beyond addressing a bully's behaviors and supporting a victim, the question of what strategies and approaches promote positive social dynamics and less hierarchical social structure in the classroom deserves careful attention from practitioners and researchers.

Although the socialization processes by parents and teachers are uniquely situated in home and classroom, we recognize tremendous potential for success by the family-school collaboration in all aspects of prevention and intervention efforts. Parents can adapt at home the anti-bullying values and strategies similar to those in the classroom, creating consistency between home and school socialization. Teachers may not be able to directly influence parenting styles, but they can model effective and respectful communication with parents. For example, teachers may notify parents when their child is involved in bullying and arrange a meeting to inform the parents of the actions the school will take. In both the conduct of the meeting and the communication style, the parents may become aware of more effective approaches. Some schools offer parenting classes, in which teachers help parents learn different approaches to their children. In addition to parent/teacher conferences and programs for parents, parents and teachers can collaborate to create a mutual understanding of bullying. If the school has an Advisory Board for their bullying program, the parent who volunteers to serve has an opportunity to voice their ideas and work with school personnel to address the problem. Parents could form relationships with teachers at the beginning of the school year, not in response to problems but to demonstrate their interest in working with the teacher, whether to help with academic issues or to solve bullying problems. Then, should a problem arise, the teacher and parent will have an established collegial relationship.

There is an urgent need for effective programs for parents and teachers that are specifically designed to address the socialization processes in the home and school contexts. Many programs for teachers have focused on increasing their awareness of bullying by highlighting prevalence and harmful effects, yielding disappointing results (e.g., Yoon, Bauman, Choi, & Hutchinson, 2011). We propose that these training programs should promote understanding of social dynamics and interactions with important socializing agents (i.e., parents, teachers, and peers) and help identify strategic approaches to develop and maintain a social climate that deters bullying and encourages prosocial behaviors.

References

Audley-Piotrowski, S., Singer, A., & Patterson, M. (2015). The role of the teacher in children's peer relations: Making the invisible hand intentional.

Translational Issues in Psychological Science, 1(2), 192–200. https://doi.org/10.1037/tps0000038.

Baier, D., Hong, J. S., Kliem, S., & Bergmann, M. C. (2018). Consequences of bullying on adolescents' mental health in Germany: Comparing face-to-face bullying and cyberbullying. *Journal of Child and Family Studies, 28,* 2347–2357. https://doi.org/10.1007/s10826-018-1181-6.

Bandura, A., & Walters, R. H. (1977). *Social learning theory* (vol. 1). Englewood Cliffs, NJ: Prentice-Hall.

Banzon-Librojo, L. A., Garabiles, M. R., & Alampay, L. P. (2017). Relations between harsh discipline from teachers, perceived teacher support, and bullying victimization among high school students. *Journal of Adolescence, 57,* 18–22. https://doi.org/10.1016/j.adolescence.2017.03.001.

Bauman, S., & Del Rio, A. (2005). Knowledge and beliefs about bullying in schools: Comparing pre-service teachers in the United States and the United Kingdom. *School Psychology International, 26,* 428–442. https://doi.org/10.1177/0143034305059019.

Bauman, S., Meter, D. J., Nixon, C., & Davis, S. (2016). Targets of peer mistreatment: Do they tell adults? What happens when they do. *Teaching and Teacher Education, 57,* 118–124. https://doi.org/10.1016/j.tate.2016.03.013.

Baumrind, D. (1971). Current patterns of parental authority. *Developmental Psychology Monographs, 4,* 1–103. https://doi.org/10.1037/h0030372.

Belsky, J. (2002). Developmental origins of attachment styles. *Attachment & Human Development, 4*(2), 166–170. https://doi.org/10.1080/14616730210157510.

Berger, C., Poteat, V. P., & Dantas, J. (2019). Should I report? The role of general and sexual orientation-specific bullying policies and teacher behavior on adolescents' reporting of victimization experiences. *Journal of School Violence, 18,* 107–120. https://doi.org/10.1080/15388220.2017.1387134.

Besag, V. E. (1989). *Bullies and victims in schools.* London: Open University Press.

Bowlby, J. (1969). *Attachment and loss, Vol. 1: Attachment.* New York: Basic Books.

Bradshaw, C. P. (2014). The roles in families in preventing and buffering the effects of bullying. *JAMA Pediatrics, 168,* 991–993. https://doi.org/10.1001/jamapediatrics.2014.1627.

Bradshaw, C. P., Sawyer, A. L., & O'Brennan, L. M. (2007). Bullying and peer victimization at school: Perceptual differences between students and school staff. *School Psychology Review, 36,* 361–382. https://doi.org/10.1080/02796015.2007.12087929.

Brendgen, M., Wanner, B., & Vitaro, F. (2006). Verbal abuse by the teacher and child adjustment from kindergarten through grade 6. *Pediatrics, 117,* 1585–1598. https://doi.org/10.1542/peds.2005-2050.

Brendgen, M., Wanner, B., Vitaro, F., Bukowski, W. M., & Tremblay, R. E. (2007). Verbal abuse by the teacher during childhood and academic, behavioral, and emotional adjustment in young adulthood. *Journal of Educational Psychology, 99*(1), 26–38. https://doi.org/10.1037/0022-0663.99.1.26.

Burger, C., Strohmeier, D., Spröber, N., Bauman, S., & Rigby, K. (2015). How teachers respond to school bullying: An examination of self-reported intervention strategy use, moderator effects, and concurrent use of multiple strategies. *Teaching and Teacher Education, 51,* 191–202. https://doi.org/10.1016/j.tate.2015.07.004.

Casarjian, B. E. (2000). Teacher psychological maltreatment and students' school-related functioning. *Dissertation Abstracts International Section A: Humanities & Social Sciences, 60*(12-A), 4314.

Casas, J. A., Ortega-Ruiz, R., & Del Rey, R. (2015). Bullying: The impact of teacher management and trait emotional intelligence. *British Journal of Educational Psychology, 85,* 407–442. https://doi.org/10.1111/bjep.12082.

Chang, L. (2003). Variable effects of children's aggression, social withdrawal, and prosocial leadership as functions of teacher beliefs and behaviors. *Child Development, 74,* 535–548. https://doi.org/10.1111/1467-8624.7402014.

Crothers, L. M., & Kolbert, J. B. (2008). Comparing middle school teachers' and students' views on bullying and anti-bullying interventions. *Journal of School Violence, 3,* 17–32. https://doi.org/10.1300/J202v03n01_03.

Crothers, L. M., Kolbert, J. B., Berbary, C., Chatlos, S., Lattanzio, L., Tiberi, A., ... Meidl, C. (2017). Teachers', LGBTQ students', and student allies' perceptions of bullying of sexually-diverse youth. *Journal of Aggression, Maltreatment & Trauma, 26,* 972–988. https://doi.org/10.1080/10926771.2017.1344344.

Curtner-Smith, M. E., Smith, P. K., & Porter, M. (2010). Family level perspective on bullies and victims. In E. M. Vernberg & B. K. Biggs (Eds.), *Preventing and treating bullying and victimization* (pp. 75–106). New York: Oxford University Press.

Darling, N. (1999). Parenting style and its correlates. *ERIC Digest (ED427896).* Retrieved from https://files.eric.ed.gov/fulltext/ED427896.pdf.

Dessel, A. B., Kulick, A., Wernick, L. J., & Sullivan, D. (2017). The importance of teacher support: Differential impacts by gender and sexuality. *Journal of Adolescence, 56,* 136–144. https://doi.org/10.1016/2017.02.002.

Doll, B., Song, S., & Siemers, E. (2004). Classroom ecologies that support or discourage bullying. In D. L. Espelage & S. Swearer (Eds.), *Bullying in North American schools* (2nd ed., pp. 161–185). New York: Routledge.

Duncan, R. (2004). The impact of family relationships on school bullies and victims. In D. L. Espelage & S. Swearer (Eds.), *Bullying in American schools: A social-ecological perspective on prevention and intervention* (pp. 227–244). New York: Routledge.

Dunst, C. J., & Kassow, D. Z. (2008). Caregiver sensitivity, contingent social responsiveness, and secure infant attachment. *Journal of Early and Intensive Behavior Intervention, 5,* 40. https://doi.org/10.1037/h0100409.

Elicker, J., Englund, M., & Sroufe, L. A. (1992). Predicting peer competence and peer relationships in childhood from early parent-child relationships. In R. D. Parker & G. W. Ladd (Eds.), *Family-peer relationships: Modes of linkage.* Hillsdale, NJ: Erlbaum.

Ellis, A. A., & Shute, R. (2007). Teacher responses to bullying in relation to moral orientation and seriousness of bullying. *British Journal of Educational Psychology, 77,* 649–663. https://doi.org/10.1348/000709906X163405.

Elsaesser, C., Russell, B., Ohannessian, C. M., & Patton, D. (2017). *Aggression and Violent Behavior, 35,* 62–72. https://doi.org/10.1348/000709906 X163405.

Etzion-Carasso, A., & Oppenheim, D. (2000). Open mother–pre-schooler communication: Relations with early secure attachment. *Attachment & Human Development, 2,* 347–370. https://doi.org/10.1080/146167300100 07914.

Farmer, T. W., Hall, C. M., Petrin, R., Hamm, J. V., & Dadisman, K. (2010). Evaluating the impact of a multicomponent intervention model on teachers' awareness of social networks at the beginning of middle school in rural communities. *School Psychology Quarterly, 25,* 94–106. https://doi.org/10.1037/a0020147.

Finnegan, R. A., Hodges, E. V. E., & Perry, D. G. (1998). Victimization by peers: Association with children's reports of mother-child interaction. *Journal of Personality and Social Psychology, 75,* 1076–1086.

Gage, N. A., Prykanowski, D. A., & Larson, A. (2014). School climate and bullying victimization: A latent class growth model analysis. *School Psychology Quarterly, 29,* 256–271. https://doi.org/10.1037/spq0000064.

Garandeau, C. F., Lee, I. A., & Salmivalli, C. (2014). Inequality matters: Classroom status hierarchy and adolescents' bullying. *Journal of Youth and Adolescence, 43*, 1123–1133. https://doi.org/10.1007/s10964-013-0040-4.

Garandeau, C. F., Vartio, A., Poskiparta, E., & Salmivalli, C. (2016). School bullies' intention to change behavior following teacher interventions: Effects of empathy arousal, condemning of bullying, and blaming of the perpetrator. *Prevention Science, 17*, 1034–1043. https://doi.org/10.1007/s11121-016-0712-x.

Gendron, B. P., Williams, K. R., & Guerra, N. G. (2011). An analysis of bullying among students within schools: Estimating the effects of individual normative beliefs, self-esteem, and school climate. *Journal of School Violence, 10*, 150–164. https://doi.org/10.1080/15388220.2010.539166.

Gest, S. D., & Rodkin, P. C. (2011). Teaching practices and elementary classroom peer ecologies. *Journal of Applied Developmental Psychology, 32*, 288–296. https://doi.org/10.1016/j.appdev.2011.02.004.

Greytak, E. A., Kosciw, J. G., & Boesen, M. J. (2013). Educating the educator: Creating supportive school personnel through professional development. *Journal of School Violence, 12*, 80–97. https://doi.org/10.1080/15388220.2012.731586.

Grusec, J. E., & Hastings, P. D. (2015). *Handbook of socialization: Theory and research* (2nd ed.). New York: Guilford Press.

Hale, R., Fox, C. L., & Murray, M. (2017). "As a parent you become a tiger": Parents talking about bullying at school. *Journal of Child and Family Studies, 26*, 2000–2015. https://doi.org/10.1007/s10826-017-0710-z.

Hamm, J. V., Farmer, T. W., Dadisman, K., Gravelle, M., & Murray, A. R. (2011). Teachers' attunement to students' peer group affiliations as a source of improved student experiences of the school social–affective context following the middle school transition. *Journal of Applied Developmental Psychology, 32*, 267–277. https://doi.org/10.1016/j.appdev.2010.06.003.

Harcourt, S., Jasperse, M., & Green, G. A. (2014). "We were sad and we were angry": A systematic review of parents' perspectives on bullying. *Child & Youth Care Forum, 43*, 373–391. https://doi.org/10.1007/s10566-014-9243-4.

Hatchel, T., Merrin, G. J., & Espelage, D. (2019). Peer victimization and suicidality among LGBTQ youth: The roles of school belonging, self-compassion, and parental support. *Journal of LGBT Youth, 16*, 134–156. https://doi.org/10.1080/19361653.2018.1543036.

Haynie, D. L., Nansel, T., Eitel, P., Crump, A. D., Saylor, K., Yu, K., & Simons-Morton, B. (2001). Bullies, victims, and bully-victims. Distinct groups of at-risk youth. *Journal of Early Adolescence, 21,* 29–49. https://doi.org/10.1177/0272431601021001002.

Hektner, J. M., & Swenson, C. A. (2012). Links from teacher beliefs to peer victimization and bystander intervention: Tests of mediating processes. *The Journal of Early Adolescence, 32,* 516–536. https://doi.org/10.1177/0272431611402502.

Hendrickx, M. M. H. G., Mainhard, T., Boor-Klip, H. J., & Brekelmans, M. (2017). Our teacher likes you, so I like you: A social network approach to social referencing. *Journal of School Psychology, 63,* 35–48. https://doi.org/10.1016/j.jsp.2017.02.004.

Hoffman, A. S., Hamm, J. V., & Farmer, T. W. (2015). Teacher attunement: Supporting early elementary students' social integration and status. *Journal of Applied Developmental Psychology, 39,* 14–23. https://doi.org/10.1016/j.appdev.2015.04.007.

Hong, J. S., & Espelage, D. L. (2012). A review of research on bullying and peer victimization in school: An ecological system analysis. *Aggression and Violent Behavior, 17,* 311–322. https://doi.org/10.1016/j.avb.2012.03.003.

Iurino, C. (2020). Examining adolescents' patterns and predictors of reporting peer victimization. *Doctoral Dissertation.* Tucson, AZ: University of Arizona.

Jungert, T., Piroddi, B., & Thornberg, R. (2016). Early adolescents' motivations to defend victims in school bullying and their perceptions of student–teacher relationships: A self-determination theory approach. *Journal of Adolescence, 53,* 75–90. https://doi.org/10.1016/j.adolescence.2016.09.001.

Kann, L., Olsen, E. O., McManus, T., Harris, W. A., Shanklin, S. L., Flint, K. H., ... Zaza, S. (2016). Sexual identity, sex of sexual contacts, and health-related behaviors among students in grades 9–12—United States and selected sites, 2015. *MMWR Surveillance Summaries, 65,* 1–202. https://doi.org/10.15585/mmwr.ss6509a1.

Khoury-Kassabri, M. (2011). Student victimization by peers in elementary schools: Individual, teacher-class, and school-level predictors. *Child Abuse and Neglect, 35,* 273–282. https://doi.org/10.1016/j.chiabu.2011.01.004.

Klein, J., Cornell, D., & Konold, T. (2012). Relationships between bullying, school climate, and student risk behaviors. *School Psychology Quarterly, 27,* 154–169. https://doi.org/10.1037/a0029350.

Kochenderfer-Ladd, B., & Pelletier, M. (2008). Teachers' views and beliefs about bullying: Influences on classroom management strategies and students' coping with peer victimization. *Journal of School Psychology, 46,* 431–453. https://doi.org/10.1016/j.jsp.2007.07.005.

Kosciw, J. G., Greytak, E. A., Zongrone, A. D., Clark, C. M., & Truong, N. L. (2018). *The 2017 national school climate survey: The experiences of lesbian, gay, bisexual and transgender youth in our nation's schools.* New York: GLSEN.

Kounin, J. (1977). *Discipline and group management in classrooms.* New York: Holt, Rinehart, and Winston.

Ladd, G. W., LeSieur, K., & Profilet, S. M. (1993). Direct parental influences on young children's peer relations. In T. S. Duck (Ed.), *Learning about relationships* (Vol. 2, pp. 152–183). London: Sage.

Larrañaga, E., Yubero, S., & Navarro, R. (2018). Parents' responses to coping with bullying: Variations by adolescents' self-reported victimization and parents' awareness of bullying involvement. *Social Sciences, 7,* 1–11. https://doi.org/10.3390/socsci7080121.

Lereya, S. T., Samara, M., & Wolke, D. (2013). Parenting behavior and the risk of becoming a victim and a bully/victim: A meta-analysis study. *Child Abuse and Neglect, 37,* 1091–1108. https://doi.org/10.1016/j.chiabu.2013.03.001.

Luckner, A. E., & Pianta, R. C. (2011). Teacher–student interactions in fifth grade classrooms: Relations with children's peer behavior. *Journal of Applied Developmental Psychology, 32,* 257–266. https://doi.org/10.1016/j.appdev.2011.02.010.

Marachi, R., Astor, R. A., & Benbenishty, R. (2007). Effects of teacher avoidance of school policies on student victimization. *School Psychology International, 28,* 501–518. https://doi.org/10.1177/0143034307084138.

McCallum, R. S., & Bracken, B. A. (1993). Interpersonal relations between school children and their peers, parents, and teachers. *Educational Psychology Review, 5,* 155–176.

McDowell, D. J., & Parke, R. D. (2009). Parental correlates of children's peer relations: An empirical test of a tripartite model. *Developmental Psychology, 45,* 224–235. https://doi.org/10.1037/a0014305.

McEvoy, A. (2005). *Teachers who bully students: Patterns and policy implications.* Retrieved August 14, 2019, from http://www.stopbullyingnow.com/teachers%20who%20bully%20students%20McEvoy.pdf.

Mercer, S. H., & DeRosier, M. (2008). A prospective investigation of teacher preference and children's perceptions of the student-teacher relationship. *Psychology in the Schools, 47,* 184–192. https://doi.org/10.1002/pits.20463.

Merritt, E. G., Wanless, S. B., Rimm-Kaufman, S. E., Cameron, C., & Peugh, J. L. (2012). The contribution of teachers' emotional support to children's social behaviors and self-regulatory skills in first grade. *School Psychology Review, 41,* 141–159. https://doi.org/10.1080/02796015.2012.12087517.

Mucherah, W., Finch, H., White, T., & Thomas, K. (2018). The relationship of school climate, teacher defending and friends on students' perceptions of bullying in high school. *Journal of Adolescence, 62,* 128–139. https://doi.org/10.1016/j.adolescence.2017.11.012.

Nappa, M., Palladino, B., Menesini, E., & Baiocco, R. (2018). Teachers' reaction in homophobic bullying incidents: The role of self-efficacy and homophobic attitudes. *Sexuality Research and Social Policy, 15,* 208–218. https://doi.org/10.1007/s13178-017-0306-9.

National Institute of Child Health and Human Development Early Child Care Research Network. (2002). The relation of global first-grade classroom environment to structural classroom features and teacher and student behaviors. *The Elementary School Journal, 102,* 367–387. https://doi.org/10.1086/499709.

Nickerson, A. B., Mele, D., & Osborne-Oliver, K. M. (2010). Parent-child relationships and bullying. In S. R. Jimerson, S. M. Swearer, & D. L. Espelage (Eds.), *Handbook of bullying in schools: An international perspective* (pp. 187–198). Routledge. https://doi.org/10.4324/9780203864968.

Nocentini, A., Fiorentini, G., DePaola, L., & Menesini, E. (2019). Parents, family characteristics and bullying behavior: A systematic review. *Aggression and Violent Behavior, 45,* 41–50. https://doi.org/10.1016/j.avb.2018.07.010.

Oldenburg, B., van Duijn, M., Sentse, M., Huitsing, G., van der Ploeg, R., Salmivalli, C., & Veenstra, R. (2015). Teacher characteristics and peer victimization in elementary schools: A classroom-level perspective. *Journal of Abnormal Child Psychology, 43,* 33–44. https://doi.org/10.1007/s10802-013-9847-4.

Olweus, D. (1980). Familial and temperamental determinants of aggressive behavior in adolescent boys: A causal analysis. *Developmental Psychology, 16*(6), 644–660.

Poteat, V. P., Mereish, E. H., DiGiovanni, C. D., & Koenig, B. W. (2011). The effects of general and homophobic victimization on adolescents' psychosocial and educational concerns: The importance of intersecting identities and parent support. *Journal of Counseling Psychology, 58,* 597–609. https://doi.org/10.1037/a0025095.

Reis, J., Trockel, M., & Mulhall, P. (2007). Individual and school predictors of middle school aggression. *Youth Society, 38,* 322–347. https://doi.org/10.1177/0044118X06287688.

Rigby, K., & Bauman, S. (2010). How school personnel tackle cases of bullying. In S. R. Jimerson, S. M. Swearer, & D. L. Espelage (Eds.), *Handbook of bullying in schools: An international perspective* (pp. 455–468). New York: Routledge.

Rodkin, P. C., & Gest, S. D. (2010). Teaching practices, classroom peer ecology, and bullying behaviors among school children. In D. L. Espelage & S. Swearer (Eds.), *Bullying in North American Schools* (2nd ed., pp. 75–90). New York, NY: Routledge.

Rodkin, P. C., & Hodges, E. V. E. (2003). Bullies and victims in the peer ecology: Four questions for psychologists and school professionals. *School Psychology Review, 32,* 384–400.

Roland, E., & Galloway, D. (2002). Classroom influences on bullying. *Educational Research, 44,* 299–312. https://doi.org/10.1080/0013188022000031597.

Saarento, S., & Salmivalli, C. (2015). The role of classroom peer ecology and bystanders' responses in bullying. *Child Development Perspectives, 9,* 201–205. https://doi.org/10.1111/cdep.12140.

Salmivalli, C., Lagerspetz, K., Björkqvist, K., Österman, K., & Kaukiainen, A. (1996). Bullying as a group process: Participant roles and their relations to social status within the group. *Aggressive Behavior, 22,* 1–15.

Sears, R. R., Maccoby, E. E., & Levin, H. (1957). *Patterns of child rearing.* Evanston: Row, Peterson & Co.

Seidel, A., & Oertel, L. (2017). A categoriztion intervention forms and goals. In L. Bilz, W. Schubarth, I. Dudziak, S. Fischer, S. Niproschke, & J. Ulbricht (Eds.), *Gewalt und Mobbing an Schulen. Wie sich Gewalt und Mobbing entwickelt haben, wie Lehrer intervenieren und welche Kompetenzen sie brauchen* (pp. 13–25). Bad Heilbrunn, Germany: Klinkardt.

Sentse, M., Veenstra, R., Kiuru, N., & Salmivalli, C. (2015). A longitudinal multilevel study of individual characteristics and classroom norms in explaining bullying behaviors. *Journal of Abnormal Child Psychology, 43,* 943–955. https://doi.org/10.1007/s10802-014-9949-7.

Serdiouk, M., Rodkin, P., Madill, R., Logis, H., & Gest, S. (2015). Rejection and victimization among elementary school children: The buffering role of classroom-level predictors. *Journal of Abnormal Child Psychology, 43,* 5–17. https://doi.org/10.1007/s10802-013-9826-9.

Smith, P. K. (2014). *Understanding school bullying.* London: Sage.

Snapp, S. D., Watson, R. J., Russell, S. T., Diaz, R. M., & Ryan, C. (2015). Social support networks for LGBT young adults: Low cost strategies for positive adjustment. *Family Relations: An Interdisciplinary Journal of Applied Family Studies, 64,* 420–430. https://doi.org/10.1111/fare.12124.

Swanson, K., & Gettinger, M. (2016). Teachers' knowledge, attitudes, and supportive behaviors toward LGBT students: Relationship to gay-straight alliances, antibullying policy, and teacher training. *Journal of LGBT Youth, 13,* 326–351. https://doi.org/10.1080/19361653.2016.1185765.

Swearer, S. M., & Espelage, D. L. (2004). Introduction: A social-ecological framework of bullying among youth. In D. L. Espelage & S. Swearer (Eds.), *Bullying in North American schools* (2nd ed., pp. 1–14). New York: Routledge. https://doi.org/10.4324/9781410609700.

Taylor, A. R. (1989). Predictors of peer rejection in early elementary grades: Roles of problem behavior, academic achievement, and teacher preference. *Journal of Clinical Child Psychology, 18,* 360–365.

Toomey, R. B., McGuire, J. K., & Russell, S. T. (2012). Heteronormativity, school climates, and perceived safety for gender nonconforming peers. *Journal of Adolescence, 35,* 187–196. https://doi.org/10.1016/j.adolescence.2011.03.001.

Toomey, R. B., & Russell, S. T. (2016). The role of sexual orientation in school-Based victimization: A meta-analysis. *Youth & Society, 48*(2), 176–201. https://doi.org/10.1177/0044118X13483778.

Troop-Gordon, W., & Ladd, G. W. (2015). Teachers' victimization-related beliefs and strategies: Associations with students' aggressive behavior and peer victimization. *Journal of Abnormal Child Psychology, 43,* 45–60. https://doi.org/10.1007/s10802-013-9840-y.

Twemlow, S. W., Fonagy, P., Sacco, F. C., & Brethour, J. R. (2006). Teachers who bully students: A hidden trauma. *International Journal of Social Psychiatry, 52,* 187–198. https://doi.org/10.1177/0020764006067234.

van Verseveld, M. D. A., Fukkink, R. G., Fekkes, M., & Oostdam, R. J. (2019). Effects of antibullying programs on teachers' interventions in bullying situations: A meta-analysis. *Psychology in Schools,* 1–18. https://doi.org/10.1002/pits.22283.

Veenstra, R., Lindenberg, S., Huitsing, G., Sainio, M., & Salmivalli, C. (2014). The role of teachers in bullying: The relation between antibullying attitudes, efficacy, and efforts to reduce bullying. *Journal of Educational Psychology, 106,* 1135–1143. https://doi.org/10.1037/a0036110.

Waasdorp, T. E., Bradshaw, C. P., & Duong, J. (2011). The link between parents' perceptions of the school and their responses to school bullying: Variation by child characteristics and the forms of victimization. *Journal of Educational Psychology, 103,* 324–335. https://doi.org/10.1037/a0022748.

Wachs, S., Bilz, L., Niproschke, S., & Schubarth, W. (2018). Bullying intervention in schools: A multilevel analysis of teachers' success in handling bullying from the students' perspective. *Journal of Early Adolescence, 39,* 642–668. https://doi.org/10.1177/0272431618780423.

Wentzel, K. R. (2003). Sociometric status and adjustment in middle school: A longitudinal study. *The Journal of Early Adolescence, 23,* 5–28. https://doi.org/10.1177/0272431602239128.

White, K. J., Sherman, M. D., & Jones, K. (1996). Children's perceptions of behavior problem peers: Effects of teacher feedback and peer reputed status. *Journal of School Psychology, 34,* 53–72. https://doi.org/10.1016/0022-4405(95)00025-9.

Yeung, R., & Leadbearer, B. (2010). Adults make a difference: The protective effects of parent and teacher emotional support on emotional and behavioral problems of peer-victimized adolescents. *Journal of Community Psychology, 38,* 80–98. https://doi.org/10.1002/jcop.20353.

Yoon, J., Bauman, S., Choi, T., & Hutchinson, A. S. (2011). How South Korean teachers handle an incident of school bullying. *School Psychology International, 32,* 312–329. https://doi.org/10.1177/0143034311402311.

Yoon, J., Sulkowski, M. L., & Bauman, S. A. (2016). Teachers' responses to bullying incidents: Effects of teacher characteristics and contexts. *Journal of School Violence, 15,* 91–113. https://doi.org/10.1080/15388220.2014.963592.

Zych, I., Farrington, D. P., & Ttofi, M. M. (2019). Protective factors against bullying and cyberbullying: A systematic review of meta-analyses. *Aggression and Violent Behavior, 45,* 4–19. https://doi.org/10.1016/j.avb.2018.06.008.

8

Bullying Through the Eyes of the Peer Group: Lessons Learned Through Multiple Vantage Points

Lisa H. Rosen, Shannon R. Scott, Samuel Y. Kim, and Meredith G. Higgins

As discussed throughout the text, systematic research on school bullying began in the 1970s (Smith, 2011), and the focus of this early work was largely centered on the bully and the victim (Salmivalli & Voeten, 2004; Sutton & Smith, 1999). The pioneering work of Christina Salmivalli framed bullying as a group process, which shifted attention beyond the bully-victim dyad (Bauman, 2010; Salmivalli, 1999, 2010). In 1996, Salmivalli and her colleagues at the University of Turku in Finland first proposed six different participant roles: bully, assistant, reinforcer, outsider, defender, and victim (Salmivalli, Lagerspetz, Björkqvist, Österman, & Kaukiainen, 1996). Since this seminal study, the view of

L. H. Rosen (✉) · S. R. Scott · S. Y. Kim · M. G. Higgins
Psychology and Philosophy, Texas Woman's University, Denton, TX, USA
e-mail: LRosen@twu.edu

S. R. Scott
e-mail: sscott@twu.edu

S. Y. Kim
e-mail: skim18@twu.edu

bullying as a group process has been widely adopted, and researchers have begun to focus on the different roles bystanders play in school bullying (Salmivalli & Voeten, 2004; Smokowski & Evans, 2019). Still, some roles such as the bully, defender, and victim have received more research attention whereas less is known about the roles of the assistant, reinforcer, and outsider. The overarching goal of this book was to synthesize this growing body of research to provide a comprehensive overview of each participant role as well as to emphasize the potential of teachers and parents to influence the peer ecology and dynamics of bullying.

Although research on participant roles has increased, many bullying prevention and intervention programs have overlooked the potential powerful role that bystanders can play in reducing bullying (Polanin, Espelage, & Pigott, 2012; Ross, Lund, Sabey, & Charlton, 2017). This lack of attention to bystanders in prevention and intervention programming is concerning because focusing only on the behavior of the bully or the victim is unlikely to have long-lasting effects (Bauman, 2010; Sutton & Smith, 1999). Bullying most often unfolds in front of an audience; peers are present for 85–88% of bullying episodes (Craig & Pepler, 1997; Hawkins, Pepler, & Craig, 2001). Bystanders can reinforce the bully by their mere presence or through active engagement, and there is a positive association between the duration of bullying episodes and the number of bystanders present (O'Connell, Pepler, & Craig, 1999). Bystander intervention may be relatively rare with peers intervening in less than 20% of all bullying episodes (Craig & Pepler, 1997; Hawkins et al., 2001). However, when peers do intervene, this is often an incredibly quick and successful deterrent to bullying; 57% of episodes of bullying halt within 10 seconds following peer intervention (Hawkins et al., 2001). Support from the bystander may serve a protective role even if the bullying does not immediately end. Salmivalli and colleagues suggest that "even if the change in bystanders' behavior would not lead (at least immediately) to changes in the bully's behavior, it is very likely to make a difference in the victim's situation" (Salmivalli, Kärnä, & Poskiparta, 2010, p. 445). Thus, bystanders have the potential to better the plight of victimized children by discouraging bullying and demonstrating their support through intervening. Our hope is that this book drew attention to the individual and contextual factors that interact to influence the adoption of each participant role.

In this concluding chapter, our goal is to draw across the different bullying roles presented to offer a road map for bullying prevention and intervention efforts. We first highlight the defining features of each participant role and describe how this approach to viewing bullying as a group process is consistent with the ecological systems framework. As each chapter presented a detailed description of the child-level factors as well as environmental factors that influence the featured participant role, we strive to synthesize this information across participant roles in this concluding chapter. Next, we discuss prevalence rates of the participant roles with attention to gender and development. Focus is then devoted to the associations between participant roles and adjustment. We end with a discussion of how adopting the participant role approach can inform anti-bullying programs and offer suggestions for future directions as the research on peer group influences continues to evolve.

Overview of Participant Roles

In Chapter 2, Mayeux and O'Mealey draw on the classic definition of bullying provided by Olweus (1993). As such, they note that the bully role is characterized by repetitive harm to a less powerful person or persons carried out with intentionality. Mayeux and O'Mealey note that bullying can take numerous forms including physical, verbal, and relational bullying, and that bullying is often targeted at a limited number of particular students. Drawing on the work of Salmivalli (2010), Mayeux and O'Mealey suggest that bullies are most often proactively aggressive, and as such their behavior is not provoked but rather in the purpose of achieving particular goals. Most often that goal is status or a central position in the peer hierarchy, which will be further described below.

In Chapter 3, Monks and O'Toole focus on the pro-bullying roles of assistant and reinforcer, both of which provide some form of social reward to the bully, and as such, encourage the bullying to continue. They describe assistants as students who join in the bullying once the ringleader bully has begun. Monks and O'Toole note that reinforcers also behave in ways that promote bullying but make the distinction that reinforcers do not actively join in on the bullying as do assistants. Rather, reinforcers can provide positive feedback to the bully in a number of ways such as laughing or offering encouraging remarks. Despite this distinction, Monks and O'Toole report that the assistant and reinforcer roles have been found to be highly correlated so that some studies jointly consider these roles under the broader term of "follower" (e.g., Goossens, Olthof, & Dekker, 2006; Pouwels, Lansu, & Cillessen, 2017).

In Chapter 4, Macheck, Bohart, Kincaid, and Hattouni differentiate the outsider role from that of other bystanders who assume either a pro-bullying role (i.e., assistant, reinforcer) or pro-victim role (e.g., defender). Machek and colleagues explain that although outsiders are often aware of bullying, they do not actively take a side when bullying episodes unfold. As such they do not condemn the bullying behavior, which may actually encourage it, as might the peer attention outsiders provide. Machek and colleagues posit that outsiders attempt to physically and emotionally distance themselves from bullying as a form of self-protection or as a result of a skill deficit that affects their ability to intervene. These and other potential correlates of the outsider role are discussed in more detail below.

In Chapter 5, Fredrick, Jenkins, and Dexter describe defenders as bystanders that engage in active and prosocial behavior during bullying episodes. Fredrick and colleagues elaborate that defending can be direct (i.e., bully-oriented) or indirect (i.e., victim-oriented). Direct defending involves active attempts to stop the bully's behavior, and these attempts may be physical or verbal in nature. Conversely, indirect defending is aimed at supporting the victim by providing comfort or offering encouragement to seek adult support. Fredrick and colleagues note that defending may be conceptualized as distinct from more general forms of altruism as there is a risk to intervening in bullying episodes in which the bully has a large amount of power.

In Chapter 6, Schwartz, Mali, and Kelleghan return to Olweus's (1993) definition. In line with this definition, victims lack power and are subject to peer maltreatment on a repeated basis. Schwartz and colleagues wisely caution against viewing victims as a homogeneous group. Further, the victim role is differentiated from all others portrayed in this book as it is the only role that is involuntary in nature. Not only are victims unwilling participants in bullying episodes, but they will also go to great lengths to avoid being bullied.

In Chapter 7, Yoon, Bauman, and Corcoran discuss the role played by adults and highlight the significant influence teachers and parents exert as socializing agents. They assert that teachers and parents are in a position of authority, and as such have the responsibility to keep children safe from bullying. However, Yoon and colleagues suggest that there are important individual differences in how teachers and parents respond to bullying. Yoon and colleagues suggest that adults can also be viewed as bystanders. Some adults may take an outsider role and not intervene in bullying whereas others may act as a defender by disciplining the bully or offering support to the victim.

As discussed throughout the previous chapters, examining different bullying roles and the influence of teachers and parents is in line with the social ecological model of bullying (Espelage, Low, & Jimerson, 2014; Espelage & Swearer, 2009). Bronfenbrenner introduced ecological systems theory, which posits that an individual interacts with different environment systems, and this shapes development (Ettekal & Mahoney, 2017). Environmental systems are nested, moving from the immediate environment (microsystem) to larger societal influences (macrosystem), and these environmental contexts interact. Peers, teachers, and parents are all central influences of the child's microsystem. However, as noted by Yoon and colleagues, it is also important to examine the mesosystem, or connections between microsystems. For instance, family-school collaborations in anti-bullying programs can be utilized to provide consistency between the school and home environments. Numerous illustrations of macrosystem influence are also provided in the preceding chapters. Schwartz and colleagues highlight one such influence; if a characteristic such as academic achievement is viewed negatively in a particular cultural context (or the macrosystem level), this can be associated with victimization in the peer group (or the microsystem level). That is, excelling in academics may be a risk factor for victimization in cultures that view academic achievement negatively, but not in other cultures that value academic achievement. In line with the social ecological model, we seek to synthesize across roles to highlight both child-level and environmental influences that would influence the efficacy of intervention.

Child-Level Factors and Participant Roles

There were several consistent patterns that emerged in the previous chapters regarding child-level correlates of participant roles. Perhaps, most importantly, great attention was devoted to power and status within the peer group across the preceding chapters. We highlight the role of social status as well as other child-level factors that were prominently featured including anti-bullying attitudes, emotion and empathy, moral disengagement, and self-efficacy with attention to implications for bullying prevention and intervention efforts.

Social Status

Bullying behavior is often motivated by the desire to increase one's status in the peer group (Salmivalli, 2010). In the vast majority of instances, bullying unfolds in front of an audience, and as such, can be seen as "an effective way to show one's might" (Juvonen & Galván, 2009, p. 301). Although bullies may be disliked by some peers, this type of behavior may be considered "cool" as bullies are commonly viewed as popular by their peers (Rodkin, 2004; Salmivalli, 2010; Sentse, Veenstra, Kiuru, & Salmivalli, 2015). Additionally, bullies are often highly visible, hold a central position in the peer group, and have large peer networks (Huitsing & Veenstra, 2012; Salmivalli, Huttunen, & Lagerspetz, 1997). Bullies may gain a socially dominant position by employing both aggressive tactics as well as prosocial strategies to reach their status goal. That is, bullies are what Hawley and colleagues refer to as bistrategic controllers, combining prosocial and coercive strategies to maximize their control of resources (i.e., popularity and social dominance; Hawley, Little, & Card, 2007). Furthermore, bullies often possess peer valued characteristics (e.g., attractive appearance, athletic competence) that may increase their social power and popularity (Pouwels, Lansu, & Cillessen, 2016; Vaillancourt, Hymel, & McDougall, 2003).

Whereas bullies have the highest status, the victim role is associated with the lowest social standing (Pouwels et al., 2016; Rambaran, Dijkstra, & Veenstra, 2019). Bullies select targets with low status, who are often rejected by their peers and are perceived as unpopular. Low status targets are unlikely to be able to successfully retaliate (Juvonen & Galván, 2009; Menesini & Salmivalli, 2017; Salmivalli, 2010). Those who assume follower roles may be trying to raise their social status by affiliating with high status bullies while distancing themselves from low status victims (Juvonen & Galván, 2009; Pouwels et al., 2017). Correspondingly, assistants and reinforcers are rated as only slightly less popular than bullies (Pouwels et al., 2016). Although their behavior is dramatically different from bullies and followers, defenders often have high status. Generally, defenders are well-liked and perceived as popular by the peer group (Lambe, Cioppa, Hong, & Craig, 2019). These status considerations hold important implications for prevention and intervention efforts because as Salmivalli (2010) notes "it is the group that assigns status to its members, so the bullies are dependent on the peer group in the realization of their status goal" (p. 113). As such, bullies are unlikely to change their behavior if it is resulting in their high status (Saarento & Salmivalli, 2015).

Anti-bullying Attitudes

Many of the preceding chapters also addressed anti-bullying attitudes. Higher levels of anti-bullying attitudes are associated with greater likelihood of assuming the defender role whereas lower levels of anti-bullying are associated with pro-bullying roles (Menesini & Salmivalli, 2017; Salmivalli, 2010; Salmivalli & Voeten, 2004). Increases in anti-bullying attitudes have been identified as one mediating mechanism that explains the success of intervention programs in reducing bullying perpetration (Saarento, Boulton, & Salmivalli, 2015).

However, it has been suggested that the association between personal anti-bullying attitudes and behavior is modest (Salmivalli & Voeten,

2004). The majority of students actually endorse anti-bullying attitudes (Pouwels et al., 2017); over 80% of students indicate wanting someone to stand up for the victim (Rigby & Slee, 1991). Salmivalli and Voeten (2004) describe this as an "interesting paradox" in that "Most students believe that bullying is wrong, and they think that one should try to help the victims. Nevertheless, most students do not express their disapproval to peers who bully, and actually do nothing to intervene or support the victim" (p. 247). This paradox may be the result of pluralistic ignorance or differences between private attitudes and group norms. Juvonen and Galván (2009) postulate that bystanders believe that their peers approve of bullying because public challenge to bullying is so rare. Based on these findings, addressing anti-bullying attitudes may be a necessary but not sufficient component of prevention and intervention efforts as many students already hold anti-bullying attitudes (Pouwels et al., 2017; Salmivalli & Voeten, 2004). In particular, it may be necessary to also equip bystanders with the tools that will enable them to successfully defend victimized peers and promote awareness that the majority of students hold anti-bullying views (Salmivalli, 2010).

Emotional Correlates

Throughout the preceding chapters, several different aspects of emotion processing were discussed in relation to bullying roles. To synthesize this information, we discuss emotions provoked during bullying episodes, the ability to detect others' emotions, and the ability to empathize with the feelings of others. Emotional responses to bullying episodes may influence behavior. Children who are saddened by witnessing bullying may be more likely to engage in defending behavior whereas children who cope by distancing may be more likely to behave as an outsider (Ettekal, Kochenderfer-Ladd, & Ladd, 2015; Lambe et al., 2019; Pozzoli & Gini, 2010). Still, some children might find witnessing bullying to be exciting, which could lead them to assume a follower role (Ettekal et al., 2015). In addition, feelings of guilt have been found to be positively related to defending but negatively related to bullying (Lambe et al., 2019; Mazzone, Camodeca, & Salmivalli, 2016). Interestingly, both Monks and O'Toole as well as Machek and colleagues highlighted the potential of fear to influence the behavior of assistants, reinforcers, and outsiders. Those who worry about becoming future victims may respond by joining forces with the bully or by attempting to avoid the situation in the hopes of self-protection (Juvonen & Galván, 2009).

In addition to one's own emotional response, examining how students understand others emotions' and respond empathically can inform the participant role approach to bullying. The extent to which children understand others' feelings is referred to as cognitive empathy whereas the extent to which children share in others' feelings is referred to as affective empathy, and both constructs have been examined in relation to bullying roles (Ettekal et al., 2015; Lambe et al., 2019; Pöyhönen, Juvonen, & Salmivalli, 2010). There has been disagreement as to whether bullies demonstrate a deficit in cognitive empathy with some researchers speculating that bullies may continue to aggress against victims because they are unaware of the distress that results from their actions. Still others suggest that bullies do not target their peers indiscriminately, but rather detect fear in their victims, which leads to the victim being perceived as more vulnerable (Ettekal et al., 2015). Although bullies may be able to detect others' emotional states, it has been suggested that they demonstrate deficits in affective empathy.

Cognitive empathy and affective empathy are both positively associated with defending. However, the association may be particularly strong for affective empathy and defending (Ettekal et al., 2015; Lambe et al., 2019; Peets, Pöyhönen, Juvonen, & Salmivalli, 2015; Pöyhönen et al., 2010). In line with these findings, interventions designed to reduce bullying and promote defending often include activities designed to evoke empathy for victims of bullying (Salmivalli et al., 2014; Twemlow et al., 2010). Although these activities may be helpful, it is critical to consider how child-level factors interact with environmental factors. Social status may moderate the association between affective empathy and defending; affective empathy is only linked to acting as a defender for popular youth (Pöyhönen et al., 2010), which points to the importance of anti-bullying efforts considering the complex implications of social status (Salmivalli et al., 2010).

Moral Disengagement

Bullying has long been framed as an issue of morality and human rights (Ettekal et al., 2015; Smith, 2011). Although bullies may understand that their behavior is hurtful, they may use moral disengagement to justify their conduct and minimize feelings of guilt. There are different cognitive mechanisms that may allow for bullies to engage in moral disengagement to rationalize their behavior including making moral justifications for the bullying, labeling the bullying as a more positive form of behavior like joking, making favorable comparisons that suggest their behavior is not really that bad, and blaming the victim (Ettekal et al., 2015; Levasseur, Desbiens, & Bowen, 2017).

In addition to its association with the bullying role, moral disengagement is associated with different forms of bystander behavior. Higher levels of moral disengagement are associated with outsider behavior. Followers also engage in higher levels of moral disengagement, and might be especially likely to employ euphemistic labeling suggesting that the bullying is really just a joke. They may also minimize the role they are playing in bullying dynamics due to higher levels of moral disengagement (Ettekal et al., 2015). Conversely, defenders show lower levels of moral disengagement (Lambe et al., 2019; Levasseur et al., 2017). Given the associations between moral disengagement and bullying behaviors, intervention and prevention programs could benefit from including components focused on moral reasoning. Specifically, anti-bullying efforts might benefit from raising awareness of the mechanisms that allow for moral disengagement in bullying episodes (Levasseur et al., 2017). Programs could do so by including opportunities for self-reflection during which students consider their own behavior as well as activities that encourage taking the perspective of the victim. Through such exercises, programs may highlight the value of supporting the victim and foster a sense of responsibility in bystanders to intervene when bullying unfolds around them (Pöyhönen, Juvonen, & Salmivalli, 2012; Salmivalli, 1999).

Self-Efficacy

Examining varying levels of self-efficacy among the different participant roles holds important implications for bystander intervention programs. Those who are confident in their ability to defend are more likely to intervene in bullying episodes (Lambe et al., 2019). In particular, Fredrick and colleagues (this volume) suggest self-efficacy may be more important for direct forms of defending such as confronting the bully than for indirect forms of defending such as comforting the victim. As Machek and colleagues (this volume) note, outsiders may hold negative self-views and perceive themselves as having physical and social forms of weakness that could prevent them from effectively intervening.

As a result of these consistent associations between self-efficacy and defending, many anti-bullying programs teach strategies for intervening (Gaffney, Farrington, & Ttofi, 2019a; Salmivalli, 1999; Salmivalli et al., 2010). Students may be able to practice these strategies through role-playing and other activities. As mastery experience promotes self-efficacy, providing multiple opportunities to rehearse these strategies may be needed (Bandura, 1994). Throughout this text, contributors have emphasized the importance of examining how child-level correlates interact with social factors. Social status has been proposed as a moderator of the association between self-efficacy and defending behavior in that self-efficacy may only predict defending for bystanders with at least medium levels of social status (Pöyhönen et al., 2010). Thus, defending may not always be an effective option for all students. Lambe and colleagues (2019) caution that "the defending strategy that works for one youth in one context may be ineffective (or even harmful) for another youth in another context" (p. 71). Given this, attention is needed to teaching a wide range of intervention strategies and promoting safe practices for defending taking into account the variability in children's characteristics and context.

Environmental Factors and Participant Roles

In line with the social ecological model of bullying (Espelage et al., 2014; Espelage & Swearer, 2009), contributors emphasized the role of environmental factors on participant roles throughout the preceding chapters. As such, contributors urged looking beyond child-level factors to consider contextual factors as well as the interaction between child-level and contextual factors. As was true for child-level factors, there were several consistent patterns that emerged in the previous chapters regarding contextual influences on participant roles. Drawing across chapters, we highlight the influence of peer groups, teachers and school, and parents on participant roles.

Peer Group Influences

The peer group exerts tremendous influence on bullying dynamics, and this is the key feature of the participant roles approach highlighted throughout the preceding chapters. When the peer group disapproves of bullying and there are consequences for bullying, this behavior decreases (Ettekal et al., 2015). Although peers can support bullying, they can also encourage defending. When there is perceived pressure to defend, bystanders are more likely to intervene (Ettekal et al., 2015; Lambe et al., 2019).

Moving focus to one's friendship group, children may befriend peers with similar participant roles (Huitsing & Veenstra, 2012; Rambaran et al., 2019; Salmivalli, 2010; Salmivalli et al., 1997). Friendship groups tend to consist of peers with similar roles such that some groups may be pro-bullying and others prosocial. This may be a result of selection effects in which children become friends with those who are similar to them (Bukowski, Buhrmester, & Underwood, 2011; Rambaran et al., 2019). However, it is likely that socialization effects are also at play (Bukowski et al., 2011; Rambaran et al., 2019; Salmivalli, 2010). Peer groups comprised of bullies, assistants, and reinforcers may encourage bullying behavior in their members. Through the process of deviancy training, group members may verbally and nonverbally reinforce the antisocial behavior of its members (Dishion, 2000; Salmivalli, 2010; Underwood, 2011). Conversely, peer groups of defenders may encourage defending behavior in its members (Lambe et al., 2019; Salmivalli, 2010).

Emotional ties to peers also influence bullying behavior (Ettekal et al., 2015). Children are more likely to defend a friend or someone that they like (Ettekal et al., 2015; Lambe et al., 2019). Conversely, children are more likely to bully someone that they do not like (Ettekal et al., 2015).

Changing peer influences and rewards for bullying is a critical component of bullying prevention and intervention programs (Salmivalli et al., 2014; Twemlow et al., 2010). This is clearly exemplified by the claim that "if the motivation to bully is related to one's social standing in the group, then the group is in the key role of regulating bullying among its members" (Salmivalli et al., 2010, p. 445). Accordingly, programs that target bystanders may offer the most promise for combatting bullying by raising awareness about the role of the peer group (Salmivalli & Voeten, 2004; Twemlow et al., 2010). The efficacy of programs may be further bolstered if teachers and school staff consider the social networks at play (Huitsing & Veenstra, 2012). For instance, teachers may be able to connect victimized youth with popular, prosocial youth who can be an important source of support (Salmivalli et al., 2014).

Classroom and School Influences

As the majority of bullying episodes occur at school (Turner, Finkelhor, Hamby, Shattuck, & Ormrod, 2011), it is critical to examine classroom and school-level influences on participant roles. We first discuss classroom-level influences, and then turn to school-level influences that also clearly affect classroom dynamics. There is wide variability in classroom bullying norms (Peets et al., 2015; Salmivalli & Voeten, 2004; Sentse et al., 2015). Descriptive norms refer to how other students in the class behave. When classes have high levels of reinforcing and low levels of defending, bullying is more likely (Lambe et al., 2019; Menesini & Salmivalli, 2017). Similarly, when classes have high rates of bullying, there tends to be low levels of defending (Peets et al., 2015). Collective bullying attitudes, or how the peer group perceives the acceptability of bullying, also has an effect on bystander behavior. Bully and follower behaviors are more likely while defending behavior is less likely when classes have high levels of pro-bullying attitudes (Ettekal et al., 2015; Salmivalli & Voeten, 2004). In addition, social prestige norms influence bullying dynamics. When social rewards are believed to be associated with bullying and bullies have high status in the classroom, there tends to be higher rates of bullying and lower levels of defending (Peets et al., 2015; Saarento & Salmivalli, 2015).

Further, bullying is more likely in classes that have greater levels of status hierarchy (Garandeau, Lee, & Salmivalli, 2014a; Menesini & Salmivalli, 2017). Status inequality is more pronounced in classes that are more hierarchical in their organization, with some students having extremely high status and other students having extremely low status. As bullying involves an imbalance of power, it is more likely to occur in classes that have greater variability in status. Moreover, status is accompanied by social rewards and those who have high status may bully in order to maintain their social position (Garandeau, Lee et al., 2014a). Teachers can influence the social dynamics of their class in important ways and work to decrease status hierarchies. For instance, teachers can foster more egalitarian classes by using small groups to promote friendships, orchestrating where students sit, and recognizing lower status students (Garandeau, Lee et al., 2014a).

Yoon and colleagues provide an excellent review of teacher-level influences in Chapter 7. Of particular note, strong classroom management and concern for students is associated with lower levels of bullying. However, there is considerable variability in how teachers address bullying, and this is likely a result of teachers' differing attitudes toward bullying (DeOrnellas & Spurgin, 2017). As Yoon and colleagues (this volume) report, the manner in which teachers respond to bullying can either increase or decrease occurrences of bullying. Some teachers are dismissive and ignore bullying. In fact, teachers may only intervene in 25% of bullying episodes that occur in their close proximity (Craig & Pepler, 1997). Regrettably, teachers' failure to respond is associated with higher rates of bullying.

Conversely, bullying levels decrease and defending levels increase both when teachers are dedicated to addressing bullying and students perceive them as effective in this endeavor (Espelage & Swearer, 2009; Veenstra, Lindenberg, Huitsing, Sainio, & Salmivalli, 2014). Fortunately, Yoon and colleagues (this volume) offer guidance on best practices for teacher intervention. Interestingly, reaching out to parents does not appear to decrease bullying. Similarly, simply reprimanding the bully does not appear to be an effective strategy and may actually encourage more secretive bullying behavior. Rather, Yoon and colleagues suggest that teachers draw attention to how the victims feel and express disapproval for the bully's behavior.

Based on these findings, effective prevention and intervention programs often include training for teachers (Ttofi & Farrington, 2011). Such training may be especially important because if students believe that teachers hold strong anti-bullying views and will effectively intervene in bullying episodes, students may be more likely to report when they are victimized (Blomqvist, Saarento-Zaprudin, & Salmivalli, 2019; Shaw et al., 2019). Another important consideration is that teachers often are the ones to implement bullying prevention and intervention programs. However, teachers differ in the effort applied and the extent to which they implement programs with fidelity (Haataja et al., 2014). Factors such as self-efficacy for implementing the program as well as burnout may influence teachers' likelihood for fully implementing an anti-bullying program (Ettekal et al., 2015; Swift et al., 2017). Thus, continued training and support throughout the academic year may be needed to assist teachers in leading intervention efforts.

Yoon and colleagues (this volume) note that teachers are largely affected by the school climate. Cohen and colleagues describe school climate as "based on patterns of people's experience of school life and reflects norms, goals, values, interpersonal relationships, teaching, learning, leadership practices, and organizational structures" (Cohen, Espelage, Berkowitz, Twemlow, & Comer, 2015, p. 8). Disciplinary structure and support of students are two key features of a school's climate. The most effective school climate may be an authoritative one, in which students know rules will be enforced but that they are supported by teachers and staff (Konold et al., 2014). School administrators, counselors, teachers, and other members of the school staff can contribute to a positive school climate, which will help deter bullying and increase defending (Rosen, DeOrnellas, & Scott, 2017).

Parental Influences

Parents are also important socializing agents who influence children's peer relations at school. Although the role of parents in bullying dynamics was a focal point of Chapter 7, many contributors discussed parental influences. For instance, parents can encourage their children to act as defenders and discourage outsider behavior. Further, high levels of parental support can help children engage in defending behavior (Lambe et al., 2019). However, the majority of research has focused on parenting in relation to bullying perpetration and victimization (Nickerson, Mele, & Osborne-Oliver, 2010). Yoon and colleagues (this volume) provide a thorough review of parent-child relationships. Here we highlight some of the key points they raised, as the home environment is a critical component of the social ecological model of bullying (Espelage & Swearer, 2009).

Parental influences on peer relationships begin in the first year of life (Nickerson et al., 2010). Yoon and colleagues (this volume) report that insecure attachment has been linked to bullying perpetration. Children with insecure attachment may come to expect others to behave inconsistently and insensitively as did their primary caregivers (Espelage & Swearer, 2009). Yoon and colleagues (this volume) also note that parenting styles have been linked to bullying involvement, with both authoritarian and permissive parenting styles serving as risk factors for aggression. If parents use harsh discipline at home, children may learn to behave aggressively via social learning mechanisms. Further, bullying is often associated with a lack of parental monitoring (see also Nickerson et al., 2010).

Drawing on family systems theory, Yoon and colleagues (this volume) suggest that there are different risk factors for victimization for boys and girls. Enmeshed family dynamics may predict victimization for boys. Being overly close to their mothers can negatively affect self-confidence and slow gains in independence. In turn, this may reduce the boys' ability to assert themselves (Espelage & Swearer, 2009). Girls who are treated in hostile ways by their parents may fear rejection, which may lead to depression and feelings of helplessness, putting girls at greater risk for victimization (Espelage & Swearer, 2009; Nickerson et al., 2010). Conversely, parental support can serve as a protective factor for victimized youth (Nickerson et al., 2010).

Given these associations, successful anti-bullying programs often involve parents in some way (Ttofi & Farrington, 2011). Importantly, positive forms of parenting (e.g., warmth, open communication) have been associated with lower levels of perpetration and victimization. Yoon and colleagues emphasize the importance of involving parents and promoting their communication with teachers. Interventions can promote parental monitoring, which may help decrease bullying (Holden, Vittrup, & Rosen, 2011; Nickerson et al., 2010). Parents of victims can help in a number of ways, including working with their children on assertive and constructive ways to respond to bullying as well as assisting their children in seeking peer support (Nickerson et al., 2010). Although interventions focused only on the family are unlikely to be effective, bullying prevention and intervention programs benefit from involving parents (Ttofi & Farrington, 2011).

Prevalence of Roles

Having discussed child-level and environmental factors that affect participant roles, we now turn our attention to prevalence. As noted by many contributors, there is a great degree of variability in reported prevalence rates for reasons such as measurement tools and age of the sample (Cook, Williams, Guerra, Kim, & Sadek, 2010; Hymel & Swearer, 2015). As did many of the contributors to this book, we turn to the original study that identified participant roles in Finnish sixth grade students. Looking at prevalence, Salmivalli et al. (1996) found that outsider was the most common role (23.7%) followed by reinforcer (19.5%) and defender (17.3%). Victims (11.7%), bullies (8.2%), and assistants (6.8%) were less common, and 12.7% of students were not assigned a role.

Gender and Participant Roles

Although boys and girls are represented in all participant roles, the text highlights various gender differences that have been found. Boys are more likely to assume the roles of bully, assistant, and reinforcer. Conversely, girls are more likely to take on the role of defender and outsider (Salmivalli et al., 1996; Salmivalli, Lappalainen, & Lagerspetz, 1998). As Schwartz and colleagues (this volume) note, gender differences in the victim role are less clear, especially when considering diverse forms of bullying. These differences are likely a result of boys and girls being socialized differently. Aggression is often considered less appropriate for girls as they are expected to be more caring and nurturing than boys (Rosen & Rubin, 2016; Underwood & Rosen, 2011).

Developmental Considerations and Stability

As noted throughout the text, there appears to be moderate stability in participant roles. Although Salmivalli et al. (1998) reported moderate stability, they also found that the bully role demonstrated greater stability in boys, whereas the defender role showed greater stability in girls. Macheck and colleagues suggest that there may be more fluidity in some roles (e.g., outsider), and that youth can transition to other participant roles (Boulton & Smith, 1994; Zych et al., 2018).

In addition to examining stability, attention was drawn in the preceding chapters to important developmental changes that hold implications for bullying dynamics. Although the majority of research has focused on middle childhood and beyond, participant roles have been examined during the preschool years (Camodeca & Coppola, 2016; Monks, Smith, & Swettenham, 2003). The prevalence rates in preschool are quite different from what Salmivalli et al. (1996) and others found with older sixth grade students. Based on peer reports, preschoolers were classified as follows: bullies (26.1%), victims (24.5%), defenders (22.2%), outsiders (12.6%), reinforcers (7.4%), and assistants (7.2%; Monks et al., 2003). Monks and colleagues (this volume) suggest that the assistant and follower roles are less pronounced during early childhood and increase in prevalence as social hierarchy grows in importance. This work with preschoolers points to the importance of beginning anti-bullying efforts at a young age.

Certain forms of participant role behavior become either more or less common with the transition to adolescence. Pro-bullying behavior becomes more prevalent while defending becomes less frequent (Lambe et al., 2019; Pouwels, van Noorden, Lansu, & Cillessen, 2018b). Interestingly, there are also changes in how the participant roles relate to social status, with bullies and followers being rated as more popular in secondary school than primary school (Pouwels, van Noorden et al., 2018b).

Helping to explain these findings are a number of developmental changes during the transition to adolescence that were outlined in the preceding chapters. As students transition to middle school, they become especially sensitive to their status in the peer group (Smith, 2010; Yeager, Dahl, & Dweck, 2018). This is in line with Sullivan's Interpersonal Theory, which posits a change in focus from friendships during childhood to popularity in the peer group during adolescence as needs for belongingness grow (Bukowski et al., 2011; Pouwels, Lansu, & Cillessen, 2018a; Sullivan, 1953). With development, adolescents better understand the peer hierarchy and recognize that not everyone can be popular. As such, youth become more likely to engage in bullying to gain and maintain status in the peer group. In addition, bullying may help to advance status with potential romantic partners as dating opportunities become of greater concern in middle school (Pouwels, Lansu et al., 2018a; Smith, 2010). As articulated by Mayeux and O'Mealy (this volume) there is a distinction between social preference (or being well-liked) and being perceived as popular, and the association between bullying and popularity intensifies during the transition to adolescence.

The increased association between bullying and popularity during adolescence may stem from growing needs for autonomy and shifting attitudes toward authority figures (Smith, 2010; Swearer, Martin, Brackett, & Palacios, 2017; Yeager et al., 2018). This is consistent with Moffitt's Developmental Taxonomy of Antisocial Behavior (Moffitt,

1993; Pouwels, Lansu et al., 2018a). Moffitt suggests that for some individuals, antisocial behavior is limited to the adolescent period during which there is a gap between biological and social maturity. With the onset of puberty, adolescents become biologically mature, but must still rely on adults. In an attempt to demonstrate maturity and independence, some youth behave antisocially. Furthermore, as bullying is increasingly associated with popularity, bullying and follower behavior becomes more common (Pouwels, Lansu et al., 2018a). In turn, defending behaviors become less likely as adolescents focus on potential social repercussions for assisting low status victims (Lambe et al., 2019; Pouwels, Lansu et al., 2018a)

These developmental changes hold vital implications for prevention and intervention efforts. A recent meta-analysis indicates that intervention programs may be more effective in childhood than adolescence (Yeager, Fong, Lee, & Espelage, 2015). Many suggest that programs may become less effective because few interventions consider adolescents' desire for peer respect and status (Pouwels, Lansu et al., 2018a; Yeager et al., 2018). As such, prevention and intervention efforts need to be tailored to the age of the students. Given the status motivations that underlie bullying in adolescence, bystander interventions may be less effective as potential defenders could fear losing status. Rather, it may be critical to raise awareness of prosocial routes to popularity (Pouwels, Lansu et al., 2018a; Pouwels, van Noorden et al., 2018b).

Participant Roles and Adjustment

Throughout the text, contributors devoted much attention to implications for prevention and intervention as effective anti-bullying efforts can positively impact youth health and adjustment. As described in this volume, a great deal of research has pointed to the negative outcomes associated with perpetration and victimization. Mayeux and O'Mealy (this volume) note that bullying perpetration is associated with internalizing and externalizing problems, low academic achievement, and risky behaviors such as substance use (see also, Feldman et al., 2014; Sigurdson, Wallander, & Sund, 2014). Similarly, as highlighted by

Schwartz and colleagues (this volume), victimization is associated with internalizing and externalizing difficulties as well as poor academic achievement (see also, McDougall & Vaillancourt, 2015). Importantly, certain protective factors have been identified for victimized youth including parental and teacher support (see Chapter 7). Furthermore, the presence of defenders can help to buffer victimized youth from adjustment problems as discussed by Fredrick and colleagues (this volume). Victims who are defended by their peers have higher social status and self-esteem as well as lower levels of social anxiety than victims who are not defended (Kärnä, Voeten, Poskiparta, & Salmivalli, 2010; Sainio, Veenstra, Huitsing, & Salmivalli, 2010). Conversely, victims may suffer greater levels of maladjustment in classes with greater numbers of reinforcers (Kärnä et al., 2010).

Less attention has been devoted to the repercussions of bullying on bystanders; as discussed throughout the text, witnessing bullying can have negative effects. Using a daily diary approach, Nishina and Juvonen (2005) found that 42% of students indicated observing at least one incident of peer harassment during the four days in which daily diaries were completed. These peer harassment experiences were associated with increased anxiety. Simply witnessing bullying may predict maladjustment including substance use, anxiety, and depression (Midgett & Doumas, 2019; Rivers, Poteat, Noret, & Ashurst, 2009; Wu, Luu, & Luh, 2016). Several explanations have been proposed to explain these findings. As noted previously, bystanders may fear becoming victims themselves in the future, which negatively affects their adjustment (Juvonen & Galván, 2009; Rivers et al., 2009, Wu et al., 2016). Furthermore, bullying can be viewed as a form of interpersonal trauma (Lambe, Hudson, Craig, & Pepler, 2017), and witnesses may experience "indirect covictimization through their empathic understanding of the suffering of the victim they observe" (Rivers et al., 2009, p. 220). Moreover, those in the outsider role may feel helpless and experience a form of cognitive dissonance as they are aware of the hurtful nature of bullying but fail to assist their victimized peers (Midgett & Doumas, 2019; Rivers et al., 2009).

There may be additional costs to defending as this form of bystander behavior increases involvement in bullying and can be risky (Lambe et al., 2017). Defending is not always successful in stopping bullying;

peer intervention was found to be ineffective for 26% of bullying episodes observed on elementary school playgrounds (Hawkins et al., 2001). As Fredrick and colleagues (this volume) discuss, there is an association between defending and internalizing problems, although the direction of effect is unclear. Defending may result in internalizing problems, or alternatively, defending may be a way to try to cope with the distressing feelings that accompany witnessing bullying (Lambe et al., 2017). Longitudinal studies are needed to better understand these associations. However, it is important that anti-bullying efforts consider the well-being of the bystander as well as the victim. Bystanders may feel pressure to defend at all times and may face backlash from those in pro-bullying roles when they do so (Wu et al., 2016). Anti-bullying programs can raise awareness about different defending strategies as assisting victimized peers does not necessarily mean "heroic acts of confronting the bullies" (Salmivalli et al., 2010, p. 444). Rather, safe strategies for intervening can be promoted (Lambe et al., 2019).

Bullying Prevention and Intervention Programs

Throughout the text we have laid out a road map for how the participant role approach to bullying can inform prevention and intervention efforts. All students have the right to not be bullied, and each of the 50 US states has anti-bullying laws that require schools to address bullying violations (Ross et al., 2017; Swearer et al., 2017). There are a wide array of anti-bullying programs, and schools try to identify the one most likely to fit the needs of their campus as well as be cost-effective (Persson, Wennberg, Beckman, Salmivalli, & Svensson, 2018; Swearer et al., 2017). Meta-analytic findings suggest that diverse programs have been successful in reducing bullying (Gaffney, Ttofi, & Farrington, 2019b; Ttofi & Farrington, 2011). However, not all programs are successful, and some may even increase bullying (Smith, 2011; Vreeman & Carroll, 2007). Based on the participant role approach, more effective programs focus beyond the bully and victim roles to include bystanders, school staff, and parents (Holt, Raczynskib, Frey, Hymel, & Limber, 2013;

Richard, Schneider, & Mallet, 2012; Rosen et al., 2017). Swearer and colleagues (2017) assert that "there are literally hundreds of bullying- and aggression-prevention programs being used in schools worldwide" (p. 23). Several programs have been found to increase bystander intervention (Polanin et al., 2012). However, here we focus on three programs that are closely in line with viewing bullying as a group process.

KiVa Program

The KiVa program was prominently featured throughout the text as it was developed based on Salmivalli's research on participant roles. The name of the program is actually an acronym for "Kiusaamista Vastaan," which means "against bullying" in Finnish while Kiva means "nice" (Salmivalli & Poskiparta, 2012, p. 42). The premise of the program is that bystander behavior can either increase or decrease the likelihood of bullying, and thus the goal is to alter bystander behavior so that bullying is less rewarding (Salmivalli, Kärnä, & Poskiparta, 2011). KiVa works at both the universal and targeted levels. At the universal level, teachers lead lessons following the KiVa manual that focus on topics such as peer pressure and how to behave in ways that help victims (Salmivalli et al., 2011, 2014; Salmivalli & Poskiparta, 2012). Lessons are designed for both primary and secondary schools and include discussion, group activities, videos, and role-play, with multiple opportunities designed to elicit empathy for victims and to allow for practice of defending strategies to promote self-efficacy. Class lessons are coupled with a virtual learning environment in which children play a game that has different levels. First, the "I Know" level addresses facts about bullying and assesses learning. Second, the "I Can" level is a virtual school environment where students can practice responding to challenging peer situations. Finally, the "I Do" level fosters application in the actual school setting letting students share how they have applied the skills in real life. The virtual learning environment has been adapted for secondary school under the name KiVa Street (Kärnä et al., 2011; Salmivalli et al., 2014).

In addition to the universal component, KiVa includes a targeted component for acute cases of bullying (Garandeau, Poskiparta et al.,

2014b: Garandeau, Vartio, Poskiparta, & Salmivalli, 2016). Each school has a KiVa team composed of teachers or school staff members that address bullying incidents. The KiVa team holds discussions first with victims and then bullies, and later follows up on these conversations. In the discussions with the bully, findings indicate it is important to evoke empathy for the victim and convey disapproval for the bullying behavior rather than the person (Garandeau et al., 2016). Additionally, teachers reach out to two to four prosocial, high status classmates of the victimized student and charge them with helping the victim. Evaluation studies suggest that KiVa may be more effective at reducing bullying and increasing bystanders' confidence in their ability to defend at the primary than secondary level (Salmivalli et al., 2011; Salmivalli & Poskiparta, 2012).

Bully Prevention in Positive Behavioral Support (BP-PSB)—Stop. Walk. Talk

Ross and Horner (2009) designed a program that was intended to make bullying less socially rewarding by decreasing peer attention for bullying. This program can work within the Bullying Prevention in Positive Behavior Support Program, which focuses on creating a positive school environment by teaching and reinforcing prosocial behavior. Ross and colleagues introduced a three-step program in which students are taught a progressive series of actions for responding to disrespectful behavior (Ross et al., 2017). The first step is for victims and bystanders to use a stop hand signal and say "stop" when they witness disrespectful behavior. If this fails, victims move to step two and walk away from the bullying. Therefore, victims ignore the bully's behavior and do not display behavior that might be perceived as rewarding to the bully such as crying. At this step, bystanders are encouraged to assist the victim in leaving the situation. If the first two steps are not effective or there is a risk for harm, students are taught to report the behavior to an adult. Evaluation of Ross and Horner's program has indicated efficacy in reducing aggression as well as bystander encouragement of bullying (Ross & Horner, 2009; Ross et al., 2017).

Meaningful Roles Intervention

The Meaningful Roles Intervention was designed to address bullying in adolescence during which popularity is of critical concern (Ellis, Volk, Gonzalez, & Embry, 2016; Pouwels, van Noorden et al., 2018b; Yeager et al., 2018). Focusing on defending during adolescence may not be an effective strategy; "as defending is not rewarded by popularity in adolescence, adolescents may refrain from it, even when they believe it is the right thing to do" (Pouwels, Lansu et al. 2018a, p. 67). Thus, it may be key for anti-bullying efforts to teach and demonstrate nonaggressive, prosocial routes to popularity, which is the goal of the Meaningful Roles Intervention. In designing the program, Ellis and colleagues (2016) recognized that bullies are often aware of the distress their behavior is causing but view it as a way to gain status in the peer group. Therefore, they designed this program on the premise that "if the methods for obtaining a goal can be altered so that it becomes prosocial rather than antisocial, then bullies should prefer using prosocial behaviors to obtain goals (so long as the cost-benefit ratios are favorable)" (Ellis et al., 2016, p. 5). Rather than bullying, the program seeks to demonstrate that adolescents can take on more adult-like roles in school to gain status. The program includes assigning roles to students that offer status in the peer group, such as homework monitor or information technology specialist. Importantly, roles can be assigned in ways that may remove bullies from challenging situations as well as partnering them with prosocial youth. Furthermore, the program focuses on reinforcing this prosocial behavior with signed or anonymous praise notes, which are posted in a public space to provide a different source of peer attention. Although this program shows promise, future evaluation studies are needed to determine its efficacy.

Future Directions and Conclusions

Our goal was to provide one of the most comprehensive accounts of participant roles surrounding bullying. As pointed out by numerous contributors, we know less about some roles such as outsiders and followers. Further research on these roles will enable more effective routes to intervention. Moreover, a great deal of attention has been devoted to reducing bullying by increasing defender behavior. As Fredrick and colleagues (this volume) urge, longitudinal investigations are needed to better understand the potential costs of defending. Given the association between defending and mental health, programs need to further focus on teaching safe ways to defend as well as coping strategies for defenders. Contributors also pointed to the importance of better examining how technology influences peer dynamics, which may be critical given that 45% of adolescents report they are online "almost constantly" (Anderson & Jiang, 2018). Cyberbullying can happen at any place or time, which can make victims feel especially vulnerable (Peebles, 2014). Accordingly, it is critical to expand on our knowledge of participant roles in online environments as well as how to effectively intervene online.

In sum, future work is needed to further apply the participant role approach to bullying in both online and offline settings. Ross and colleagues (2017) suggest that bullying can be viewed using a candle and flame analogy.

> Disrespectful, bullying behavior is like a flame that is hurtful to those around it. However, in order for a flame to burn it needs the oxygen for fuel. This is similar to bullying, which needs peer attention to keep burning. Consequently, if you take a glass cup and cover the flame, removing the oxygen fueling it, the flame goes out. This is what happens when bystanders use a stop response, help victims walk away, or otherwise remove peer attention from bullying situations. Like a burning candle, the bullying flame does not go out right away, but over time as students learn their inappropriate behavior will not achieve the peer attention they desire. (pp. 40–41)

Our hope is that this book will help inspire future research on how peers can help extinguish the bullying flame.

References

Anderson, M., & Jiang, J. (2018). Teens, social media, & technology 2018. *Pew Research Center*. http://www.pewinternet.org/2018/05/31/teens-social-media-technology-2018/.

Bandura, A. (1994). *Self-efficacy*. In V. S. Ramachaudran (Ed.), Encyclopedia of human behavior (Vol. 4, pp. 71–81). New York: Academic Press.

Bauman, S. (2010). Groups and bullying. *The Journal for Specialists in Group Work, 35,* 321–323. https://doi.org/10.1080/01933922.2010.515177.

Blomqvist, K., Saarento-Zaprudin, S., & Salmivalli, C. (2019). Telling adults about one's plight as a victim of bullying: Student- and context-related factors predicting disclosure. *Scandinavian Journal of Psychology, 61,* 151–159. https://doi.org/10.1111/sjop.12521.

Boulton, M. J., & Smith, P. K. (1994). Bully/victim problems in middle school children: Stability, self-perceived competence, peer perceptions and peer acceptance. *British Journal of Developmental Psychology, 12,* 315–329. https://doi.org/10.1111/j.2044-835X.1994.tb00637.x.

Bukowski, W. M., Buhrmester, D., & Underwood, M. K. (2011). Peer relations as a developmental context. In M. K. Underwood & L. H. Rosen (Eds.), *Social development: Relationships in infancy, childhood, and adolescence* (pp. 153–179). New York: Guilford.

Camodeca, M., & Coppola, G. (2016). Bullying, empathic concern, and internalization of rules among preschool children: The role of emotion understanding. *International Journal of Behavioral Development, 40,* 459–465. https://doi.org/10.1177/016502.

Cohen, J., Espelage, D. L., Berkowitz, M., Twemlow, S., & Comer, J. (2015). Rethinking effective bully and violence prevention efforts: Promoting healthy school climates, positive youth development, and preventing bully-victim-bystander behavior. *International Journal of Violence and Schools, 15,* 2–40.

Cook, C. R., Williams, K. R., Guerra, N. G., Kim, T. E., & Sadek, S. (2010). Predictors of bullying and victimization in childhood and adolescence: A meta-analytic investigation. *School Psychology Quarterly, 25,* 65–83. https://doi.org/10.1037/a0020149.

Craig, W., & Pepler, D. J. (1997). Observations of bullying and victimization in the schoolyard. *Canadian Journal of School Psychology, 13,* 41–60. https://doi.org/10.1177/082957359801300205.

DeOrnellas, K., & Spurgin, A. (2017). Teachers' perspectives on bullying. In L. H. Rosen, K. DeOrnellas, & S. R. Scott (Eds.), *Bullying in schools: Perspectives from school staff, students, and parents* (pp. 49–68). New York: Palgrave Macmillan.

Dishion, T. J. (2000). Cross-setting consistency in early adolescent psychopathology: Deviant friendships and problem behavior sequelae. *Journal of Personality, 68,* 1109–1126. https://doi.org/10.1111/1467-6494.00128.

Ellis, B., Volk, A., Gonzalez, J., & Embry, D. (2016). The meaningful roles intervention: An evolutionary approach to reducing bullying and increasing prosocial behavior. *Journal of Research on Adolescence, 26*. https://doi.org/10.1111/jora.12243.

Espelage, D. L., Low, S. K., & Jimerson, S. R. (2014). Understanding school climate, aggression, peer victimization, and bully perpetration: Contemporary science, practice, and policy. *School Psychology Quarterly, 29,* 233–237. https://doi.org/10.1037/spq0000090.

Espelage, D. L., & Swearer, S. M. (2009). Contributions of three social theories to understanding bullying perpetration and victimization among school-aged youth. In M. J. Harris (Ed.), *Bullying, rejection, and peer victimization: A social cognitive neuroscience perspective* (pp. 151–170). New York: Springer.

Ettekal, A., & Mahoney, J. L. (2017). Ecological systems theory. Invited chapter to appear in K. Peppler (Ed.), *The SAGE encyclopedia of out-of-school learning* (pp. 239–241). Thousand Oaks, CA: SAGE.

Ettekal, I., Kochenderfer-Ladd, B., & Ladd, G. W. (2015). A synthesis of person- and relational-level factors that influence bullying and bystanding behaviors: Toward an integrative framework. *Aggression and Violent Behavior, 23,* 75–86. https://doi.org/10.1016/j.avb.2015.05.011.

Feldman, M. A., Ojanen, T., Gesten, E. L., Smith-Schrandt, H., Brannick, M., Totura, C. M. W., ... Brown, K. (2014). The effects of middle school bullying and victimization on adjustment through high school: Growth modeling of achievement, school attendance, and disciplinary trajectories. *Psychology in the Schools, 51,* 1046–1062. https://doi.org/10.1002/pits.21799.

Gaffney, H., Farrington, D. P. & Ttofi, M. M. (2019a). Examining the effectiveness of school-bullying intervention programs globally: A meta-analysis. *International Journal of Bullying Prevention 1,* 14–31. https://doi.org/10.1007/s42380-019-0007-4.

Gaffney, H., Ttofi, M. M., & Farrington, D. P. (2019b). Evaluating the effectiveness of school-bullying prevention programs: An updated meta-analytical review. *Aggression and Violent Behavior, 45*, 111–133. https://doi.org/10.1016/j.avb.2018.07.001.

Garandeau, C. F., Lee, I. A. & Salmivalli, C. (2014a). Inequality matters: Classroom status hierarchy and adolescents' bullying. *Journal of Youth and Adolescence, 43*, 1123–1133. https://doi.org/10.1007/s10964-013-0040-4.

Garandeau, C. F., Poskiparta, E., & Salmivalli, C. (2014b). Tackling acute cases of school bullying in the KiVa anti-bullying program: A comparison of two approaches. *Journal of Abnormal Child Psychology, 42*, 981–991. https://doi.org/10.1007/s10802-014-9861-1.

Garandeau, C. F., Vartio, A., Poskiparta, E., & Salmivalli, C. (2016). School bullies' intention to change behavior following teacher interventions: Effects of empathy arousal, condemning of bullying, and blaming of the perpetrator. *Prevention Science, 17*, 1034–1043. https://doi.org/10.1007/s11121-016-0712-x.

Goossens, F. A., Olthof, T., & Dekker, P. H. (2006). New participant role scales: Comparison between various criteria for assigning roles and indications for their validity. *Aggressive Behavior, 32*, 343–357. https://doi.org/10.1002/ab.20133.

Haataja, A., Voeten, M., Boulton, A. J., Ahtola, A., Poskiparta, E., & Salmivalli, C. (2014). The KiVa anti-bullying curriculum and outcome: Does fidelity matter? *Journal of School Psychology, 52*, 479–493. https://doi.org/10.1016/j.jsp.2014.07.001.

Hawkins, D. L., Pepler, D. J., & Craig, W. M. (2001). Naturalistic observations of peer interventions in bullying. *Social Development, 10*, 512–527. https://doi.org/10.1111/1467-9507.00178.

Hawley, P. H., Little, T. D., & Card, N. A. (2007). The allure of a mean friend: Relationship quality and processes of aggressive adolescents with prosocial skills. *International Journal of Behavioral Development, 31*, 170–180. https://doi.org/10.1177/0165025407074630.

Holden, G. W., Vittrup, B., & Rosen, L. H. (2011). Families, parenting, and discipline. In M. K. Underwood & L. H. Rosen (Eds.), *Social development: Relationships in infancy, childhood, and adolescence* (pp. 127–152). New York: Guilford.

Holt, M. K., Raczynskib, K., Frey, K. S., Hymel, S., & Limber, S. P. (2013). School and community-based approaches for preventing bullying. *Journal of School Violence, 12*, 238–252. https://doi.org/10.1080/15388220.2013.792271.

Huitsing, G., & Veenstra, R. (2012). Bullying in the classrooms: Participant roles from a social network perspective. *Aggressive Behavior, 38,* 494–509. https://doi.org/10.1002/ab.21438.

Hymel, S., & Swearer, S. M. (2015). Four decades of research on school bullying. *American Psychologist, 70,* 293–299. https://doi.org/10.1037/a0038928.

Juvonen, J., & Galván, A. (2009). Bullying as a means to foster compliance. In M. J. Harris (Ed.), *Bullying, rejection, and peer victimization: A social cognitive neuroscience perspective* (pp. 299–318). New York: Springer.

Kärnä, A., Voeten, M., Little, T. D., Poskiparta, E., Kaljonen, A., & Salmivalli, C. (2011). A large-scale evaluation of the KiVa anti-bullying program: Grades 4–6. *Child Development, 82,* 311–330. https://doi.org/10.1111/j.1467-8624.2010.01557.x.

Kärnä, A., Voeten, M., Poskiparta, E., & Salmivalli, C. (2010). Vulnerable children in varying classroom contexts: Bystanders' behaviors moderate the effects of risk factors on victimization. *Merrill-Palmer Quarterly, 56*(3), 261–282. https://doi.org/10.1353/mpq.0.0052.

Konold, T., Cornell, D., Huang, F., Meyer, P., Lacey, A., Nekvasil, E., ... Shukla, K. (2014). Multilevel multi-informant structure of the authoritative school climate survey. *School Psychology Quarterly, 29,* 238–255. https://doi.org/10.1037/spq0000062, https://doi.org/10.1037/spq0000062.supp.

Lambe, L. J., Cioppa, V. D., Hong, I. K., & Craig, W. M. (2019). Standing up to bullying: A social ecological review of peer defending in offline and online contexts. *Aggression and Violent Behavior, 45,* 51–74. https://doi.org/10.1016/j.avb.2018.05.007.

Lambe, L. J., Hudson, C. C., Craig, W. M., & Pepler, D. J. (2017). Does defending come with a cost? Examining the psychosocial correlates of defending behaviour among bystanders of bullying in a Canadian sample. *Child Abuse and Neglect, 65,* 112–123. https://doi.org/10.1016/j.chiabu.2017.01.012.

Levasseur, C., Desbiens, N., & Bowen, F. (2017). Moral reasoning about school bullying in involved adolescents. *Journal of Moral Education, 46,* 158–176. https://doi.org/10.1080/03057240.2016.1268113.

Mazzone, A., Camodeca, M., & Salmivalli, C. (2016). Stability and change of outsider behavior in school bullying: The role of shame and guilt in a longitudinal perspective. *The Journal of Early Adolescence, 38,* 164–177. https://doi.org/10.1177/0272431616659560.

McDougall, P., & Vaillancourt, T. (2015). Long-term adult outcomes of peer victimization in childhood and adolescence: Pathways to adjustment

and maladjustment. *American Psychologist, 70,* 300–310. https://doi.org/10.1037/a0039174.
Menesini, E., & Salmivalli, C. (2017). Bullying in schools: The state of knowledge and effective interventions. *Psychology, Health & Medicine, 22,* 240–253. https://doi.org/10.1080/13548506.2017.1279740.
Midgett, A., & Doumas, D. M. (2019). Witnessing bullying at school: The association between being a bystander and anxiety and depressive symptoms. *School Mental Health.* Advance online publication. https://doi.org/10.1007/s12310-019-09312-6.
Moffitt, T. E. (1993). Adolescence-limited and life-course-persistent antisocial behavior: A developmental taxonomy. *Psychological Review, 100,* 674–701. https://doi.org/10.1037/0033-295X.100.4.674.
Monks, C. P., Smith, P. K., & Swettenham, J. (2003). Aggressors, victims, and defenders in preschool: Peer, self-, and teacher reports. *Merrill-Palmer Quarterly, 49,* 453–469. https://doi.org/10.1353/mpq.2003.0024.
Nickerson, A. B., Mele, D., & Osborne-Oliver, K. M. (2010). Parent-child relationships and bullying. In S. R. Jimerson, S. M. Swearer, & D. L. Espelage (Eds.), *Handbook of bullying in schools: An international perspective* (pp. 187–197). New York: Routledge.
Nishina, A., & Juvonen, J. (2005). Daily reports of witnessing and experiencing peer harassment in middle school. *Child Development, 76,* 435–450. https://doi.org/10.1111/j.1467-8624.2005.00855.x.
O'Connell, P., Pepler, D., & Craig, W. (1999). Peer involvement in bullying: Insights and challenges for intervention. *Journal of Adolescence, 22,* 437–452. https://doi.org/10.1006/jado.1999.0238.
Olweus, D. (1993). *Bullying at school: What we know and what we can do.* Malden: Blackwell.
Peebles, E. (2014). Cyberbullying: Hiding behind the screen. *Paediatrics & Child Health, 19,* 527–528. https://doi.org/10.1093/pch/19.10.527.
Peets, K., Pöyhönen, V., Juvonen, J., & Salmivalli, C. (2015). Classroom norms of bullying alter the degree to which children defend in response to their affective empathy and power. *Developmental Psychology, 51,* 913–920. https://doi.org/10.1037/a0039287.
Persson, M., Wennberg, L., Beckman, L., Salmivalli, C., & Svensson, M. (2018). The cost-effectiveness of the Kiva anti-bullying program: Results from a decision-analytic model. *Prevention Science, 19,* 728–737. https://doi.org/10.1007/s11121-018-0893-6.

Polanin, J. R., Espelage, D. L., & Pigott, T. D. (2012). A meta-analysis of school-based bullying prevention programs' effects on bystander intervention behavior. *School Psychology Review, 41,* 47–65.

Pouwels, J. L., Lansu, T. A. M., & Cillessen, A. H. N. (2016). Participant roles of bullying in adolescence: Status characteristics, social behavior, and assignment criteria. *Aggressive Behavior, 42,* 239–253. https://doi.org/10.1002/ab.21614.

Pouwels, J. L., Lansu, T. A. M., & Cillessen, A. H. N. (2017). Adolescents' explicit and implicit evaluations of hypothetical and actual peers with different bullying participant roles. *Journal of Experimental Child Psychology, 159,* 219–241. https://doi.org/10.1016/j.jecp.2017.02.008.

Pouwels, J. L., Lansu, T. A. M., & Cillessen, A. H. N. (2018a). A developmental perspective on popularity and the group process of bullying. *Aggression and Violent Behavior, 43,* 64–70. https://doi.org/10.1016/j.avb.2018.10.003.

Pouwels, J. L., van Noorden, T. H. J., Lansu, T. A. M., & Cillessen, A. H. N. (2018b). The participant roles of bullying in different grades: Prevalence and social status profiles. *Social Development, 27,* 732–747. https://doi.org/10.1111/sode.12294.

Pöyhönen, V., Juvonen, J., & Salmivalli, C. (2010). What does it take to stand up for the victim of bullying? The interplay between personal and social factors. *Merrill-Palmer Quarterly, 56,* 143–163. https://doi.org/10.1353/mpq.0.0046.

Pöyhönen, V., Juvonen, J., & Salmivalli, C. (2012). Standing up for the victim, siding with the bully or standing by? Bystander responses in bullying situations. *Social Development, 21,* 722–741. https://doi.org/10.1111/j.1467-9507.2012.00662.x.

Pozzoli, T., & Gini, G. (2010). Active defending and passive bystanding behavior in bullying: The role of personal characteristics and perceived peer pressure. *Journal of Abnormal Child Psychology, 38,* 815–827. https://doi.org/10.1007/s10802-010-939909.

Rambaran, J., Dijkstra, J., & Veenstra, R. (2019). Bullying as a group process in childhood: A longitudinal social network analysis. *Child Development.* https://doi.org/10.1111/cdev.13298.

Richard, J. F., Schneider, B. H., & Mallet, P. (2012). Revisiting the whole-school approach to bullying: Really looking at the whole school. *School Psychology International, 33,* 263–284. https://doi.org/10.1177/0143034311415906.

Rigby, K., & Slee, P. T. (1991). Bullying among Australian school children: Reported behavior and attitudes toward victims. *The Journal of Social Psychology, 131*(5), 615–627. https://doi.org/10.1080/00224545.1991.992 4646.
Rivers, I., Poteat, V. P., Noret, N., & Ashurst, N. (2009). Observing bullying at school: The mental health implications of witness status. *School Psychology Quarterly, 24,* 211–223. https://doi.org/10.1037/a0018164.
Rodkin, P. C. (2004). Peer ecologies of aggression and bullying. In D. L. Espelage & S. M. Swearer (Eds.), *Bullying in American schools: A social-ecological perspective on prevention and intervention* (pp. 87–106). Hillsdale: Lawrence Erlbaum Associates Publishers.
Rosen, L. H., DeOrnellas, K., & Scott, S. R. (2017). Drawing across perspectives: Implications for prevention and intervention. In L. H. Rosen, K. DeOrnellas, & S. R. Scott (Eds.), *Bullying in schools: Perspectives from school staff, students, and parents* (pp. 159–177). New York: Palgrave Macmillan.
Rosen, L. H., & Rubin, L. J. (2016). Bullying. In N. Naples (Ed.), *Encyclopedia of gender and sexuality studies*. Malden: Wiley.
Ross, S. W., & Horner, R. H. (2009). Bully prevention in positive behavior support. *Journal of Applied Behavior Analysis, 42,* 747–759. https://doi.org/10.1901/jaba.2009.42-747.
Ross, S. W., Lund, E. M., Sabey, C., & Charlton, C. (2017). Students' perspectives on bullying. In L. H. Rosen, K. DeOrnellas, & S. R. Scott (Eds.), *Bullying in schools: Perspectives from school staff, students, and parents* (pp. 23–47). New York: Palgrave Macmillan.
Saarento, S., Boulton, A. J., & Salmivalli, C. (2015). Reducing bullying and victimization: Student- and classroom-level mechanisms of change. *Journal of Abnormal Child Psychology, 43,* 61–76. https://doi.org/10.1007/s10802-013-9841-x.
Saarento, S., & Salmivalli, C. (2015). The role of classroom peer ecology and bystanders' responses in bullying. *Child Development Perspectives, 9,* 201–205. https://doi.org/10.1111/cdep.12140.
Sainio, M., Veenstra, R., Huitsing, G., & Salmivalli, C. (2010). Victims and their defenders: A dyadic approach. *International Journal of Behavioral Development, 35,* 144–151. https://doi.org/10.1177/0165025410378068.
Salmivalli, C. (1999). Participant role approach to school bullying: Implications for interventions. *Journal of Adolescence, 22,* 453–459. https://doi.org/10.1006/jado.1999.0239.
Salmivalli, C. (2010). Bullying and the peer group: A review. *Aggression and Violent Behavior, 15,* 112–120. https://doi.org/10.1016/j.avb.2009.08.007.

Salmivalli, C., Huttunen, A., & Lagerspetz, K. (1997). Peer networks and bullying in schools. *Scandinavian Journal of Psychology, 38,* 305–312. https://doi.org/10.1111/1467-9450.00040.

Salmivalli, C., Kärnä, A., & Poskiparta, E. (2010). From peer putdowns to peer support: A theoretical model and how it translated into a national antibullying program. In S. R. Jimerson, S. M. Swearer & D. L. Espelage (Eds.), *Handbook of bullying in schools: An international perspective* (pp. 441–454). New York: Routledge.

Salmivalli, C., Kärnä, A., & Poskiparta, E. (2011). Counteracting bullying in Finland: The KiVa program and its effects on different forms of being bullied. *International Journal of Behavioral Development, 35,* 405–411. https://doi.org/10.1177/0165025411407457.

Salmivalli, C., Lagerspetz, K., Björkqvist, K., Österman, K., & Kaukiainen, A. (1996). Bullying as group process: Participant roles and their relations to social status within the group. *Aggressive Behavior, 22,* 1–15. https://doi.org/10.1002/(SICI)1098-2337(1996)22:1.

Salmivalli, C., Lappalainen, M., & Lagerspetz, K. M. J. (1998). Stability and change of behavior in connection with bullying in schools: A two-year follow-up. *Aggressive Behavior, 24,* 205–218. https://doi.org/10.1002/(SICI)1098-2337.

Salmivalli, C., Peets, K., & Hodges, E. V. E. (2014). Bullying. In P. K. Smith & C. H. Hart (Eds.), *Wiley Blackwell handbooks of developmental psychology: The Wiley Blackwell handbook of childhood social development* (pp. 510–528). Hoboken: Wiley-Blackwell.

Salmivalli, C., & Poskiparta, E. (2012). Making bullying prevention a priority in Finnish schools: The KiVa anti-bullying program. *New Directions for Youth Development, 2012,* 41–53. https://doi.org/10.1002/yd.20006.

Salmivalli, C., & Voeten, M. (2004). Connections between attitudes, group norms, and behaviour in bullying situations. *International Journal of Behavioral Development, 28,* 246–258. https://doi.org/10.1080/01650250344000488.

Sentse, M., Veenstra, R., Kiuru, N., & Salmivalli, C. (2015). A longitudinal multilevel study of individual characteristics and classroom norms in explaining bullying behaviors. *Journal of Abnormal Child Psychology, 43,* 943–955. https://doi.org/10.1007/s10802-014-9949-7.

Shaw, T., Campbell, M. A., Eastham, J., Runions, K. C., Salmivalli, C., & Cross, D. (2019). Telling an adult at school about bullying: Subsequent victimization and internalizing problems. *Journal of Child and Family Studies, 28,* 2594–2605. https://doi.org/10.1007/s10826-019-01507-4.

Sigurdson, J. F., Wallander, J., & Sund, A. M. (2014). Is involvement in school bullying associated with general health and psychosocial adjustment outcomes in adulthood? *Child Abuse and Neglect, 38,* 1607–1617. https://doi.org/10.1016/j.chiabu.2014.06.001.

Smith, P. K. (2010). Bullying in primary and secondary schools: Psychological and organizational comparisons. In S. R. Jimerson, S. M. Swearer, & D. L. Espelage (Eds.), *Handbook of bullying in schools: An international perspective* (pp. 137–150). New York: Routledge.

Smith, P. K. (2011). Why interventions to reduce bullying and violence in schools may (or may not) succeed: Comments on this special section. *International Journal of Behavioral Development, 35,* 419–423. https://doi.org/10.1177/0165025411407459.

Smokowski, P., & Evans, C. (2019). *Bullying and victimization across the lifespan: Playground politics and power.* New York: Springer Nature.

Sullivan, H. S. (1953). *Interpersonal theory of psychiatry.* New York: Norton.

Sutton, J., & Smith, P. K. (1999). Bullying as a group process: An adaptation of the participant role approach. *Aggressive Behavior, 25,* 97–111. https://doi.org/10.1002/(sici)1098-2337.

Swearer, S. M., Martin, M., Brackett, M., & Palacios, R. A. (2017). Bullying intervention in adolescence: The intersection of legislation, policies, and behavioral change. *Adolescent Research Review, 2,* 23–35. https://doi.org/10.1007/s40894-016-0037-9.

Swift, L. E., Hubbard, J. A., Bookhout, M. K., Grassetti, S. N., Smith, M. A., & Morrow, M. T. (2017). Teacher factors contributing to dosage of the KiVa anti-bullying program. *Journal of School Psychology, 65,* 102–115. https://doi.org/10.1016/j.jsp.2017.07.005.

Ttofi, M. M., & Farrington, D. P. (2011). Effectiveness of school-based programs to reduce bullying: A systematic and meta-analytic review. *Journal of Experimental Criminology, 7,* 27–56. https://doi.org/10.1007/s11292-010-9109-1.

Turner, H. A., Finkelhor, D., Hamby, S. L., Shattuck, A., & Ormrod, R. K. (2011). Specifying type and location of peer victimization in a national sample of children and youth. *Journal of Youth and Adolescence, 40,* 1052–1067. https://doi.org/10.1007/s10964-011-9639-5.

Twemlow, S., Vernberg, E., Fonagy, P., Biggs, B., Nelson, J. M., Nelson, T. D., & Sacco, F. (2010). A school climate intervention that reduces bullying by a focus on the bystander audience rather than the bully and victim: The Peaceful Schools Project of the Menninger Clinic and Baylor College of

Medicine. In S. R. Jimerson, S. M. Swearer, & D. L. Espelage (Eds.), *Handbook of bullying in schools: An international perspective* (pp. 365–376). New York: Routledge.

Underwood, M. K. (2011). Aggression. In M. K. Underwood & L. H. Rosen (Eds.), *Social development* (pp. 207–234). New York: Guilford.

Underwood, M. K., & Rosen, L. H. (2011). Gender and bullying: Moving beyond mean differences to consider conceptions of bullying, processes by which bullying unfolds, and cyber bullying. In D. Espelage & S. Swearer (Eds.), *Bullying in American schools: An update* (pp. 13–22). Mahwah: Lawrence Erlbaum.

Vaillancourt, T., Hymel, S., & McDougall, P. (2003). Bullying is power: Implications for school-based intervention strategies. *Journal of Applied School Psychology, 19,* 157–176. https://doi.org/10.1300/J008v19n02_10.

Veenstra, R., Lindenberg, S., Huitsing, G., Sainio, M., & Salmivalli, C. (2014). The role of teachers in bullying: The relation between anti-bullying attitudes, efficacy, and efforts to reduce bullying. *Journal of Educational Psychology, 106,* 1135–1143. https://doi.org/10.1037/a0036110.

Vreeman, R. C., & Carroll, A. E. (2007). Do school-based interventions prevent bullying? A systematic review. *Archives of Pediatric and Adolescent Medicine, 161,* 78–88. https://doi.org/10.1001/archpedi.161.1.78.

Wu, W., Luu, S., & Luh, D. (2016). Defending behaviors, bullying roles, and their associations with mental health in junior high school students: A population-based study. *BMC Public Health, 16,* 1–10. https://doi.org/10.1186/s12889-016-3721-6.

Yeager, D. S., Dahl, R. E., & Dweck, C. S. (2018). Why interventions to influence adolescent behavior often fail but could succeed. *Perspectives on Psychological Science, 13,* 101–122. https://doi.org/10.1177/1745691617722620.

Yeager, D. S., Fong, C. J., Lee, H. Y., & Espelage, D. L. (2015). Declines in efficacy of anti-bullying programs among older adolescents: Theory and a three-level meta-analysis. *Journal of Applied Developmental Psychology, 37,* 36–51. https://doi.org/10.1016/j.appdev.2014.11.005.

Zych, I., Ttofi, M., Llorent, V., Farrington, D., Ribeaud, D., & Eisner, M. (2018). A longitudinal study on stability and transitions among bullying roles. *Child Development.* https://doi.org/10.1111/cdev.13195.

Index

A
anti-bullying attitudes 219

B
bullying
 associated traits/behaviors 3–4
 assistants/reinforcers 52–56
 bullies/perpetrators 20, 222
 outsiders/bystanders 80, 86, 96–97, 222
 victims 147–152
 definition 2, 18
 effects on
  assistants/reinforcers 61–62
  bullies/perpetrators 6, 28–29, 232
  defenders 127–129, 233
  outsiders/bystanders 7, 85–86, 94–95, 233
 victims 6, 157–158, 233
 roles
  assistants/reinforcers 45, 46–47, 215
  bullies/perpetrators 17, 215
  defenders 117, 216, 221, 223
  outsiders/bystanders 80, 214–215, 216
  teachers 181, 192–199, 226–228
  victims 143–147, 216
bystander effect 89–90

C
cognitive patterns/processes 24, 91–93
cultural differences 50, 121, 156–157

cyberbullying 4, 18–20, 29, 31–32, 49, 55, 60, 102–104, 153–154, 162–163

D

developmental/age differences 22, 26, 47–49, 83, 87, 90, 120–121, 154–155, 157, 230–232

E

emotional correlates 94–95, 220–221
empathy 25, 93, 122–123, 221

L

LGBTQ 197–199

M

moral disengagement 25, 96, 54–55, 123–124, 222
motivation to bully 20–25, 50–52

P

parent/family influences 90–91, 182–191, 199, 228–229

peer relationships 18–19, 48, 56–57, 86–88, 158–159, 192–193, 224–225
prevalence 4–5, 18, 45, 47, 81, 118, 229
prevention/intervention 29–31, 62–65, 81–82, 100–102, 129–132, 223, 227, 234–237

R

racial/ethnic differences 27, 155–156

S

school/classroom climate 19, 57–60, 86, 118, 126–127, 191–192, 225–227
self-efficacy 99–100, 124, 223
severity 88–90
sex/gender differences 25, 49–50, 83, 84, 119–120, 123, 127, 153–154, 228, 230
social ecological framework 7–8, 56, 217–218, 224
social status/popularity 21–23, 51, 88, 125–126, 146–147, 150, 218–219
socioeconomic differences 27

Printed in the United States
By Bookmasters